MW01296912

PINHOK™
LANGUAGES

www.pinhok.com

Introduction

This Book

This vocabulary book contains more than 3000 words and phrases and is organized by topic to make it easier for you to pick what to learn first. On top of that, the second half of the book contains two index sections that can be used as basic dictionaries to look up words in either of the two languages. This book is well suited for learners of all levels who are looking for an extensive resource to improve their vocabulary or are interested in learning vocabularies in one particular area of interest.

Learning Community

If you find this book helpful, do us and other fellow learners a favour and leave a comment wherever you bought this book explaining how you use this book in your learning process. Your thoughts and experiences can help and have a positive impact on numerous other language learners around the world. We are looking forward to your stories and thank you in advance for your insights!

Pinhok Languages

Pinhok Languages strives to create language learning products that support learners around the world in their mission of learning a new language. In doing so, we combine best practice from various fields and industries to come up with innovative products and material.

The Pinhok Team hopes this book can help you with your learning process and gets you to your goal faster. Should you be interested in finding out more about us, please go to our website www.pinhok.com. For feedback, error reports, criticism or simply a quick "hi", please also go to our website and use the contact form.

Disclaimer of Liability

THIS BOOK IS PROVIDED "AS IS", WITHOUT WARRANTY OF ANY KIND, EXPRESS OR IMPLIED, INCLUDING BUT NOT LIMITED TO THE WARRANTIES OF MERCHANTABILITY, FITNESS FOR A PARTICULAR PURPOSE AND NONINFRINGEMENT. IN NO EVENT SHALL THE AUTHORS OR COPYRIGHT HOLDERS BE LIABLE FOR ANY CLAIM, DAMAGES OR OTHER LIABILITY, WHETHER IN AN ACTION OF CONTRACT, TORT OR OTHERWISE, ARISING FROM, OUT OF OR IN CONNECTION WITH THE BOOK OR THE USE OR OTHER DEALINGS IN THE BOOK.

Copyright © 2018 Pinhok.com. All Rights Reserved

4

Table of Contents

Topics

Index

Animals

Mammals

dog	개 (gae)
cat	고양이 (goyang-i)
rabbit	토끼 (tokki)
cow	암소 (amso)
sheep	양 (yang)
pig	돼지 (dwaeji)
horse	말 (mal)
monkey	원숭이 (wonsung-i)
bear	곰 (gom)
lion	사자 (saja)
tiger	호랑이 (holang-i)
panda	판다 (panda)
giraffe	기린 (gilin)
camel	낙타 (nagta)
elephant	코끼리 (kokkili)
wolf	늑대 (neugdae)
rat	쥐 (jwi)
mouse (animal)	생쥐 (saengjwi)
zebra	얼룩말 (eollugmal)
hippo	하마 (hama)
polar bear	북극곰 (buggeuggom)
rhino	코뿔소 (koppulso)
kangaroo	캥거루 (kaeng-geolu)
leopard	표범 (pyobeom)
cheetah	치타 (chita)
donkey	당나귀 (dangnagwi)
ant-eater	개미핥기 (gaemihaltgi)
buffalo	물소 (mulso)
deer	사슴 (saseum)
squirrel	다람쥐 (dalamjwi)

elk	엘크 (elkeu)
piglet	새끼돼지 (saekkidwaeji)
bat	박쥐 (bagjwi)
fox	여우 (yeou)
hamster	햄스터 (haemseuteo)
guinea pig	기니피그 (ginipigeu)
koala	코알라 (koalla)
lemur	여우원숭이 (yeouwonsung-i)
meerkat	미어캣 (mieokaes)
raccoon	미국너구리 (migugneoguli)
tapir	맥 (maeg)
bison	들소 (deulso)
goat	염소 (yeomso)
llama	라마 (lama)
red panda	레서판다 (leseopanda)
bull	황소 (hwangso)
hedgehog	고슴도치 (goseumdochi)
otter	수달 (sudal)

Birds

pigeon	비둘기 (bidulgi)
duck	오리 (oli)
seagull	갈매기 (galmaegi)
chicken (animal)	닭 (dalg)
cockerel	어린 수탉 (eolin sutalg)
goose	거위 (geowi)
owl	부엉이 (bueong-i)
swan	백조 (baegjo)
penguin	펭귄 (peng-gwin)
crow	까마귀 (kkamagwi)
turkey	칠면조 (chilmyeonjo)
ostrich	타조 (tajo)
stork	황새 (hwangsae)

chick	병아리 (byeong-ali)
eagle	독수리 (dogsuli)
raven	큰까마귀 (keunkkamagwi)
peacock	공작새 (gongjagsae)
pelican	펠리컨 (pellikeon)
parrot	앵무새 (aengmusae)
magpie	까치 (kkachi)
flamingo	홍학 (honghag)
falcon	매 (mae)

Insects

fly	파리 (pali)
butterfly	나비 (nabi)
bug	벌레 (beolle)
bee	꿀벌 (kkulbeol)
mosquito	모기 (mogi)
ant	개미 (gaemi)
dragonfly	잠자리 (jamjali)
grasshopper	메뚜기 (mettugi)
caterpillar	애벌레 (aebeolle)
wasp	말벌 (malbeol)
moth	나방 (nabang)
bumblebee	호박벌 (hobagbeol)
termite	흰개미 (huingaemi)
cricket	귀뚜라미 (gwittulami)
ladybird	무당벌레 (mudangbeolle)
praying mantis	사마귀 (samagwi)

Marine Animals

fish (animal)	물고기 (mulgogi)
whale	고래 (golae)
shark	상어 (sang-eo)
dolphin	돌고래 (dolgolae)

seal	바다표범 (badapyobeom)
jellyfish	해파리 (haepali)
squid	오징어 (ojing-eo)
octopus	문어 (mun-eo)
turtle	바다 거북 (bada geobug)
sea horse	해마 (haema)
sea lion	바다사자 (badasaja)
walrus	바다코끼리 (badakokkili)
shell	조개 (jogae)
starfish	불가사리 (bulgasali)
killer whale	범고래 (beomgolae)
crab	게 (ge)
lobster	바닷가재 (badasgajae)

Reptiles & More

snail	달팽이 (dalpaeng-i)
spider	거미 (geomi)
frog	개구리 (gaeguli)
snake	뱀 (baem)
crocodile	악어 (ag-eo)
tortoise	거북이 (geobug-i)
scorpion	전갈 (jeongal)
lizard	도마뱀 (domabaem)
chameleon	카멜레온 (kamelle-on)
tarantula	타란튤라 (talantyulla)
gecko	도마뱀붙이 (domabaembut-i)
dinosaur	공룡 (gonglyong)

Sport

Summer

tennis	테니스 (teniseu)
badminton	배드민턴 (baedeuminteon)
boxing	권투 (gwontu)
golf	골프 (golpeu)
running	달리기 (dalligi)
cycling	사이클링 (saikeulling)
gymnastics	체조 (chejo)
table tennis	탁구 (taggu)
weightlifting	역도 (yeogdo)
long jump	멀리뛰기 (meollittwigi)
triple jump	3단뛰기 (3danttwigi)
modern pentathlon	근대 5종 경기 (geundae 5jong gyeong-gi)
rhythmic gymnastics	리듬 체조 (lideum chejo)
hurdles	허들 경기 (heodeul gyeong-gi)
marathon	마라톤 (malaton)
pole vault	장대높이뛰기 (jangdaenop-ittwigi)
high jump	높이뛰기 (nop-ittwigi)
shot put	포환던지기 (pohwandeonjigi)
javelin throw	창던지기 (changdeonjigi)
discus throw	원반 던지기 (wonban deonjigi)
karate	가라데 (galade)
triathlon	철인3종경기 (cheol-in3jong-gyeong-gi)
taekwondo	태권도 (taegwondo)
sprint	단거리 달리기 (dangeoli dalligi)
show jumping	장애물 경주 (jang-aemul gyeongju)
shooting	사격 (sagyeog)
wrestling	레슬링 (leseulling)
mountain biking	산악 자전거 타기 (san-ag jajeongeo tagi)
judo	유도 (yudo)
hammer throw	해머 던지기 (haemeo deonjigi)

fencing	펜싱 (pensing)
archery	양궁 (yang-gung)
track cycling	트랙 사이클링 (teulaeg saikeulling)

Winter

skiing	스키 (seuki)
snowboarding	스노보드 (seunobodeu)
ice skating	아이스 스케이팅 (aiseu seukeiting)
ice hockey	아이스하키 (aiseuhaki)
figure skating	피겨 스케이팅 (pigyeo seukeiting)
curling	컬링 (keolling)
Nordic combined	노르딕 복합 (noleudig boghab)
biathlon	바이애슬론 (baiaeseullon)
luge	루지 (luji)
bobsleigh	봅슬레이 (bobseullei)
short track	쇼트트랙 (syoteuteulaeg)
skeleton	스켈레톤 (seukelleton)
ski jumping	스키 점프 (seuki jeompeu)
cross-country skiing	크로스컨트리 스키 (keuloseukeonteuli seuki)
ice climbing	빙벽 등반 (bingbyeog deungban)
freestyle skiing	프리스타일 스키 (peuliseutail seuki)
speed skating	스피드 스케이팅 (seupideu seukeiting)

Team

football	축구 (chuggu)
basketball	농구 (nong-gu)
volleyball	배구 (baegu)
cricket	크리켓 (keulikes)
baseball	야구 (yagu)
rugby	럭비 (leogbi)
handball	핸드볼 (haendeubol)
polo	폴로 (pollo)
lacrosse	라크로스 (lakeuloseu)

field hockey	필드하키 (pildeuhaki)
beach volleyball	비치 발리볼 (bichi ballibol)
Australian football	호주식 축구 (hojusig chuggu)
American football	미식 축구 (misig chuggu)

Water

swimming	수영 (suyeong)
water polo	수구 (sugu)
diving (into the water)	다이빙 (daibing)
surfing	서핑 (seoping)
rowing	조정 (jojeong)
synchronized swimming	수중 발레 (sujung balle)
diving (under the water)	다이빙 (daibing)
windsurfing	윈드 서핑 (windeu seoping)
sailing	세일링 (seilling)
waterskiing	수상스키 (susangseuki)
rafting	래프팅 (laepeuting)
cliff diving	암벽 다이빙 (ambyeog daibing)
canoeing	카누 타기 (kanu tagi)

Motor

car racing	자동차 경주 (jadongcha gyeongju)
rally racing	랠리 경주 (laelli gyeongju)
motorcycle racing	오토바이 경주 (otobai gyeongju)
motocross	모터크로스 (moteokeuloseu)
Formula 1	포뮬러 원 (pomyulleo won)
kart	레이싱 카트 (leising kateu)
jet ski	제트 스키 (jeteu seuki)

Other

hiking	하이킹 (haiking)
mountaineering	등산 (deungsan)
snooker	스누커 (seunukeo)

parachuting	낙하산 (naghasan)
poker	포커 (pokeo)
dancing	춤 (chum)
bowling	볼링 (bolling)
skateboarding	스케이트보드 타기 (seukeiteubodeu tagi)
chess	체스 (cheseu)
bodybuilding	보디빌딩 (bodibilding)
yoga	요가 (yoga)
ballet	발레 (balle)
bungee jumping	번지 점프 (beonji jeompeu)
climbing	등반 (deungban)
roller skating	롤러 스케이팅 (lolleo seukeiting)
breakdance	브레이크댄싱 (beuleikeudaensing)
billiards	당구 (dang-gu)

Gym

warm-up	준비운동 (junbiundong)
stretching	스트레칭 (seuteuleching)
sit-ups	윗몸 일으키기 (wismom il-eukigi)
push-up	팔굽혀 펴기 (palgubhyeo pyeogi)
squat	스쿼트 (seukwoteu)
treadmill	밟아 돌리는 바퀴 (balb-a dollineun bakwi)
bench press	벤치 프레스 (benchi peuleseu)
exercise bike	실내 운동용 자전거 (silnae undong-yong jajeongeo)
cross trainer	크로스 트레이너 (keuloseu teuleineo)
circuit training	서킷 트레이닝 (seokis teuleining)
Pilates	필라테스 (pillateseu)
leg press	레그 프레스 (legeu peuleseu)
aerobics	에어로빅 (eeolobig)
dumbbell	아령 (alyeong)
barbell	역기 (yeoggi)
sauna	사우나 (sauna)

Geography

Europe

United Kingdom	영국 (yeong-gug)
Spain	스페인 (seupein)
Italy	이탈리아 (itallia)
France	프랑스 (peulangseu)
Germany	독일 (dog-il)
Switzerland	스위스 (seuwiseu)
Albania	알바니아 (albania)
Andorra	안도라 (andola)
Austria	오스트리아 (oseuteulia)
Belgium	벨기에 (belgie)
Bosnia	보스니아 (boseunia)
Bulgaria	불가리아 (bulgalia)
Denmark	덴마크 (denmakeu)
Estonia	에스토니아 (eseutonia)
Faroe Islands	페로 제도 (pelo jedo)
Finland	핀란드 (pinlandeu)
Gibraltar	지브롤터 (jibeulolteo)
Greece	그리스 (geuliseu)
Ireland	아일랜드 (aillaendeu)
Iceland	아이스랜드 (aiseulaendeu)
Kosovo	코소보 (kosobo)
Croatia	크로아티아 (keuloatia)
Latvia	라트비아 (lateubia)
Liechtenstein	리히텐슈타인 (lihitensyutain)
Lithuania	리투아니아 (lituania)
Luxembourg	룩셈부르크 (lugsembuleukeu)
Malta	몰타 (molta)
Macedonia	마케도니아 (makedonia)
Moldova	몰도바 (moldoba)
Monaco	모나코 (monako)

Montenegro	몬테네그로 (montenegeulo)
Netherlands	네덜란드 (nedeollandeu)
Norway	노르웨이 (noleuwei)
Poland	폴란드 (pollandeu)
Portugal	포르투갈 (poleutugal)
Romania	루마니아 (lumania)
San Marino	산마리노 (sanmalino)
Sweden	스웨덴 (seuweden)
Serbia	세르비아 (seleubia)
Slovakia	슬로바키아 (seullobakia)
Slovenia	슬로베니아 (seullobenia)
Czech Republic	체코 (cheko)
Turkey	터키 (teoki)
Ukraine	우크라이나 (ukeulaina)
Hungary	헝가리 (heong-gali)
Vatican City	바티칸 시국 (batikan sigug)
Belarus	벨라루스 (bellaluseu)
Cyprus	키프로스 (kipeuloseu)

Asia

China	중국 (jung-gug)
Russia	러시아 (leosia)
India	인도 (indo)
Singapore	싱가포르 (sing-gapoleu)
Japan	일본 (ilbon)
South Korea	대한민국 (daehanmingug)
Afghanistan	아프가니스탄 (apeuganiseutan)
Armenia	아르메니아 (aleumenia)
Azerbaijan	아제르바이잔 (ajeleubaijan)
Bahrain	바레인 (balein)
Bangladesh	방글라데시 (bang-geulladesi)
Bhutan	부탄 (butan)
Brunei	브루나이 (beulunai)

Georgia	그루지아 (geulujia)
Hong Kong	홍콩 (hongkong)
Indonesia	인도네시아 (indonesia)
Iraq	이라크 (ilakeu)
Iran	이란 (ilan)
Israel	이스라엘 (iseula-el)
Yemen	예멘 (yemen)
Jordan	요르단 (yoleudan)
Cambodia	캄보디아 (kambodia)
Kazakhstan	카자흐스탄 (kajaheuseutan)
Qatar	카타르 (kataleu)
Kyrgyzstan	키르기스스탄 (kileugiseuseutan)
Kuwait	쿠웨이트 (kuweiteu)
Laos	라오스 (laoseu)
Lebanon	레바논 (lebanon)
Macao	마카오 (makao)
Malaysia	말레이시아 (malleisia)
Maldives	몰디브 (moldibeu)
Mongolia	몽골 (mong-gol)
Burma	버마 (beoma)
Nepal	네팔 (nepal)
North Korea	북한 (bughan)
Oman	오만 (oman)
East Timor	동티모르 (dongtimoleu)
Pakistan	파키스탄 (pakiseutan)
Palestine	팔레스타인 (palleseutain)
Philippines	필리핀 (pillipin)
Saudi Arabia	사우디아라비아 (saudialabia)
Sri Lanka	스리랑카 (seulilangka)
Syria	시리아 (silia)
Tajikistan	타지키스탄 (tajikiseutan)
Taiwan	대만 (daeman)
Thailand	태국 (taegug)

Turkmenistan	투르크메니스탄 (tuleukeumeniseutan)
Uzbekistan	우즈베키스탄 (ujeubekiseutan)
United Arab Emirates	아랍에미리트 (alab-emiliteu)
Vietnam	베트남 (beteunam)

America

The United States of America	미국 (migug)
Mexico	멕시코 (megsiko)
Canada	캐나다 (kaenada)
Brazil	브라질 (beulajil)
Argentina	아르헨티나 (aleuhentina)
Chile	칠레 (chille)
Antigua and Barbuda	앤티가 바부다 (aentiga babuda)
Aruba	아루바 (aluba)
The Bahamas	바하마 (bahama)
Barbados	바베이도스 (babeidoseu)
Belize	벨리즈 (bellijeu)
Bolivia	볼리비아 (bollibia)
Cayman Islands	케이맨 제도 (keimaen jedo)
Costa Rica	코스타리카 (koseutalika)
Dominica	도미니카 (dominika)
Dominican Republic	도미니카 공화국 (dominika gonghwagug)
Ecuador	에콰도르 (ekwadoleu)
El Salvador	엘살바도르 (elsalbadoleu)
Falkland Islands	포클랜드 제도 (pokeullaendeu jedo)
Grenada	그레나다 (geulenada)
Greenland	그린란드 (geulinlandeu)
Guatemala	과테말라 (gwatemalla)
Guyana	가이아나 (gaiana)
Haiti	아이티 (aiti)
Honduras	온두라스 (ondulaseu)
Jamaica	자메이카 (jameika)
Colombia	콜롬비아 (kollombia)

Cuba	쿠바 (kuba)
Montserrat	몬세라트 (monselateu)
Nicaragua	니카라과 (nikalagwa)
Panama	파나마 (panama)
Paraguay	파라과이 (palagwai)
Peru	페루 (pelu)
Puerto Rico	푸에르토리코 (pueleutoliko)
Saint Kitts and Nevis	세인트키츠 네비스 (seinteukicheu nebiseu)
Saint Lucia	세인트루시아 (seinteulusia)
Saint Vincent and the Grenadines	세인트빈센트 그레나딘 (seinteubinsenteu geulenadin)
Suriname	수리남 (sulinam)
Trinidad and Tobago	트리니다드 토바고 (teulinidadeu tobago)
Uruguay	우루과이 (ulugwai)
Venezuela	베네수엘라 (benesuella)

Africa

South Africa	남아프리카 공화국 (nam-apeulika gonghwagug)
Nigeria	나이지리아 (naijilia)
Morocco	모로코 (moloko)
Libya	리비아 (libia)
Kenya	케냐 (kenya)
Algeria	알제리 (aljeli)
Egypt	이집트 (ijibteu)
Ethiopia	에티오피아 (etiopia)
Angola	앙골라 (ang-golla)
Benin	베냉 (benaeng)
Botswana	보츠와나 (bocheuwana)
Burkina Faso	부르키나파소 (buleukinapaso)
Burundi	부룬디 (bulundi)
Democratic Republic of the Congo	콩고 민주 공화국 (kong-go minju gonghwagug)
Djibouti	지부티 (jibuti)
Equatorial Guinea	적도 기니 (jeogdo gini)
Ivory Coast	코트디부아르 (koteudibualeu)

Eritrea	에리트레아 (eliteulea)
Gabon	가봉 (gabong)
The Gambia	감비아 (gambia)
Ghana	가나 (gana)
Guinea	기니 (gini)
Guinea-Bissau	기니비사우 (ginibisau)
Cameroon	카메룬 (kamelun)
Cape Verde	카보베르데 (kabobeleude)
Comoros	코모로 (komolo)
Lesotho	레소토 (lesoto)
Liberia	라이베리아 (laibelia)
Madagascar	마다가스카르 (madagaseukaleu)
Malawi	말라위 (mallawi)
Mali	말리 (malli)
Mauritania	모리타니 (molitani)
Mauritius	모리셔스 (molisyeoseu)
Mozambique	모잠비크 (mojambikeu)
Namibia	나미비아 (namibia)
Niger	니제르 (nijeleu)
Republic of the Congo	콩고 공화국 (kong-go gonghwagug)
Rwanda	르완다 (leuwanda)
Zambia	잠비아 (jambia)
São Tomé and Príncipe	상투메 프린시페 (sangtume peulinsipe)
Senegal	세네갈 (senegal)
Seychelles	세이셸 (seisyel)
Sierra Leone	시에라리온 (sielalion)
Zimbabwe	짐바브웨 (jimbabeuwe)
Somalia	소말리아 (somallia)
Sudan	수단 (sudan)
South Sudan	남수단 (namsudan)
Swaziland	스와질란드 (seuwajillandeu)
Tanzania	탄자니아 (tanjania)
Togo	토고 (togo)

Chad	차드 (chadeu)
Tunisia	튀니지 (twiniji)
Uganda	우간다 (uganda)
Central African Republic	중앙아프리카 공화국 (jung-ang-apeulika gonghwagug)

Oceania

Australia	호주 (hoju)
New Zealand	뉴질랜드 (nyujillaendeu)
Fiji	피지 (piji)
American Samoa	아메리칸 사모아 (amelikan samoa)
Cook Islands	쿡 제도 (kug jedo)
French Polynesia	프랑스령 폴리네시아 (peulangseulyeong pollinesia)
Kiribati	키리바시 (kilibasi)
Marshall Islands	마셜 제도 (masyeol jedo)
Micronesia	미크로네시아 (mikeulonesia)
Nauru	나우루 (naulu)
New Caledonia	뉴칼레도니아 (nyukalledonia)
Niue	니우에 (niue)
Palau	팔라우 (pallau)
Papua New Guinea	파푸아뉴기니 (papuanyugini)
Solomon Islands	솔로몬 제도 (sollomon jedo)
Samoa	사모아 (samoa)
Tonga	통가 (tong-ga)
Tuvalu	투발루 (tuballu)
Vanuatu	바누아투 (banuatu)

Numbers

0-20

0	영 (yeong)
1	일 (il)
2	이 (i)
3	삼 (sam)
4	사 (sa)
5	오 (o)
6	육 (yug)
7	칠 (chil)
8	팔 (pal)
9	구 (gu)
10	십 (sib)
11	십일 (sib-il)
12	십이 (sib-i)
13	십삼 (sibsam)
14	십사 (sibsa)
15	십오 (sib-o)
16	십육 (sib-yug)
17	십칠 (sibchil)
18	십팔 (sibpal)
19	십구 (sibgu)
20	이십 (isib)

21-100

21	이십일 (isib-il)
22	이십이 (isib-i)
26	이십육 (isib-yug)
30	삼십 (samsib)
31	삼십일 (samsib-il)
33	삼십삼 (samsibsam)
37	삼삽칠 (samsabchil)

40	사십 (sasib)
41	사십일 (sasib-il)
44	사십사 (sasibsa)
48	사십팔 (sasibpal)
50	오십 (osib)
51	오십일 (osib-il)
55	오십오 (osib-o)
59	오십구 (osibgu)
60	육십 (yugsib)
61	육십일 (yugsib-il)
62	육십이 (yugsib-i)
66	육십육 (yugsib-yug)
70	칠십 (chilsib)
71	칠십일 (chilsib-il)
73	칠십삼 (chilsibsam)
77	칠십칠 (chilsibchil)
80	팔십 (palsib)
81	팔십일 (palsib-il)
84	팔십사 (palsibsa)
88	팔십팔 (palsibpal)
90	구십 (gusib)
91	구십일 (gusib-il)
95	구십오 (gusib-o)
99	구십구 (gusibgu)
100	백 (baeg)

101-1000

101	백일 (baeg-il)
105	백오 (baeg-o)
110	백십 (baegsib)
151	백오십일 (baeg-osib-il)
200	이백 (ibaeg)
202	이백이 (ibaeg-i)

206	이백육 (ibaeg-yug)
220	이백이십 (ibaeg-isib)
262	이백육십이 (ibaeg-yugsib-i)
300	삼백 (sambaeg)
303	삼백삼 (sambaegsam)
307	삼백칠 (sambaegchil)
330	삼백삼십 (sambaegsamsib)
373	삼백칠십삼 (sambaegchilsibsam)
400	사백 (sabaeg)
404	사백사 (sabaegsa)
408	사백팔 (sabaegpal)
440	사백사십 (sabaegsasib)
484	사백팔십사 (sabaegpalsibsa)
500	오백 (obaeg)
505	오백오 (obaeg-o)
509	오백구 (obaeggu)
550	오백오십 (obaeg-osib)
595	오백구십오 (obaeggusib-o)
600	육백 (yugbaeg)
601	육백일 (yugbaeg-il)
606	육백육 (yugbaeg-yug)
616	육백십육 (yugbaegsib-yug)
660	육백육십 (yugbaeg-yugsib)
700	칠백 (chilbaeg)
702	칠백이 (chilbaeg-i)
707	칠백칠 (chilbaegchil)
727	칠백이십칠 (chilbaeg-isibchil)
770	칠백칠십 (chilbaegchilsib)
800	팔백 (palbaeg)
803	팔백삼 (palbaegsam)
808	팔백팔 (palbaegpal)
838	팔백삼십팔 (palbaegsamsibpal)
880	팔백팔십 (palbaegpalsib)

900	구백 (gubaeg)
904	구백사 (gubaegsa)
909	구백구 (gubaeggu)
949	구백사십구 (gubaegsasibgu)
990	구백구십 (gubaeggusib)
1000	천 (cheon)

1001-10000

1001	천일 (cheon-il)
1012	천십이 (cheonsib-i)
1234	천이백삼십사 (cheon-ibaegsamsibsa)
2000	이천 (icheon)
2002	이천이 (icheon-i)
2023	이천이십삼 (icheon-isibsam)
2345	이천삼백사십오 (icheonsambaegsasib-o)
3000	삼천 (samcheon)
3003	삼천삼 (samcheonsam)
3034	삼천삼십사 (samcheonsamsibsa)
3456	삼천사백오십육 (samcheonsabaeg-osib-yug)
4000	사천 (sacheon)
4004	사천사 (sacheonsa)
4045	사천사십오 (sacheonsasib-o)
4567	사천오백육십칠 (sacheon-obaeg-yugsibchil)
5000	오천 (ocheon)
5005	오천오 (ocheon-o)
5056	오천오십육 (ocheon-osib-yug)
5678	오천육백칠십팔 (ocheon-yugbaegchilsibpal)
6000	육천 (yugcheon)
6006	육천육 (yugcheon-yug)
6067	육천육십칠 (yugcheon-yugsibchil)
6789	육천칠백팔십구 (yugcheonchilbaegpalsibgu)
7000	칠천 (chilcheon)
7007	칠천칠 (chilcheonchil)

7078	칠천칠십팔 (chilcheonchilsibpal)
7890	칠천팔백구십 (chilcheonpalbaeggusib)
8000	팔천 (palcheon)
8008	팔천팔 (palcheonpal)
8089	팔천팔십구 (palcheonpalsibgu)
8901	팔천구백일 (palcheongubaeg-il)
9000	구천 (gucheon)
9009	구천구 (gucheongu)
9012	구천십이 (gucheonsib-i)
9090	구천구십 (gucheongusib)
10.000	만 (man)

> 10000

10.001	만일 (man-il)
20.020	이만이십 (iman-isib)
30.300	삼만삼백 (sammansambaeg)
44.000	사만사천 (samansacheon)
100.000	십만 (sibman)
500.000	오십만 (osibman)
1.000.000	백만 (baegman)
6.000.000	육백만 (yugbaegman)
10.000.000	천만 (cheonman)
70.000.000	칠천만 (chilcheonman)
100.000.000	일억 (il-eog)
800.000.000	팔억 (pal-eog)
1.000.000.000	십억 (sib-eog)
9.000.000.000	구십억 (gusib-eog)
10.000.000.000	백억 (baeg-eog)
20.000.000.000	이백억 (ibaeg-eog)
100.000.000.000	천억 (cheon-eog)
300.000.000.000	삼천억 (samcheon-eog)
1.000.000.000.000	일조 (iljo)

Body

Head

nose	코 (ko)
eye	눈 (nun)
ear	귀 (gwi)
mouth	입 (ib)
tooth	치아 (chia)
lip	입술 (ibsul)
hair	머리카락 (meolikalag)
beard	턱수염 (teogsuyeom)
forehead	이마 (ima)
eyebrow	눈썹 (nunsseob)
eyelashes	속눈썹 (sognunsseob)
pupil	동공 (dong-gong)
cheek	빰 (ppyam)
chin	턱 (teog)
dimple	보조개 (bojogae)
wrinkle	주름 (juleum)
freckles	주근깨 (jugeunkkae)
tongue	혀 (hyeo)
nostril	콧구멍 (kosgumeong)
temple	관자놀이 (gwanjanol-i)

Body Parts

head	머리 (meoli)
arm	팔 (pal)
hand	손 (son)
leg	다리 (dali)
knee	무릎 (muleup)
foot	발 (bal)
belly	배 (bae)
belly button	배꼽 (baekkob)

bosom	유방 (yubang)
chest	가슴 (gaseum)
elbow	팔꿈치 (palkkumchi)
nipple	유두 (yudu)
shoulder	어깨 (eokkae)
neck	목 (mog)
bottom	엉덩이 (eongdeong-i)
nape	목덜미 (mogdeolmi)
back (part of body)	등 (deung)
waist	허리 (heoli)

Hand & Foot

finger	손가락 (songalag)
thumb	엄지 (eomji)
fingernail	손톱 (sontob)
toe	발가락 (balgalag)
heel	발꿈치 (balkkumchi)
palm	손바닥 (sonbadag)
wrist	손목 (sonmog)
fist	주먹 (jumeog)
Achilles tendon	아킬레스건 (akilleseugeon)
index finger	집게 손가락 (jibge songalag)
middle finger	가운데 손가락 (gaunde songalag)
ring finger	약손가락 (yagsongalag)
little finger	새끼 손가락 (saekki songalag)

Bones & More

bone (part of body)	뼈 (ppyeo)
muscle	근육 (geun-yug)
tendon	힘줄 (himjul)
vertebra	척추뼈 (cheogchuppyeo)
pelvis	골반 (golban)
breastbone	흉골 (hyung-gol)

rib	늑골 (neuggol)
collarbone	쇄골 (swaegol)
skeleton	골격 (golgyeog)
skull	두개골 (dugaegol)
shoulder blade	어깨뼈 (eokkaeppyeo)
kneecap	슬개골 (seulgaegol)
cartilage	연골 (yeongol)
jawbone	턱뼈 (teogppyeo)
nasal bone	코뼈 (koppyeo)
spine	척추 (cheogchu)
ankle	발목 (balmog)
bone marrow	골수 (golsu)

Organs

heart	심장 (simjang)
lung	허파 (heopa)
liver	간 (gan)
kidney	신장 (sinjang)
vein	정맥 (jeongmaeg)
artery	동맥 (dongmaeg)
stomach	위 (wi)
intestine	장 (jang)
bladder	방광 (bang-gwang)
brain	뇌 (noe)
anus	항문 (hangmun)
appendix	맹장 (maengjang)
spleen	비장 (bijang)
oesophagus	식도 (sigdo)
nerve	신경 (singyeong)
spinal cord	척수 (cheogsu)
pancreas	췌장 (chwejang)
gall bladder	쓸개 (sseulgae)
colon	결장 (gyeoljang)

small intestine	소장 (sojang)
windpipe	기관 (gigwan)
diaphragm	횡경막 (hoeng-gyeongmag)
duodenum	십이지장 (sib-ijijang)

Reproduction

testicle	고환 (gohwan)
penis	음경 (eumgyeong)
prostate	전립샘 (jeonlibsaem)
ovary	난소 (nanso)
oviduct	나팔관 (napalgwan)
uterus	자궁 (jagung)
ovum	난자 (nanja)
sperm	정액 (jeong-aeg)
scrotum	음낭 (eumnang)
clitoris	음핵 (eumhaeg)
vagina	질 (jil)

Adjective

Colours

white	하얀색 (hayansaeg)
black	검정색 (geomjeongsaeg)
grey	회색 (hoesaeg)
green	초록색 (chologsaeg)
blue	파랑색 (palangsaeg)
red	빨간색 (ppalgansaeg)
pink	분홍색 (bunhongsaeg)
orange (colour)	주황색 (juhwangsaeg)
purple	보라색 (bolasaeg)
yellow	노랑색 (nolangsaeg)
brown	갈색 (galsaeg)
beige	베이지 (beiji)

Basics

heavy	무거운 (mugeoun)
light (weight)	가벼운 (gabyeoun)
correct	옳은 (olh-eun)
difficult	어려운 (eolyeoun)
easy	쉬운 (swiun)
wrong	틀린 (teullin)
many	많은 (manh-eun)
few	적은 (jeog-eun)
new	새로운 (saeloun)
old (not new)	오래된 (olaedoen)
slow	느린 (neulin)
quick	빠른 (ppaleun)
poor	가난한 (gananhan)
rich	부유한 (buyuhan)
funny	재미있는 (jaemiissneun)
boring	지루한 (jiluhan)

fair	공평한 (gongpyeonghan)
unfair	불공평한 (bulgongpyeonghan)

Feelings

good	좋은 (joh-eun)
bad	나쁜 (nappeun)
weak	약한 (yaghan)
happy	행복한 (haengboghan)
sad	슬픈 (seulpeun)
strong	강한 (ganghan)
angry	화난 (hwanan)
healthy	건강한 (geonganghan)
sick	아픈 (apeun)
hungry	배고픈 (baegopeun)
thirsty	목마른 (mogmaleun)
full (from eating)	배부른 (baebuleun)
proud	자랑스러운 (jalangseuleoun)
lonely	외로운 (oeloun)
tired	피곤한 (pigonhan)
safe (adjective)	안전한 (anjeonhan)

Space

short (length)	짧은 (jjalb-eun)
long	긴 (gin)
round	둥근 (dung-geun)
small	작은 (jag-eun)
big	큰 (keun)
square (adjective)	각진 (gagjin)
twisting	비틀림 (biteullim)
straight (line)	직진 (jigjin)
high	높은 (nop-eun)
low	낮은 (naj-eun)
steep	가파른 (gapaleun)

flat	평평한 (pyeongpyeonghan)
shallow	얕은 (yat-eun)
deep	깊은 (gip-eun)
broad	넓은 (neolb-eun)
narrow	좁은 (job-eun)
huge	큰 (keun)

Place

right	오른쪽 (oleunjjog)
left	왼쪽 (oenjjog)
above	위 (wi)
back (position)	뒤 (dwi)
front	앞 (ap)
below	아래 (alae)
here	여기 (yeogi)
there	저기 (jeogi)
close	가까운 (gakkaun)
far	먼 (meon)
inside	안 (an)
outside	밖 (bakk)
beside	옆 (yeop)
north	북 (bug)
east	동 (dong)
south	남 (nam)
west	서 (seo)

Things

cheap	싼 (ssan)
expensive	비싼 (bissan)
full (not empty)	가득찬 (gadeugchan)
hard	딱딱한 (ttagttaghan)
soft	부드러운 (budeuleoun)
empty	빈 (bin)

light (colour)	밝은 (balg-eun)
dark	어두운 (eoduun)
clean	깨끗한 (kkaekkeushan)
dirty	더러운 (deoleoun)
boiled	삶은 (salm-eun)
raw	날것의 (nalgeos-ui)
strange	이상한 (isanghan)
sour	사워 (sawo)
sweet	단 (dan)
salty	짠 (jjan)
hot (spicy)	매운 (maeun)
juicy	즙이 많은 (jeub-i manh-eun)

People

short (height)	키가 작은 (kiga jag-eun)
tall	키가 큰 (kiga keun)
slim	날씬한 (nalssinhan)
young	젊은 (jeolm-eun)
old (not young)	늙은 (neulg-eun)
plump	통통한 (tongtonghan)
skinny	마른 (maleun)
chubby	통통한 (tongtonghan)
cute	귀여운 (gwiyeoun)
clever	영리한 (yeonglihan)
evil	악한 (aghan)
well-behaved	행실이 바른 (haengsil-i baleun)
cool	멋진 (meosjin)
worried	걱정하는 (geogjeonghaneun)
surprised	놀란 (nollan)
sober	냉정한 (naengjeonghan)
drunk	술취한 (sulchwihan)
blind	맹인 (maeng-in)
mute	농아자 (nong-aja)

deaf	귀머거리의 (gwimeogeoliui)
guilty	유죄의 (yujoeui)
friendly	친절한 (chinjeolhan)
busy	바쁜 (bappeun)
bloody	피투성이의 (pituseong-iui)
pale	창백한 (changbaeghan)
strict	엄격한 (eomgyeoghan)
holy	신성한 (sinseonghan)
beautiful	아름다운 (aleumdaun)
silly	바보 같은 (babo gat-eun)
crazy	미친 (michin)
ugly	못생긴 (mos-saeng-gin)
handsome	잘생긴 (jalsaeng-gin)
greedy	탐욕스러운 (tam-yogseuleoun)
generous	관대한 (gwandaehan)
brave	용감한 (yong-gamhan)
shy	수줍은 (sujub-eun)
lazy	게으른 (geeuleun)
sexy	섹시한 (segsihan)
stupid	바보 (babo)

Outside

cold (adjective)	추운 (chuun)
hot (temperature)	더운 (deoun)
warm	따뜻한 (ttatteushan)
silent	고요한 (goyohan)
quiet	조용한 (joyonghan)
loud	시끄러운 (sikkeuleoun)
wet	젖은 (jeoj-eun)
dry	건조한 (geonjohan)
windy	바람이 부는 (balam-i buneun)
cloudy	구름 낀 (guleum kkin)
foggy	안개 낀 (angae kkin)

rainy	비가 오는 (biga oneun)
sunny	화창한 (hwachanghan)

Verb

Basics

to open (e.g. a door)	열다 (yeolda)
to close	닫다 (dadda)
to sit	앉다 (anjda)
to turn on	켜다 (kyeoda)
to turn off	끄다 (kkeuda)
to stand	서다 (seoda)
to lie	눕다 (nubda)
to come	오다 (oda)
to think	생각하다 (saeng-gaghada)
to know	알다 (alda)
to fail	실패하다 (silpaehada)
to win	이기다 (igida)
to lose	지다 (jida)
to live	살다 (salda)
to die	죽다 (jugda)

Action

to take	가지고 가다 (gajigo gada)
to put	놓다 (nohda)
to find	찾다 (chajda)
to smoke	피우다 (piuda)
to steal	훔치다 (humchida)
to kill	죽이다 (jug-ida)
to fly	날다 (nalda)
to carry	들다 (deulda)
to rescue	구조하다 (gujohada)
to burn	태우다 (taeuda)
to injure	다치다 (dachida)
to attack	공격하다 (gong-gyeoghada)
to defend	방어하다 (bang-eohada)

to fall	떨어지다 (tteol-eojida)
to vote	투표를 하다 (tupyoleul hada)
to choose	선택하다 (seontaeghada)
to gamble	도박을 하다 (dobag-eul hada)
to shoot	쏘다 (ssoda)
to saw	톱질하다 (tobjilhada)
to drill	드릴질하다 (deuliljilhada)
to hammer	망치질하다 (mangchijilhada)

Body

to eat	먹다 (meogda)
to drink	마시다 (masida)
to talk	말하다 (malhada)
to laugh	웃다 (usda)
to cry	울다 (ulda)
to sing	노래하다 (nolaehada)
to walk	걷다 (geodda)
to watch	지켜보다 (jikyeoboda)
to work	일하다 (ilhada)
to breathe	숨을 쉬다 (sum-eul swida)
to smell	냄새 맡다 (naemsae matda)
to listen	듣다 (deudda)
to lose weight	체중을 빼다 (chejung-eul ppaeda)
to gain weight	체중을 늘리다 (chejung-eul neullida)
to shrink	줄어들다 (jul-eodeulda)
to grow	자라다 (jalada)
to smile	미소를 짓다 (misoleul jisda)
to whisper	속삭이다 (sogsag-ida)
to touch	만지다 (manjida)
to shiver	몸을 떨다 (mom-eul tteolda)
to bite	깨물다 (kkaemulda)
to swallow	삼키다 (samkida)
to faint	기절하다 (gijeolhada)

to stare	쳐다보다 (chyeodaboda)
to kick	발로 차다 (ballo chada)
to shout	소리지르다 (solijileuda)
to spit	침을 뱉다 (chim-eul baetda)
to vomit	구토하다 (gutohada)

Interaction

to ask	질문하다 (jilmunhada)
to answer	답변하다 (dabbyeonhada)
to help	돕다 (dobda)
to like	좋아하다 (joh-ahada)
to love	사랑하다 (salanghada)
to give (somebody something)	주다 (juda)
to marry	결혼하다 (gyeolhonhada)
to meet	만나다 (mannada)
to kiss	키스하다 (kiseuhada)
to argue	언쟁하다 (eonjaenghada)
to share	나누다 (nanuda)
to warn	경고하다 (gyeong-gohada)
to follow	따르다 (ttaleuda)
to hide	숨다 (sumda)
to bet	내기하다 (naegihada)
to feed	먹이를 주다 (meog-ileul juda)
to threaten	협박하다 (hyeobbaghada)
to give a massage	마사지를 해주다 (masajileul haejuda)

Movements

to run	달리다 (dallida)
to swim	수영하다 (suyeonghada)
to jump	점프하다 (jeompeuhada)
to lift	들어올리다 (deul-eoollida)
to pull (... open)	당기다 (dang-gida)
to push (... open)	밀다 (milda)

to press (a button)	누르다 (nuleuda)
to throw	던지다 (deonjida)
to crawl	포복 (pobog)
to fight	싸우다 (ssauda)
to catch	잡다 (jabda)
to hit	때리다 (ttaelida)
to climb	오르다 (oleuda)
to roll	구르다 (guleuda)
to dig	파다 (pada)

Business

to buy	구매하다 (gumaehada)
to pay	지불하다 (jibulhada)
to sell	판매하다 (panmaehada)
to study	공부하다 (gongbuhada)
to practice	연습하다 (yeonseubhada)
to call	전화하다 (jeonhwahada)
to read	읽다 (ilgda)
to write	쓰다 (sseuda)
to calculate	계산하다 (gyesanhada)
to measure	재다 (jaeda)
to earn	돈을 벌다 (don-eul beolda)
to look for	찾다 (chajda)
to cut	자르다 (jaleuda)
to count	세다 (seda)
to scan	스캔하다 (seukaenhada)
to print	출력하다 (chullyeoghada)
to copy	복사하다 (bogsahada)
to fix	수리하다 (sulihada)
to quote	인용하다 (in-yonghada)
to deliver	전달하다 (jeondalhada)

Home

to sleep	잠을 자다 (jam-eul jada)
to dream	꿈을 꾸다 (kkum-eul kkuda)
to wait	기다리다 (gidalida)
to clean	청소하다 (cheongsohada)
to wash	씻다 (ssisda)
to cook	요리하다 (yolihada)
to play	놀다 (nolda)
to travel	여행을 하다 (yeohaeng-eul hada)
to enjoy	즐기다 (jeulgida)
to bake	굽다 (gubda)
to fry	튀기다 (twigida)
to boil	끓이다 (kkeulh-ida)
to pray	기도하다 (gidohada)
to rest	쉬다 (swida)
to lock	잠그다 (jamgeuda)
to open (unlock)	열다 (yeolda)
to celebrate	기념하다 (ginyeomhada)
to dry	말리다 (mallida)
to fish	낚시를 하다 (nakksileul hada)
to take a shower	샤워를 하다 (syawoleul hada)
to iron	다림질 하다 (dalimjil hada)
to vacuum	청소기를 돌리다 (cheongsogileul dollida)
to paint	그리다 (geulida)

House

Parts

door	문 (mun)
window (building)	창문 (changmun)
wall	벽 (byeog)
roof	지붕 (jibung)
elevator	엘리베이터 (ellibeiteo)
stairs	계단 (gyedan)
toilet (at home)	화장실 (hwajangsil)
attic	다락 (dalag)
basement	지하 (jiha)
solar panel	태양 전지판 (taeyang jeonjipan)
chimney	굴뚝 (gulttug)
fifth floor	5층 (5cheung)
first floor	1층 (1cheung)
ground floor	지상층 (jisangcheung)
first basement floor	지하1층 (jiha1cheung)
second basement floor	지하2층 (jiha2cheung)
living room	거실 (geosil)
bedroom	침실 (chimsil)
kitchen	부엌 (bueok)
corridor	복도 (bogdo)
front door	현관문 (hyeongwanmun)
bathroom	욕실 (yogsil)
workroom	작업실 (jag-eobsil)
nursery	아기 방 (agi bang)
floor	바닥 (badag)
ceiling	천장 (cheonjang)
garage door	차고 문 (chago mun)
garage	차고 (chago)
garden	정원 (jeong-won)
balcony	발코니 (balkoni)

| terrace | 테라스 (telaseu) |

Devices

TV set	텔레비전 (tellebijeon)
remote control	리모컨 (limokeon)
security camera	보안카메라 (boankamela)
rice cooker	전기 밥솥 (jeongi babsot)
router	공유기 (gong-yugi)
heating	난방 (nanbang)
washing machine	세탁기 (setaggi)
fridge	냉장고 (naengjang-go)
freezer	냉동실 (naengdongsil)
microwave	전자레인지 (jeonjaleinji)
oven	오븐 (obeun)
cooker	가스레인지 (gaseuleinji)
cooker hood	가스레인지 후드 (gaseuleinji hudeu)
dishwasher	식기세척기 (siggisecheoggi)
kettle	주전자 (jujeonja)
mixer	믹서기 (migseogi)
electric iron	전기다리미 (jeongidalimi)
toaster	토스터 (toseuteo)
hairdryer	헤어 드라이어 (heeo deulaieo)
ironing table	다리미판 (dalimipan)
vacuum cleaner	진공청소기 (jingongcheongsogi)
coffee machine	커피머신 (keopimeosin)
air conditioner	에어컨 (eeokeon)
satellite dish	위성방송 수신 안테나 (wiseongbangsong susin antena)
fan	선풍기 (seonpung-gi)
radiator	라디에이터 (ladieiteo)
sewing machine	재봉틀 (jaebongteul)

Kitchen

| spoon | 숟가락 (sudgalag) |

fork	포크 (pokeu)
knife	칼 (kal)
plate	접시 (jeobsi)
bowl	그릇 (geuleus)
glass	유리컵 (yulikeob)
cup (for cold drinks)	컵 (keob)
garbage bin	쓰레기통 (sseulegitong)
chopstick	젓가락 (jeosgalag)
light bulb	전구 (jeongu)
pan	후라이팬 (hulaipaen)
pot	냄비 (naembi)
ladle	국자 (gugja)
cup (for hot drinks)	머그컵 (meogeukeob)
teapot	차주전자 (chajujeonja)
grater	강판 (gangpan)
cutlery	식기도구 (siggidogu)
tap	수도꼭지 (sudokkogji)
sink	싱크대 (singkeudae)
wooden spoon	나무 숟가락 (namu sudgalag)
chopping board	도마 (doma)
sponge	스폰지 (seuponji)
corkscrew	타래 송곳 (talae song-gos)

Bedroom

bed	침대 (chimdae)
alarm clock	알람시계 (allamsigye)
curtain	커튼 (keoteun)
bedside lamp	침실등 (chimsildeung)
wardrobe	옷장 (osjang)
drawer	서랍 (seolab)
bunk bed	이층침대 (icheungchimdae)
desk	책상 (chaegsang)
cupboard	찬장 (chanjang)

shelf	선반 (seonban)
blanket	담요 (dam-yo)
pillow	베개 (begae)
mattress	메트리스 (meteuliseu)
night table	침실용 탁자 (chimsil-yong tagja)
cuddly toy	봉제 인형 (bongje inhyeong)
bookshelf	책장 (chaegjang)
lamp	램프 (laempeu)
safe (for money)	금고 (geumgo)
baby monitor	아기 감시용 모니터 (agi gamsiyong moniteo)

Bathroom

broom	빗자루 (bisjalu)
shower	샤워기 (syawogi)
mirror	거울 (geoul)
scale	체중계 (chejung-gye)
bucket	양동이 (yangdong-i)
toilet paper	화장지 (hwajangji)
basin	세면기 (semyeongi)
towel	수건 (sugeon)
tile	타일 (tail)
toilet brush	변기청소솔 (byeongicheongsosol)
soap	비누 (binu)
bath towel	목욕수건 (mog-yogsugeon)
bathtub	욕조 (yogjo)
shower curtain	샤워커튼 (syawokeoteun)
laundry	빨래 (ppallae)
laundry basket	빨래통 (ppallaetong)
peg	빨래집게 (ppallaejibge)
washing powder	가루비누 (galubinu)

Living room

chair	의자 (uija)

table	식탁 (sigtag)
clock	시계 (sigye)
calendar	달력 (dallyeog)
picture	그림 (geulim)
carpet	카페트 (kapeteu)
sofa	소파 (sopa)
power outlet	콘센트 (konsenteu)
coffee table	탁자 (tagja)
houseplant	화초 (hwacho)
shoe cabinet	신발장 (sinbaljang)
light switch	스위치 (seuwichi)
stool	스툴 (seutul)
rocking chair	흔들의자 (heundeul-uija)
door handle	문손잡이 (munsonjab-i)
tablecloth	식탁보 (sigtagbo)
blind	블라인드 (beullaindeu)
keyhole	열쇠구멍 (yeolsoegumeong)
smoke detector	연기감지기 (yeongigamjigi)

Garden

neighbour	이웃 (ius)
axe	도끼 (dokki)
saw	톱 (tob)
ladder	사다리 (sadali)
fence	울타리 (ultali)
swimming pool (garden)	수영장 (suyeongjang)
deck chair	갑판의자 (gabpan uija)
mailbox (for letters)	우편함 (upyeonham)
pond	연못 (yeonmos)
shed	오두막 (odumag)
flower bed	화단 (hwadan)
lawn mower	잔디깎이 (jandikkakk-i)
rake	갈퀴 (galkwi)

shovel	삽 (sab)
water can	물뿌리개 (mulppuligae)
wheelbarrow	외바퀴 손수레 (oebakwi sonsule)
hose	호스 (hoseu)
pitchfork	쇠스랑 (soeseulang)
loppers	절단기 (jeoldangi)
flower pot	화분 (hwabun)
hedge	산울타리 (san-ultali)
tree house	트리하우스 (teulihauseu)
hoe	괭이 (gwaeng-i)
chainsaw	전기톱 (jeongitob)
kennel	개집 (gaejib)
bell	초인종 (choinjong)
greenhouse	온실 (onsil)

Food

Dairy Products

egg	계란 (gyelan)
milk	우유 (uyu)
cheese	치즈 (chijeu)
butter	버터 (beoteo)
yoghurt	요구르트 (yoguleuteu)
ice cream	아이스크림 (aiseukeulim)
cream (food)	크림 (keulim)
sour cream	사워크림 (sawokeulim)
whipped cream	생크림 (saengkeulim)
egg white	달걀 흰자 (dalgyal huinja)
yolk	달걀 노른자 (dalgyal noleunja)
boiled egg	삶은계란 (salm-eungyelan)
buttermilk	버터밀크 (beoteomilkeu)
feta	페타 (peta)
mozzarella	모차렐라 (mochalella)
parmesan	파르메산 치즈 (paleumesan chijeu)
milk powder	분유 (bun-yu)

Meat & Fish

meat	고기 (gogi)
fish (to eat)	생선 (saengseon)
steak	스테이크 (seuteikeu)
sausage	소시지 (sosiji)
bacon	베이컨 (beikeon)
ham	햄 (haem)
lamb	양고기 (yang-gogi)
pork	돼지고기 (dwaejigogi)
beef	쇠고기 (soegogi)
chicken (meat)	닭고기 (dalg-gogi)
turkey	칠면조 고기 (chilmyeonjo gogi)

salami	살라미 (sallami)
game	사슴고기 (saseumgogi)
veal	송아지고기 (song-ajigogi)
fat meat	지방이 많은 고기 (jibang-i manh-eun gogi)
lean meat	지방이 적은 고기 (jibang-i jeog-eun gogi)
minced meat	다진고기 (dajingogi)
salmon	연어 (yeon-eo)
tuna	참치 (chamchi)
sardine	정어리 (jeong-eoli)
fishbone	생선 가시 (saengseon gasi)
bone (food)	뼈 (ppyeo)

Vegetables

lettuce	상추 (sangchu)
potato	감자 (gamja)
mushroom	버섯 (beoseos)
garlic	마늘 (maneul)
cucumber	오이 (oi)
onion	양파 (yangpa)
corn	옥수수 (ogsusu)
pea	완두콩 (wandukong)
bean	콩 (kong)
celery	셀러리 (selleoli)
okra	오크라 (okeula)
bamboo (food)	대나무 (daenamu)
Brussels sprouts	방울양배추 (bang-ul-yangbaechu)
spinach	시금치 (sigeumchi)
turnip cabbage	콜라비 (kollabi)
broccoli	브로콜리 (beulokolli)
cabbage	배추 (baechu)
artichoke	아티초크 (atichokeu)
cauliflower	콜리플라워 (kollipeullawo)
pepper (vegetable)	고추류 (gochulyu)

chili	고추 (gochu)
courgette	애호박 (aehobag)
radish	무 (mu)
carrot	당근 (dang-geun)
sweet potato	고구마 (goguma)
aubergine	가지 (gaji)
ginger	생강 (saeng-gang)
spring onion	파 (pa)
leek	골파 (golpa)
truffle	트러플 (teuleopeul)
pumpkin	호박 (hobag)
lotus root	연근 (yeongeun)

Fruits & More

apple	사과 (sagwa)
banana	바나나 (banana)
pear	배 (bae)
tomato	토마토 (tomato)
orange (food)	오렌지 (olenji)
lemon	레몬 (lemon)
strawberry	딸기 (ttalgi)
pineapple	파인애플 (pain-aepeul)
water melon	수박 (subag)
grapefruit	자몽 (jamong)
lime	라임 (laim)
peach	복숭아 (bogsung-a)
apricot	살구 (salgu)
plum	자두 (jadu)
cherry	체리 (cheli)
blackberry	블랙베리 (beullaegbeli)
cranberry	크랜베리 (keulaenbeli)
blueberry	블루베리 (beullubeli)
raspberry	라즈베리 (lajeubeli)

currant	까막까치밥나무 열매 (kkamagkkachibabnamu yeolmae)
sugar melon	멜론 (mellon)
grape	포도 (podo)
avocado	아보카도 (abokado)
kiwi	키위 (kiwi)
lychee	리치 (lichi)
papaya	파파야 (papaya)
mango	망고 (mang-go)
pistachio	피스타치오 (piseutachio)
cashew	캐슈 (kaesyu)
peanut	땅콩 (ttangkong)
hazelnut	헤이즐넛 (heijeulneos)
walnut	호두 (hodu)
almond	아몬드 (amondeu)
coconut	코코넛 (kokoneos)
date (food)	대추 (daechu)
fig	무화과 (muhwagwa)
raisin	건포도 (geonpodo)
olive	올리브 (ollibeu)
pit	심지 (simji)
peel	껍질을 까다 (kkeobjil-eul kkada)
jackfruit	잭푸르트 (jaegpuleuteu)

Spices

salt	소금 (sogeum)
pepper (spice)	후추 (huchu)
curry	커리 (keoli)
vanilla	바닐라 (banilla)
nutmeg	육두구 (yugdugu)
paprika	파프리카 (papeulika)
cinnamon	시나몬 (sinamon)
lemongrass	레몬그라스 (lemongeulaseu)
fennel	회향 (hoehyang)

thyme	백리향 (baeglihyang)
mint	민트 (minteu)
chive	골파 (golpa)
marjoram	마저럼 (majeoleom)
basil	바질 (bajil)
rosemary	로즈마리 (lojeumali)
dill	딜 (dil)
coriander	고수 (gosu)
oregano	오레가노 (olegano)

Products

flour	밀가루 (milgalu)
sugar	설탕 (seoltang)
rice	쌀 (ssal)
bread	빵 (ppang)
noodle	국수 (gugsu)
oil	기름 (gileum)
soy	콩 (kong)
wheat	밀 (mil)
oat	귀리 (gwili)
sugar beet	사탕무 (satangmu)
sugar cane	사탕수수 (satangsusu)
rapeseed oil	유채씨유 (yuchaessiyu)
sunflower oil	해바라기유 (haebalagiyu)
olive oil	올리브유 (ollibeuyu)
peanut oil	땅콩기름 (ttangkong-gileum)
soy milk	두유 (duyu)
corn oil	옥수수기름 (ogsusugileum)
vinegar	식초 (sigcho)
yeast	효모 (hyomo)
baking powder	베이킹파우더 (beikingpaudeo)
gluten	글루텐 (geulluten)
tofu	두부 (dubu)

icing sugar	가루 설탕 (galu seoltang)
granulated sugar	입자가 굵은 설탕 (ibjaga gulg-eun seoltang)
vanilla sugar	바닐라 설탕 (banilla seoltang)
tobacco	담배 (dambae)

Breakfast

honey	꿀 (kkul)
jam	잼 (jaem)
peanut butter	땅콩버터 (ttangkongbeoteo)
nut	견과 (gyeongwa)
oatmeal	오트밀 (oteumil)
cereal	씨리얼 (ssilieol)
maple syrup	메이플 시럽 (meipeul sileob)
chocolate cream	초콜릿 크림 (chokollis keulim)
porridge	죽 (jug)
baked beans	구운 콩 (guun kong)
scrambled eggs	스크램블드 에그 (seukeulaembeuldeu egeu)
muesli	뮤즐리 (myujeulli)
fruit salad	과일 샐러드 (gwail saelleodeu)
dried fruit	말린과일 (mallingwail)

Sweet Food

cake	케이크 (keikeu)
cookie	쿠키 (kuki)
muffin	머핀 (meopin)
biscuit	비스킷 (biseukis)
chocolate	초콜릿 (chokollis)
candy	사탕 (satang)
doughnut	도넛 (doneos)
brownie	브라우니 (beulauni)
pudding	푸딩 (puding)
custard	커스터드 (keoseuteodeu)
cheesecake	치즈케이크 (chijeukeikeu)

crêpe	크레페 (keulepe)
croissant	크루아상 (keuluasang)
pancake	팬케익 (paenkeig)
waffle	와플 (wapeul)
apple pie	애플파이 (aepeulpai)
marshmallow	마시멜로 (masimello)
chewing gum	껌 (kkeom)
fruit gum	과일 껌 (gwail kkeom)
liquorice	감초사탕 (gamchosatang)
caramel	카라멜 (kalamel)
candy floss	솜사탕 (somsatang)
nougat	누가 (nuga)

Drinks

water	물 (mul)
tea	차 (cha)
coffee	커피 (keopi)
coke	콜라 (kolla)
milkshake	밀크쉐이크 (milkeusweikeu)
orange juice	오렌지 주스 (olenji juseu)
soda	탄산수 (tansansu)
tap water	수돗물 (sudosmul)
black tea	홍차 (hongcha)
green tea	녹차 (nogcha)
milk tea	밀크티 (milkeuti)
hot chocolate	핫초콜릿 (haschokollis)
cappuccino	카푸치노 (kapuchino)
espresso	에스프레소 (eseupeuleso)
mocha	모카 (moka)
iced coffee	아이스커피 (aiseukeopi)
lemonade	레모네이드 (lemoneideu)
apple juice	사과 주스 (sagwa juseu)
smoothie	스무디 (seumudi)

energy drink	에너지 드링크 (eneoji deulingkeu)

Alcohol

wine	와인 (wain)
beer	맥주 (maegju)
champagne	샴페인 (syampein)
red wine	적포도주 (jeogpodoju)
white wine	백포도주 (baegpodoju)
gin	진 (jin)
vodka	보드카 (bodeuka)
whiskey	위스키 (wiseuki)
rum	럼 (leom)
brandy	브랜디 (beulaendi)
cider	사이다 (saida)
tequila	테킬라 (tekilla)
cocktail	칵테일 (kagteil)
martini	마티니 (matini)
liqueur	리큐어 (likyueo)
sake	사케 (sake)
sparkling wine	스파클링 와인 (seupakeulling wain)

Meals

soup	수프 (supeu)
salad	샐러드 (saelleodeu)
dessert	디저트 (dijeoteu)
starter	전채 요리 (jeonchae yoli)
side dish	사이드 디쉬 (saideu diswi)
snack	간식 (gansig)
breakfast	아침식사 (achimsigsa)
lunch	점심식사 (jeomsimsigsa)
dinner	저녁식사 (jeonyeogsigsa)
picnic	피크닉 (pikeunig)
seafood	해산물 요리 (haesanmul yoli)

street food	길거리 음식 (gilgeoli eumsig)
menu	메뉴판 (menyupan)
tip	팁 (tib)
buffet	뷔페 (bwipe)

Western Food

pizza	피자 (pija)
spaghetti	스파게티 (seupageti)
potato salad	감자샐러드 (gamjasaelleodeu)
mustard	머스타드 (meoseutadeu)
barbecue	바비큐 (babikyu)
steak	스테이크 (seuteikeu)
roast chicken	로스트치킨 (loseuteuchikin)
pie	파이 (pai)
meatball	미트볼 (miteubol)
lasagne	라자냐 (lajanya)
fried sausage	튀긴소시지 (twiginsosiji)
skewer	꼬치 (kkochi)
goulash	굴라시 (gullasi)
roast pork	구운 돼지고기 (guun dwaejigogi)
mashed potatoes	으깬 감자 (eukkaen gamja)

Asian Food

sushi	스시 (seusi)
spring roll	춘권 (chungwon)
instant noodles	인스턴트 면류 (inseuteonteu myeonlyu)
fried noodles	볶음면 (bokk-eummyeon)
fried rice	볶음밥 (bokk-eumbab)
ramen	라멘 (lamen)
dumpling	만두 (mandu)
dim sum	딤섬 (dimseom)
hot pot	전골 (jeongol)
Beijing duck	북경오리 (buggyeong-oli)

Fast Food

burger	버거 (beogeo)
French fries	프렌치 프라이 (peulenchi peulai)
chips	감자칩 (gamjachib)
tomato sauce	토마토소스 (tomatososeu)
mayonnaise	마요네즈 (mayonejeu)
popcorn	팝콘 (pabkon)
hamburger	햄버거 (haembeogeo)
cheeseburger	치즈버거 (chijeubeogeo)
hot dog	핫도그 (hasdogeu)
sandwich	샌드위치 (saendeuwichi)
chicken nugget	치킨너겟 (chikinneoges)
fish and chips	피시 앤 칩스 (pisi aen chibseu)
kebab	케밥 (kebab)
chicken wings	치킨 윙 (chikin wing)
onion ring	어니언링 (eonieonling)
potato wedges	웨지감자 (wejigamja)
nachos	나쵸 (nachyo)

Life

Holiday

luggage	짐 (jim)
hotel	호텔 (hotel)
passport	여권 (yeogwon)
tent	텐트 (tenteu)
sleeping bag	침낭 (chimnang)
backpack	배낭 (baenang)
room key	방열쇠 (bang-yeolsoe)
guest	손님 (sonnim)
lobby	로비 (lobi)
room number	방번호 (bangbeonho)
single room	1인실 (1insil)
double room	2인실 (2insil)
dorm room	도미토리 룸 (domitoli lum)
room service	룸서비스 (lumseobiseu)
minibar	미니바 (miniba)
reservation	예약 (yeyag)
membership	회원권 (hoewongwon)
beach	해변 (haebyeon)
parasol	파라솔 (palasol)
camping	캠핑 (kaemping)
camping site	캠프장 (kaempeujang)
campfire	캠프파이어 (kaempeupaieo)
air mattress	에어메트리스 (eeometeuliseu)
postcard	엽서 (yeobseo)
diary	일기 (ilgi)
visa	비자 (bija)
hostel	호스텔 (hoseutel)
booking	예약 (yeyag)
member	회원 (hoewon)

Time

second (time)	초 (cho)
minute	분 (bun)
hour	시 (si)
morning (6:00-9:00)	아침 (achim)
noon	정오 (jeong-o)
evening	저녁 (jeonyeog)
morning (9:00-11:00)	오전 (ojeon)
afternoon	오후 (ohu)
night	밤 (bam)
1:00	한시 (hansi)
2:05	두시 오분 (dusi obun)
3:10	세시 십분 (sesi sibbun)
4:15	네시 십오분 (nesi sib-obun)
5:20	다섯시 이십분 (daseos-si isibbun)
6:25	여섯시 이십오분 (yeoseos-si isib-obun)
7:30	일곱시 반 (ilgobsi ban)
8:35	여덟시 삼십오분 (yeodeolbsi samsib-obun)
9:40	열시 이십분전 (yeolsi isibbunjeon)
10:45	열한시 십오분전 (yeolhansi sib-obunjeon)
11:50	열두시 십분전 (yeoldusi sibbunjeon)
12:55	한시 오분전 (hansi obunjeon)
one o'clock in the morning	새벽 한시 (saebyeog hansi)
two o'clock in the afternoon	오후 두시 (ohu dusi)
half an hour	삼십분 (samsibbun)
quarter of an hour	십오분 (sib-obun)
three quarters of an hour	사십오분 (sasib-obun)
midnight	자정 (jajeong)
now	지금 (jigeum)

Date

the day before yesterday	그저께 (geujeokke)
yesterday	어제 (eoje)

today	오늘 (oneul)
tomorrow	내일 (naeil)
the day after tomorrow	모레 (mole)
spring	봄 (bom)
summer	여름 (yeoleum)
autumn	가을 (ga-eul)
winter	겨울 (gyeoul)
Monday	월요일 (wol-yoil)
Tuesday	화요일 (hwayoil)
Wednesday	수요일 (suyoil)
Thursday	목요일 (mog-yoil)
Friday	금요일 (geum-yoil)
Saturday	토요일 (toyoil)
Sunday	일요일 (il-yoil)
day	일 (il)
week	주 (ju)
month	달 (dal)
year	년 (nyeon)
January	1월 (1wol)
February	2월 (2wol)
March	3월 (3wol)
April	4월 (4wol)
May	5월 (5wol)
June	6월 (6wol)
July	7월 (7wol)
August	8월 (8wol)
September	9월 (9wol)
October	10월 (10wol)
November	11월 (11wol)
December	12월 (12wol)
century	백년 (baegnyeon)
decade	십년 (sibnyeon)
millennium	천년 (cheonnyeon)

2014-01-01	이천십사년 일월 일일 (icheonsibsanyeon il-wol il-il)
2015-04-03	이천십오년 사월 삼일 (icheonsib-onyeon sawol sam-il)
2016-05-17	이천십육년 오월 십칠일 (icheonsib-yugnyeon owol sibchil-il)
1988-04-12	천구백팔십팔년 사월 십이일 (cheongubaegpalsibpalnyeon sawol sib-iil)
1899-10-13	천팔백구십구년 시월 십삼일 (cheonpalbaeggusibgunyeon siwol sibsam-il)
2000-12-12	이천년 십이월 십이일 (icheonnyeon sib-iwol sib-iil)
1900-11-11	천구백년 십일월 십일일 (cheongubaegnyeon sib-il-wol sib-il-il)
2010-07-14	이천십년 칠월 십사일 (icheonsibnyeon chil-wol sibsail)
1907-09-30	천구백칠년 구월 삼십일 (cheongubaegchilnyeon guwol samsib-il)
2003-02-25	이천삼년 이월 이십오일 (icheonsamnyeon iwol isib-oil)
last week	지난주 (jinanju)
this week	이번주 (ibeonju)
next week	다음주 (da-eumju)
last year	작년 (jagnyeon)
this year	올해 (olhae)
next year	내년 (naenyeon)
last month	지난달 (jinandal)
this month	이번달 (ibeondal)
next month	다음달 (da-eumdal)
birthday	생일 (saeng-il)
Christmas	크리스마스 (keuliseumaseu)
New Year	새해 (saehae)
Ramadan	라마단 (lamadan)
Halloween	할로윈 (hallowin)
Thanksgiving	추수감사절 (chusugamsajeol)
Easter	부활절 (buhwaljeol)

Relatives

daughter	딸 (ttal)

son	아들 (adeul)
mother	어머니 (eomeoni)
father	아버지 (abeoji)
wife	아내 (anae)
husband	남편 (nampyeon)
grandfather (paternal)	친할아버지 (chinhal-abeoji)
grandfather (maternal)	외할아버지 (oehal-abeoji)
grandmother (paternal)	친할머니 (chinhalmeoni)
grandmother (maternal)	외할머니 (oehalmeoni)
aunt	이모 (imo)
uncle	삼촌 (samchon)
cousin (male)	사촌 (sachon)
cousin (female)	사촌 (sachon)
big brother	형/오빠 (hyeong/oppa)
little brother	남동생 (namdongsaeng)
big sister	누나/언니 (nuna/eonni)
little sister	여동생 (yeodongsaeng)
niece	조카딸 (jokattal)
nephew	조카 (joka)
daughter-in-law	며느리 (myeoneuli)
son-in-law	사위 (sawi)
grandson	손자 (sonja)
granddaughter	손녀 (sonnyeo)
brother-in-law	매형 (maehyeong)
sister-in-law	시누이 (sinu-i)
father-in-law	장인어른 (jang-in-eoleun)
mother-in-law	장모 (jangmo)
parents	부모님 (bumonim)
parents-in-law	시부모 (sibumo)
siblings	형제 (hyeongje)
grandchild	손주 (sonju)
stepfather	새아버지 (saeabeoji)
stepmother	새어머니 (saeeomeoni)

stepdaughter	의붓딸 (uibusttal)
stepson	의붓아들 (uibus-adeul)
dad	아빠 (appa)
mum	엄마 (eomma)

Life

man	남자 (namja)
woman	여자 (yeoja)
child	아이 (ai)
boy	소년 (sonyeon)
girl	소녀 (sonyeo)
baby	아기 (agi)
love	사랑 (salang)
job	직업 (jig-eob)
death	죽음 (jug-eum)
birth	탄생 (tansaeng)
infant	유아 (yua)
birth certificate	출생증명서 (chulsaengjeungmyeongseo)
nursery	보육원 (boyug-won)
kindergarten	유치원 (yuchiwon)
primary school	초등학교 (chodeunghaggyo)
twins	쌍둥이 (ssangdung-i)
triplets	세쌍둥이 (sessangdung-i)
junior school	중학교 (junghaggyo)
high school	고등학교 (godeunghaggyo)
friend	친구 (chingu)
girlfriend	여자친구 (yeojachingu)
boyfriend	남자친구 (namjachingu)
university	대학교 (daehaggyo)
vocational training	직업학교 (jig-eobhaggyo)
graduation	졸업 (jol-eob)
engagement	약혼 (yaghon)
fiancé	약혼자 (yaghonja)

fiancée	약혼녀 (yaghonnyeo)
lovesickness	상사병 (sangsabyeong)
sex	섹스 (segseu)
engagement ring	약혼반지 (yaghonbanji)
kiss	키스 (kiseu)
wedding	결혼식 (gyeolhonsig)
divorce	이혼 (ihon)
groom	신랑 (sinlang)
bride	신부 (sinbu)
wedding dress	웨딩드레스 (wedingdeuleseu)
wedding ring	결혼반지 (gyeolhonbanji)
wedding cake	웨딩 케이크 (weding keikeu)
honeymoon	신혼여행 (sinhon-yeohaeng)
funeral	장례식 (janglyesig)
retirement	은퇴 (euntoe)
coffin	관 (gwan)
corpse	시체 (siche)
urn	유골 단지 (yugol danji)
grave	무덤 (mudeom)
widow	과부 (gwabu)
widower	홀아비 (hol-abi)
orphan	고아 (goa)
testament	유언 (yueon)
heir	상속인 (sangsog-in)
heritage	유산 (yusan)
gender	성별 (seongbyeol)
cemetery	묘지 (myoji)

Transport

Car

tyre	타이어 (taieo)
steering wheel	핸들 (haendeul)
throttle	조절판 (jojeolpan)
brake	브레이크 (beuleikeu)
clutch	클러치 (keulleochi)
horn	경적 (gyeongjeog)
windscreen wiper	와이퍼 (waipeo)
battery	배터리 (baeteoli)
rear trunk	트렁크 (teuleongkeu)
wing mirror	사이드미러 (saideumileo)
rear mirror	백미러 (baegmileo)
windscreen	앞유리 (ap-yuli)
bonnet	보닛 (bonis)
side door	옆문 (yeopmun)
front light	전방라이트 (jeonbanglaiteu)
bumper	범퍼 (beompeo)
seatbelt	안전벨트 (anjeonbelteu)
diesel	디젤 (dijel)
petrol	휘발유 (hwibal-yu)
back seat	뒷좌석 (dwisjwaseog)
front seat	앞좌석 (apjwaseog)
gear shift	변속 기어 (byeonsog gieo)
automatic	자동 (jadong)
dashboard	계기판 (gyegipan)
airbag	에어백 (eeobaeg)
GPS	GPS (GPS)
speedometer	속도계 (sogdogye)
gear lever	변속 레버 (byeonsog lebeo)
motor	모터 (moteo)
exhaust pipe	배기관 (baegigwan)

hand brake	핸드 브레이크 (haendeu beuleikeu)
shock absorber	완충기 (wanchung-gi)
rear light	후미등 (humideung)
brake light	브레이크 등 (beuleikeu deung)

Bus & Train

train	기차 (gicha)
bus	버스 (beoseu)
tram	트램 (teulaem)
subway	지하철 (jihacheol)
bus stop	버스정류장 (beoseujeonglyujang)
train station	기차역 (gichayeog)
timetable	시간표 (siganpyo)
fare	요금 (yogeum)
minibus	소형 버스 (sohyeong beoseu)
school bus	스쿨버스 (seukulbeoseu)
platform	승강장 (seung-gangjang)
locomotive	기관차 (gigwancha)
steam train	증기 기관차 (jeung-gi gigwancha)
high-speed train	고속열차 (gosog-yeolcha)
monorail	모노레일 (monoleil)
freight train	화물 기차 (hwamul gicha)
ticket office	매표소 (maepyoso)
ticket vending machine	매표기기 (maepyogigi)
railtrack	선로 (seonlo)

Plane

airport	공항 (gonghang)
emergency exit (on plane)	비상출구 (bisangchulgu)
helicopter	헬리콥터 (hellikobteo)
wing	날개 (nalgae)
engine	엔진 (enjin)
life jacket	구명조끼 (gumyeongjokki)

cockpit	조종석 (jojongseog)
row	열 (yeol)
window (in plane)	창문 (changmun)
aisle	복도 (bogdo)
glider	글라이더 (geullaideo)
cargo aircraft	화물수송기 (hwamulsusong-gi)
business class	비즈니스석 (bijeuniseuseog)
economy class	이코노미석 (ikonomiseog)
first class	일등석 (ildeungseog)
carry-on luggage	기내 휴대 수하물 (ginae hyudae suhamul)
check-in desk	체크인 데스크 (chekeu-in deseukeu)
airline	항공사 (hang-gongsa)
control tower	관제탑 (gwanjetab)
customs	관세 (gwanse)
arrival	도착 (dochag)
departure	출발 (chulbal)
runway	활주로 (hwaljulo)

Ship

harbour	항구 (hang-gu)
container	컨테이너 (keonteineo)
container ship	컨테이너선 (keonteineoseon)
yacht	요트 (yoteu)
ferry	연락선 (yeonlagseon)
anchor	닻 (dach)
rowing boat	노 젓는 배 (no jeosneun bae)
rubber boat	고무보트 (gomuboteu)
mast	돛대 (dochdae)
life buoy	구명 부표 (gumyeong bupyo)
sail	항해하다 (hanghaehada)
radar	레이더 (leideo)
deck	갑판 (gabpan)
lifeboat	구명보트 (gumyeongboteu)

bridge	다리 (dali)
engine room	기관실 (gigwansil)
cabin	객실 (gaegsil)
sailing boat	돛단배 (dochdanbae)
submarine	잠수함 (jamsuham)
aircraft carrier	항공모함 (hang-gongmoham)
cruise ship	유람선 (yulamseon)
fishing boat	어선 (eoseon)
pier	부두 (budu)
lighthouse	등대 (deungdae)
canoe	카누 (kanu)

Infrastructure

road	도로 (dolo)
motorway	고속도로 (gosogdolo)
petrol station	주유소 (juyuso)
traffic light	신호등 (sinhodeung)
construction site	공사현장 (gongsahyeonjang)
car park	주차장 (juchajang)
traffic jam	교통체증 (gyotongchejeung)
intersection	교차로 (gyochalo)
toll	통행료 (tonghaenglyo)
overpass	고가도로 (goga dolo)
underpass	지하도 (jihado)
one-way street	일방통행 (ilbangtonghaeng)
pedestrian crossing	횡단보도 (hoengdanbodo)
speed limit	속도제한 (sogdojehan)
roundabout	로터리 (loteoli)
parking meter	주차 요금 미터기 (jucha yogeum miteogi)
car wash	세차 (secha)
pavement	보도 (bodo)
rush hour	러시아워 (leosiawo)
street light	가로등 (galodeung)

Others

car	승용차 (seung-yongcha)
ship	선박 (seonbag)
plane	비행기 (bihaeng-gi)
bicycle	자전거 (jajeongeo)
taxi	택시 (taegsi)
lorry	대형 트럭 (daehyeong teuleog)
snowmobile	설상차 (seolsangcha)
cable car	케이블카 (keibeulka)
classic car	고전차 (gojeoncha)
limousine	리무진 (limujin)
motorcycle	오토바이 (otobai)
motor scooter	스쿠터 (seukuteo)
tandem	2인용 자전거 (2in-yong jajeongeo)
racing bicycle	경주용 자전거 (gyeongjuyong jajeongeo)
hot-air balloon	열기구 (yeolgigu)
caravan	여행 트레일러 (yeohaeng teuleilleo)
trailer	트레일러 (teuleilleo)
child seat	유아용 안전시트 (yuayong anjeonsiteu)
antifreeze fluid	부동액 (budong-aeg)
jack	잭 (jaeg)
chain	체인 (chein)
air pump	공기 펌프 (gong-gi peompeu)
tractor	트랙터 (teulaegteo)
combine harvester	콤바인 수확기 (kombain suhwaggi)
excavator	굴착기 (gulchaggi)
road roller	로드 롤러 (lodeu lolleo)
crane truck	기중기 트럭 (gijung-gi teuleog)
tank	탱크 (taengkeu)
concrete mixer	콘크리트 혼합기 (konkeuliteu honhabgi)
forklift truck	지게차 (jigecha)

Culture

Cinema & TV

TV	텔레비전 (tellebijeon)
cinema	영화관 (yeonghwagwan)
ticket	표 (pyo)
comedy	코미디 (komidi)
thriller	스릴러 (seulilleo)
horror movie	공포 영화 (gongpo yeonghwa)
western film	서부 (seobu)
science fiction	공상 과학 (gongsang gwahag)
cartoon	만화 (manhwa)
screen (cinema)	스크린 (seukeulin)
seat	자리 (jali)
news	뉴스 (nyuseu)
channel	채널 (chaeneol)
TV series	티비 시리즈 (tibi silijeu)

Instruments

violin	바이올린 (baiollin)
keyboard (music)	건반 (geonban)
piano	피아노 (piano)
trumpet	트럼펫 (teuleompes)
guitar	기타 (gita)
flute	플루트 (peulluteu)
harp	하프 (hapeu)
double bass	더블베이스 (deobeulbeiseu)
viola	비올라 (biolla)
cello	첼로 (chello)
oboe	오보에 (obo-e)
saxophone	색소폰 (saegsopon)
bassoon	바순 (basun)
clarinet	클라리넷 (keullalines)

tambourine	탬버린 (taembeolin)
cymbals	심벌즈 (simbeoljeu)
snare drum	스네어 드럼 (seuneeo deuleom)
kettledrum	케틀 드럼 (keteul deuleom)
triangle	트라이앵글 (teulaiaeng-geul)
trombone	트럼본 (teuleombon)
French horn	프렌치 호른 (peulenchi holeun)
tuba	튜바 (tyuba)
bass guitar	베이스 기타 (beiseu gita)
electric guitar	일렉트릭 기타 (illegteulig gita)
drums	드럼 (deuleom)
organ	오르간 (oleugan)
xylophone	실로폰 (sillopon)
accordion	아코디언 (akodieon)
ukulele	우쿨렐레 (ukullelle)
harmonica	하모니카 (hamonika)

Music

opera	오페라 (opela)
orchestra	오케스트라 (okeseuteula)
concert	콘서트 (konseoteu)
classical music	클래식 음악 (keullaesig eum-ag)
pop	팝 (pab)
jazz	재즈 (jaejeu)
blues	블루스 (beulluseu)
punk	펑크 (peongkeu)
rock (music)	록 (log)
folk music	민요 (min-yo)
heavy metal	헤비메탈 (hebimetal)
rap	랩 (laeb)
reggae	레게 (lege)
lyrics	가사 (gasa)
melody	멜로디 (mellodi)

note (music)	음표 (eumpyo)
clef	음자리표 (eumjalipyo)
symphony	심포니 (simponi)

Arts

theatre	극장 (geugjang)
stage	무대 (mudae)
audience	관객 (gwangaeg)
painting	그림 (geulim)
drawing	그림 (geulim)
palette	팔레트 (palleteu)
brush (to paint)	붓 (bus)
oil paint	오일 페인트 (oil peinteu)
origami	종이접기 (jong-ijeobgi)
pottery	도기류 (dogilyu)
woodwork	목세공 (mogsegong)
sculpting	조각하다 (jogaghada)
cast	출연진 (chul-yeonjin)
play	연극 (yeongeug)
script	대본 (daebon)
portrait	초상화 (chosanghwa)

Dancing

ballet	발레 (balle)
Viennese waltz	비엔나 왈츠 (bienna walcheu)
tango	탱고 (taeng-go)
Ballroom dance	사교 댄스 (sagyo daenseu)
Latin dance	라틴 댄스 (latin daenseu)
rock 'n' roll	록큰롤 (logkeunlol)
waltz	왈츠 (walcheu)
quickstep	퀵스텝 (kwigseuteb)
cha-cha	차차차 (chachacha)
jive	자이브 (jaibeu)

salsa	살사 (salsa)
samba	삼바 (samba)
rumba	룸바 (lumba)

Writing

newspaper	신문 (sinmun)
magazine	잡지 (jabji)
advertisement	광고 (gwang-go)
letter (like a, b, c)	글자 (geulja)
character	글자 (geulja)
text	본문 (bonmun)
flyer	광고지 (gwang-goji)
leaflet	전단지 (jeondanji)
comic book	만화책 (manhwachaeg)
article	기사 (gisa)
photo album	사진첩 (sajincheob)
newsletter	뉴스레터 (nyuseuleteo)
joke	농담 (nongdam)
Sudoku	스도쿠 (seudoku)
crosswords	십자말풀이 (sibjamalpul-i)
caricature	캐리커쳐 (kaelikeochyeo)
table of contents	목차 (mogcha)
preface	서문 (seomun)
content	내용 (naeyong)
heading	머리말 (meolimal)
publisher	출판사 (chulpansa)
novel	소설 (soseol)
textbook	교과서 (gyogwaseo)
alphabet	알파벳 (alpabes)

School

Basics

book	책 (chaeg)
dictionary	사전 (sajeon)
library	도서관 (doseogwan)
exam	시험 (siheom)
blackboard	칠판 (chilpan)
desk	책상 (chaegsang)
chalk	분필 (bunpil)
schoolyard	학교 운동장 (haggyo undongjang)
school uniform	교복 (gyobog)
schoolbag	책가방 (chaeggabang)
notebook	공책 (gongchaeg)
lesson	수업 (sueob)
homework	숙제 (sugje)
essay	수필 (supil)
term	학기 (haggi)
sports ground	체육관 (cheyuggwan)
reading room	독서실 (dogseosil)

Subjects

history	역사 (yeogsa)
science	과학 (gwahag)
physics	물리학 (mullihag)
chemistry	화학 (hwahag)
art	미술 (misul)
English	영어 (yeong-eo)
Latin	라틴어 (latin-eo)
Spanish	스페인어 (seupein-eo)
Mandarin	북경어 (buggyeong-eo)
Japanese	일본어 (ilbon-eo)
French	불어 (bul-eo)

German	독일어 (dog-il-eo)
Arabic	아랍어 (alab-eo)
literature	문학 (munhag)
geography	지리 (jili)
mathematics	수학 (suhag)
biology	생물학 (saengmulhag)
physical education	체육 (cheyug)
economics	경제학 (gyeongjehag)
philosophy	철학 (cheolhag)
politics	정치학 (jeongchihag)
geometry	기하학 (gihahag)

Stationery

pen	펜 (pen)
pencil	연필 (yeonpil)
rubber	지우개 (jiugae)
scissors	가위 (gawi)
ruler	자 (ja)
hole puncher	펀치 (peonchi)
paperclip	클립 (keullib)
ball pen	볼펜 (bolpen)
glue	풀 (pul)
adhesive tape	테이프 (teipeu)
stapler	호치키스 (hochikiseu)
oil pastel	오일 파스텔 (oil paseutel)
ink	잉크 (ingkeu)
coloured pencil	색연필 (saeg-yeonpil)
pencil sharpener	연필깎이 (yeonpilkkakk-i)
pencil case	필통 (piltong)

Mathematics

result	결과 (gyeolgwa)
addition	덧셈 (deos-sem)

subtraction	뺄셈 (ppaelsem)
multiplication	곱셈 (gobsem)
division	나눗셈 (nanus-sem)
fraction	분수 (bunsu)
numerator	분자 (bunja)
denominator	분모 (bunmo)
arithmetic	산수 (sansu)
equation	방정식 (bangjeongsig)
first	첫째 (cheosjjae)
second (2nd)	둘째 (duljjae)
third	셋째 (sesjjae)
fourth	넷째 (nesjjae)
millimeter	밀리미터 (millimiteo)
centimeter	센티미터 (sentimiteo)
decimeter	데시미터 (desimiteo)
yard	야드 (yadeu)
meter	미터 (miteo)
mile	마일 (mail)
square meter	제곱미터 (jegobmiteo)
cubic meter	세제곱미터 (sejegobmiteo)
foot	풋 (pus)
inch	인치 (inchi)
0%	영 퍼센트 (yeong peosenteu)
100%	백 퍼센트 (baeg peosenteu)
3%	삼 퍼센트 (sam peosenteu)

Geometry

circle	원 (won)
square (shape)	정사각형 (jeongsagaghyeong)
triangle	삼각형 (samgaghyeong)
height	높이 (nop-i)
width	폭 (pog)
vector	벡터 (begteo)

diagonal	대각선 (daegagseon)
radius	반지름 (banjileum)
tangent	접선 (jeobseon)
ellipse	타원 (tawon)
rectangle	직사각형 (jigsagaghyeong)
rhomboid	평행사변형 (pyeonghaengsabyeonhyeong)
octagon	팔각형 (palgaghyeong)
hexagon	육각형 (yuggaghyeong)
rhombus	마름모 (maleummo)
trapezoid	사다리꼴 (sadalikkol)
cone	원뿔 (wonppul)
cylinder	원기둥 (wongidung)
cube	정육면체 (jeong-yugmyeonche)
pyramid	피라미드 (pilamideu)
straight line	직선 (jigseon)
right angle	직각 (jiggag)
angle	각도 (gagdo)
curve	곡선 (gogseon)
volume	부피 (bupi)
area	면적 (myeonjeog)
sphere	구 (gu)

Science

gram	그램 (geulaem)
kilogram	킬로그램 (killogeulaem)
ton	톤 (ton)
liter	리터 (liteo)
volt	볼트 (bolteu)
watt	와트 (wateu)
ampere	암페어 (ampeeo)
laboratory	실험실 (silheomsil)
funnel	깔때기 (kkalttaegi)
Petri dish	페트리 접시 (peteuli jeobsi)

microscope	현미경 (hyeonmigyeong)
magnet	자석 (jaseog)
pipette	피펫 (pipes)
filter	필터 (pilteo)
pound	파운드 (paundeu)
ounce	온스 (onseu)
milliliter	밀리리터 (milliliteo)
force	힘 (him)
gravity	중력 (junglyeog)
theory of relativity	상대성 이론 (sangdaeseong ilon)

University

lecture	강의 (gang-ui)
canteen	구내식당 (gunaesigdang)
scholarship	장학금 (janghaggeum)
graduation ceremony	졸업식 (jol-eobsig)
lecture theatre	계단식 강의실 (gyedansig gang-uisil)
bachelor	학사 학위 (hagsa hag-wi)
master	석사 학위 (seogsa hag-wi)
PhD	박사 학위 (bagsa hag-wi)
diploma	졸업장 (jol-eobjang)
degree	학위 (hag-wi)
thesis	논문 (nonmun)
research	연구 (yeongu)
business school	경영대학 (gyeong-yeongdaehag)

Characters

full stop	마침표 (machimpyo)
question mark	물음표 (mul-eumpyo)
exclamation mark	느낌표 (neukkimpyo)
space	공간 (gong-gan)
colon	콜론 (kollon)
comma	쉼표 (swimpyo)

hyphen	하이픈 (haipeun)
underscore	밑줄 (mitjul)
apostrophe	아포스트로피 (aposeuteulopi)
semicolon	세미콜론 (semikollon)
()	괄호 (gwalho)
/	빗금 (bisgeum)
&	그리고 (geuligo)
...	기타 (gita)
1 + 2	일 더하기 이 (il deohagi i)
2 x 3	이 곱하기 삼 (i gobhagi sam)
3 - 2	삼 빼기 이 (sam ppaegi i)
1 + 1 = 2	일 더하기 일은 이 (il deohagi il-eun i)
4 / 2	사 나누기 이 (sa nanugi i)
4^2	사의 제곱 (saui jegob)
6^3	육의 세제곱 (yug-ui sejegob)
3 to the power of 5	삼의 오제곱 (sam-ui ojegob)
3.4	삼 점 사 (sam jeom sa)
www.pinhok.com	더블유 더블유 더블유 닷 핀혹 닷 컴 (deobeul-yu deobeul-yu deobeul-yu das pinhog das keom)
contact@pinhok.com	컨택트 골뱅이 핀혹 닷 컴 (keontaegteu golbaeng-i pinhog das keom)
x < y	x는 y보다 작다 (xneun yboda jagda)
x > y	x는 y보다 크다 (xneun yboda keuda)
x >= y	x는 y보다 크거나 같다 (xneun yboda keugeona gatda)
x <= y	x는 y보다 작거나 같다 (xneun yboda jaggeona gatda)

Nature

Elements

fire (general)	불 (bul)
soil	흙 (heulg)
ash	재 (jae)
sand	모래 (molae)
coal	석탄 (seogtan)
diamond	다이아몬드 (daiamondeu)
clay	찰흙 (chalheulg)
chalk	분필 (bunpil)
limestone	석회석 (seoghoeseog)
granite	화강암 (hwagang-am)
ruby	루비 (lubi)
opal	오팔 (opal)
jade	옥 (og)
sapphire	사파이어 (sapaieo)
quartz	석영 (seog-yeong)
calcite	방해석 (banghaeseog)
graphite	흑연 (heug-yeon)
lava	용암 (yong-am)
magma	마그마 (mageuma)

Universe

planet	행성 (haengseong)
star	별 (byeol)
sun	태양 (taeyang)
earth	지구 (jigu)
moon	달 (dal)
rocket	로켓 (lokes)
Mercury	수성 (suseong)
Venus	금성 (geumseong)
Mars	화성 (hwaseong)

Jupiter	목성 (mogseong)
Saturn	토성 (toseong)
Neptune	해왕성 (haewangseong)
Uranus	천왕성 (cheon-wangseong)
Pluto	명왕성 (myeong-wangseong)
comet	혜성 (hyeseong)
asteroid	소행성 (sohaengseong)
galaxy	은하계 (eunhagye)
Milky Way	우리은하 (ulieunha)
lunar eclipse	월식 (wolsig)
solar eclipse	일식 (ilsig)
meteorite	운석 (unseog)
black hole	블랙홀 (beullaeghol)
satellite	위성 (wiseong)
space station	우주 정거장 (uju jeong-geojang)
space shuttle	우주 왕복선 (uju wangbogseon)
telescope	망원경 (mang-wongyeong)

Earth (1)

equator	적도 (jeogdo)
North Pole	북극 (buggeug)
South Pole	남극 (namgeug)
tropics	열대 (yeoldae)
northern hemisphere	북반구 (bugbangu)
southern hemisphere	남반구 (nambangu)
longitude	경도 (gyeongdo)
latitude	위도 (wido)
Pacific Ocean	태평양 (taepyeong-yang)
Atlantic Ocean	대서양 (daeseoyang)
Mediterranean Sea	지중해 (jijunghae)
Black Sea	흑해 (heughae)
Sahara	사하라 (sahala)
Himalayas	히말라야 (himallaya)

Indian Ocean	인도양 (indoyang)
Red Sea	홍해 (honghae)
Amazon	아마존 (amajon)
Andes	안데스 산맥 (andeseu sanmaeg)
continent	대륙 (daelyug)

Earth (2)

sea	바다 (bada)
island	섬 (seom)
mountain	산 (san)
river	강 (gang)
forest	숲 (sup)
desert (dry place)	사막 (samag)
lake	호수 (hosu)
volcano	화산 (hwasan)
cave	동굴 (dong-gul)
pole	극 (geug)
ocean	해양 (haeyang)
peninsula	반도 (bando)
atmosphere	대기 (daegi)
earth's crust	지각 (jigag)
earth's core	지구핵 (jiguhaeg)
mountain range	산맥 (sanmaeg)
crater	분화구 (bunhwagu)
earthquake	지진 (jijin)
tidal wave	해일 (haeil)
glacier	빙하 (bingha)
valley	계곡 (gyegog)
slope	경사면 (gyeongsamyeon)
shore	해안 (haean)
waterfall	폭포 (pogpo)
rock (stone)	바위 (bawi)
hill	언덕 (eondeog)

canyon	협곡 (hyeobgog)
marsh	습지 (seubji)
rainforest	우림 (ulim)
stream	시내 (sinae)
geyser	간헐 온천 (ganheol oncheon)
coast	해안가 (haeanga)
cliff	절벽 (jeolbyeog)
coral reef	산호초 (sanhocho)
aurora	오로라 (olola)

Weather

rain	비 (bi)
snow	눈 (nun)
ice	얼음 (eol-eum)
wind	바람 (balam)
storm	폭풍 (pogpung)
cloud	구름 (guleum)
thunderstorm	뇌우 (noeu)
lightning	번개 (beongae)
thunder	천둥 (cheondung)
sunshine	햇빛 (haesbich)
hurricane	허리케인 (heolikein)
typhoon	태풍 (taepung)
temperature	온도 (ondo)
humidity	습도 (seubdo)
air pressure	기압 (giab)
rainbow	무지개 (mujigae)
fog	안개 (angae)
flood	홍수 (hongsu)
monsoon	우기 (ugi)
tornado	토네이도 (toneido)
centigrade	섭씨 (seobssi)
Fahrenheit	화씨 (hwassi)

-2 °C	섭씨 영하 이도 (seobssi yeongha ido)
0 °C	섭씨 영도 (seobssi yeongdo)
12 °C	섭씨 십이도 (seobssi sib-ido)
-4 °F	화씨 영하 사도 (hwassi yeongha sado)
0 °F	화씨 영도 (hwassi yeongdo)
30 °F	화씨 삼십도 (hwassi samsibdo)

Trees

tree	나무 (namu)
trunk	줄기 (julgi)
root	뿌리 (ppuli)
leaf	잎 (ip)
branch	나뭇가지 (namusgaji)
bamboo (plant)	대나무 (daenamu)
oak	오크 (okeu)
eucalyptus	유칼립투스 (yukallibtuseu)
pine	소나무 (sonamu)
birch	자작나무 (jajagnamu)
larch	낙엽송 (nag-yeobsong)
beech	너도밤나무 (neodobamnamu)
palm tree	야자수 (yajasu)
maple	단풍나무 (danpungnamu)
willow	버드나무 (beodeunamu)

Plants

flower	꽃 (kkoch)
grass	잔디 (jandi)
cactus	선인장 (seon-injang)
stalk	줄기 (julgi)
blossom	꽃 (kkoch)
seed	씨앗 (ssias)
petal	꽃잎 (kkoch-ip)
nectar	꽃꿀 (kkochkkul)

sunflower	해바라기 (haebalagi)
tulip	튤립 (tyullib)
rose	장미 (jangmi)
daffodil	수선화 (suseonhwa)
dandelion	민들레 (mindeulle)
buttercup	미나리아재비 (minaliajaebi)
reed	갈대 (galdae)
fern	양치식물 (yangchisigmul)
weed	잡초 (jabcho)
bush	관목 (gwanmog)
acacia	아카시아 (akasia)
daisy	데이지 (deiji)
iris	붓꽃 (buskkoch)
gladiolus	글라디올러스 (geulladiolleoseu)
clover	클로버 (keullobeo)
seaweed	미역 (miyeog)

Chemistry

gas	기체 (giche)
fluid	액체 (aegche)
solid	고체 (goche)
atom	원자 (wonja)
metal	금속 (geumsog)
plastic	플라스틱 (peullaseutig)
atomic number	원자 번호 (wonja beonho)
electron	전자 (jeonja)
neutron	중성자 (jungseongja)
proton	양성자 (yangseongja)
non-metal	비금속 (bigeumsog)
metalloid	반금속 (bangeumsog)
isotope	동위 원소 (dong-wi wonso)
molecule	분자 (bunja)
ion	이온 (ion)

chemical reaction	화학 반응 (hwahag ban-eung)
chemical compound	화합물 (hwahabmul)
chemical structure	화학 구조 (hwahag gujo)
periodic table	주기율표 (jugiyulpyo)
carbon dioxide	이산화탄소 (isanhwatanso)
carbon monoxide	일산화탄소 (ilsanhwatanso)
methane	메탄 (metan)

Periodic Table (1)

hydrogen	수소 (suso)
helium	헬륨 (hellyum)
lithium	리튬 (lityum)
beryllium	베릴륨 (belillyum)
boron	붕소 (bungso)
carbon	탄소 (tanso)
nitrogen	질소 (jilso)
oxygen	산소 (sanso)
fluorine	플루오르 (peulluoleu)
neon	네온 (ne-on)
sodium	나트륨 (nateulyum)
magnesium	마그네슘 (mageunesyum)
aluminium	알루미늄 (alluminyum)
silicon	규소 (gyuso)
phosphorus	인 (in)
sulphur	황 (hwang)
chlorine	염소 (yeomso)
argon	아르곤 (aleugon)
potassium	칼륨 (kallyum)
calcium	칼슘 (kalsyum)
scandium	스칸듐 (seukandyum)
titanium	타이타늄 (taitanyum)
vanadium	바나듐 (banadyum)
chromium	크로뮴 (keulomyum)

manganese	망간 (mang-gan)
iron	철 (cheol)
cobalt	코발트 (kobalteu)
nickel	니켈 (nikel)
copper	구리 (guli)
zinc	아연 (ayeon)
gallium	갈륨 (gallyum)
germanium	게르마늄 (geleumanyum)
arsenic	비소 (biso)
selenium	셀레늄 (sellenyum)
bromine	브로민 (beulomin)
krypton	크립톤 (keulibton)
rubidium	루비듐 (lubidyum)
strontium	스트론튬 (seuteulontyum)
yttrium	이트륨 (iteulyum)
zirconium	지르코늄 (jileukonyum)

Periodic Table (2)

niobium	나이오븀 (naiobyum)
molybdenum	몰리브데넘 (mollibeudeneom)
technetium	테크네튬 (tekeunetyum)
ruthenium	루테늄 (lutenyum)
rhodium	로듐 (lodyum)
palladium	팔라듐 (palladyum)
silver	은 (eun)
cadmium	카드뮴 (kadeumyum)
indium	인듐 (indyum)
tin	주석 (juseog)
antimony	안티모니 (antimoni)
tellurium	텔루륨 (tellulyum)
iodine	요오드 (yoodeu)
xenon	제논 (jenon)
caesium	세슘 (sesyum)

barium	바륨 (balyum)
lanthanum	란타넘 (lantaneom)
cerium	세륨 (selyum)
praseodymium	프라세오디뮴 (peulase-odimyum)
neodymium	네오디뮴 (ne-odimyum)
promethium	프로메튬 (peulometyum)
samarium	사마륨 (samalyum)
europium	유로퓸 (yulopyum)
gadolinium	가돌리늄 (gadollinyum)
terbium	터븀 (teobyum)
dysprosium	디스프로슘 (diseupeulosyum)
holmium	홀뮴 (holmyum)
erbium	어븀 (eobyum)
thulium	툴륨 (tullyum)
ytterbium	이터븀 (iteobyum)
lutetium	루테튬 (lutetyum)
hafnium	하프늄 (hapeunyum)
tantalum	탄탈럼 (tantalleom)
tungsten	텅스텐 (teongseuten)
rhenium	레늄 (lenyum)
osmium	오스뮴 (oseumyum)
iridium	이리듐 (ilidyum)
platinum	백금 (baeggeum)
gold	금 (geum)
mercury	수은 (sueun)

Periodic Table (3)

thallium	탈륨 (tallyum)
lead	납 (nab)
bismuth	비스무트 (biseumuteu)
polonium	폴로늄 (pollonyum)
astatine	아스타틴 (aseutatin)
radon	라돈 (ladon)

francium	프란슘 (peulansyum)
radium	라듐 (ladyum)
actinium	악티늄 (agtinyum)
thorium	토륨 (tolyum)
protactinium	프로트악티늄 (peuloteuagtinyum)
uranium	우라늄 (ulanyum)
neptunium	넵투늄 (nebtunyum)
plutonium	플루토늄 (peullutonyum)
americium	아메리슘 (amelisyum)
curium	퀴륨 (kwilyum)
berkelium	버클륨 (beokeullyum)
californium	칼리포르늄 (kallipoleunyum)
einsteinium	아인슈타이늄 (ainsyutainyum)
fermium	페르뮴 (peleumyum)
mendelevium	멘델레븀 (mendellebyum)
nobelium	노벨륨 (nobellyum)
lawrencium	로렌슘 (lolensyum)
rutherfordium	러더포듐 (leodeopodyum)
dubnium	더브늄 (deobeunyum)
seaborgium	시보귬 (sibogyum)
bohrium	보륨 (bolyum)
hassium	하슘 (hasyum)
meitnerium	마이트너륨 (maiteuneolyum)
darmstadtium	다름스타튬 (daleumseutatyum)
roentgenium	뢴트게늄 (loenteugenyum)
copernicium	코페르니슘 (kopeleunisyum)
ununtrium	우눈트륨 (ununteulyum)
flerovium	플레로븀 (peullelobyum)
ununpentium	우눈펜튬 (ununpentyum)
livermorium	리버모륨 (libeomolyum)
ununseptium	우눈셉튬 (ununsebtyum)
ununoctium	우누녹튬 (ununogtyum)

Clothes

Shoes

flip-flops	쪼리 (jjoli)
high heels	하이힐 (haihil)
trainers	운동화 (undonghwa)
wellington boots	장화 (janghwa)
sandals	샌들 (saendeul)
leather shoes	가죽신발 (gajugsinbal)
heel	굽 (gub)
sole	구두밑창 (gudumitchang)
lace	신발 끈 (sinbal kkeun)
slippers	슬리퍼 (seullipeo)
bathroom slippers	화장실슬리퍼 (hwajangsilseullipeo)
football boots	축구화 (chugguhwa)
skates	스케이트 (seukeiteu)
hiking boots	등산화 (deungsanhwa)
ballet shoes	발레화 (ballehwa)
dancing shoes	댄스화 (daenseuhwa)

Clothes

T-shirt	티셔츠 (tisyeocheu)
shorts	반바지 (banbaji)
trousers	바지 (baji)
jeans	청바지 (cheongbaji)
sweater	스웨터 (seuweteo)
shirt	셔츠 (syeocheu)
suit	양복 (yangbog)
dress	드레스 (deuleseu)
skirt	치마 (chima)
coat	코트 (koteu)
anorak	아노락 (anolag)
jacket	자켓 (jakes)

leggings	레깅스 (legingseu)
sweatpants	트레이닝바지 (teuleiningbaji)
tracksuit	운동복 (undongbog)
polo shirt	폴로셔츠 (pollosyeocheu)
jersey	저지 (jeoji)
diaper	기저귀 (gijeogwi)
wedding dress	웨딩드레스 (wedingdeuleseu)
bathrobe	목욕가운 (mog-yoggaun)
cardigan	가디건 (gadigeon)
blazer	블레이저 (beulleijeo)
raincoat	우비 (ubi)
evening dress	이브닝 드레스 (ibeuning deuleseu)
ski suit	스키복 (seukibog)
space suit	우주복 (ujubog)

Underwear

bra	브라 (beula)
thong	티팬티 (tipaenti)
panties	팬티 (paenti)
underpants	팬티 (paenti)
undershirt	속셔츠 (sogsyeocheu)
sock	양말 (yangmal)
pantyhose	팬티스타킹 (paentiseutaking)
stocking	스타킹 (seutaking)
thermal underwear	내복 (naebog)
pyjamas	잠옷 (jam-os)
jogging bra	스포츠브라 (seupocheubeula)
negligee	네글리제 (negeullije)
little black dress	리틀 블랙 드레스 (liteul beullaeg deuleseu)
nightie	잠옷 (jam-os)
lingerie	란제리 (lanjeli)

Accessory

glasses	안경 (angyeong)
sunglasses	선글라스 (seongeullaseu)
umbrella	우산 (usan)
ring	반지 (banji)
earring	귀걸이 (gwigeol-i)
wallet	지갑 (jigab)
watch	손목시계 (sonmogsigye)
belt	벨트 (belteu)
handbag	핸드백 (haendeubaeg)
glove	장갑 (jang-gab)
scarf	스카프 (seukapeu)
hat	모자 (moja)
necklace	목걸이 (moggeol-i)
purse	여성용 지갑 (yeoseong-yong jigab)
knit cap	비니 (bini)
tie	넥타이 (negtai)
bow tie	나비넥타이 (nabinegtai)
baseball cap	야구 모자 (yagu moja)
brooch	브로치 (beulochi)
bracelet	팔찌 (paljji)
pearl necklace	진주목걸이 (jinjumoggeol-i)
briefcase	서류가방 (seolyugabang)
contact lens	콘택트 렌즈 (kontaegteu lenjeu)
sun hat	모자 (moja)
sleeping mask	수면 마스크 (sumyeon maseukeu)
earplug	귀마개 (gwimagae)
tattoo	타투 (tatu)
bib	턱받이 (teogbad-i)
shower cap	샤워캡 (syawokaeb)
medal	훈장 (hunjang)
crown	왕관 (wang-gwan)

Sport

helmet	헬멧 (helmes)
boxing glove	권투장갑 (gwontujang-gab)
fin	오리발 (olibal)
swim trunks	남성용 사각 수영복 (namseong-yong sagag suyeongbog)
bikini	비키니 (bikini)
swimsuit	수영복 (suyeongbog)
shinpad	신 패드 (sin paedeu)
sweatband	땀흡수밴드 (ttamheubsubaendeu)
swim goggles	고글 (gogeul)
swim cap	수영모 (suyeongmo)
wetsuit	잠수복 (jamsubog)
diving mask	다이빙 마스크 (daibing maseukeu)

Hairstyle

curly	곱슬곱슬한 (gobseulgobseulhan)
straight (hair)	직모의 (jigmoui)
bald head	대머리 (daemeoli)
blond	금발의 (geumbal-ui)
brunette	갈색머리의 (galsaegmeoliui)
ginger	붉은머리의 (bulg-eunmeoliui)
scrunchy	헤어밴드 (heeobaendeu)
barrette	머리핀 (meolipin)
dreadlocks	레게머리 (legemeoli)
hair straightener	고데기 (godegi)
dandruff	비듬 (bideum)
dyed	염색머리 (yeomsaegmeoli)
wig	가발 (gabal)
ponytail	포니테일 (poniteil)

Others

button	단추 (danchu)
zipper	지퍼 (jipeo)
pocket	주머니 (jumeoni)

sleeve	소매 (somae)
collar	깃 (gis)
tape measure	줄자 (julja)
mannequin	마네킹 (maneking)
cotton	솜 (som)
fabric	천 (cheon)
silk	비단 (bidan)
nylon	나일론 (naillon)
polyester	폴리에스테르 (pollieseuteleu)
wool	양모 (yangmo)
dress size	드레스 사이즈 (deuleseu saijeu)
changing room	탈의실 (tal-uisil)

Chemist

Women

perfume	향수 (hyangsu)
tampon	탐폰 (tampon)
panty liner	팬티라이너 (paentilaineo)
face mask	얼굴 마스크 (eolgul maseukeu)
sanitary towel	생리대 (saenglidae)
curling iron	컬 고데기 (keol godegi)
antiwrinkle cream	노화방지 크림 (nohwabangji keulim)
pedicure	페디큐어 (pedikyueo)
manicure	매니큐어 (maenikyueo)

Men

razor	면도기 (myeondogi)
shaving foam	면도용 거품 (myeondoyong geopum)
shaver	전기 면도기 (jeongi myeondogi)
condom	콘돔 (kondom)
shower gel	샤워젤 (syawojel)
nail clipper	손톱깎이 (sontobkkakk-i)
aftershave	애프터셰이브 (aepeuteosyeibeu)
lubricant	윤활제 (yunhwalje)
hair gel	헤어 젤 (heeo jel)
nail scissors	손톱가위 (sontobgawi)
lip balm	립밤 (libbam)
razor blade	면도날 (myeondonal)

Daily Use

toothbrush	칫솔 (chis-sol)
toothpaste	치약 (chiyag)
comb	빗 (bis)
tissue	휴지 (hyuji)
cream (pharmaceutical)	크림 (keulim)
shampoo	샴푸 (syampu)

brush (for cleaning)	빗 (bis)
body lotion	바디로션 (badilosyeon)
face cream	얼굴로션 (eolgullosyeon)
sunscreen	자외선 차단제 (jaoeseon chadanje)
insect repellent	방충제 (bangchungje)

Cosmetics

lipstick	립스틱 (libseutig)
mascara	마스카라 (maseukala)
nail polish	매니큐어 (maenikyueo)
foundation	파운데이션 (paundeisyeon)
nail file	손톱 다듬는 줄 (sontob dadeumneun jul)
eye shadow	아이섀도우 (aisyaedou)
eyeliner	아이라이너 (ailaineo)
eyebrow pencil	브로우 펜슬 (beulou penseul)
facial toner	토너 (toneo)
nail varnish remover	매니큐어 리무버 (maenikyueo limubeo)
tweezers	족집게 (jogjibge)
lip gloss	립글로스 (libgeulloseu)
concealer	컨실러 (keonsilleo)
face powder	얼굴 파우더 (eolgul paudeo)
powder puff	파우더 퍼프 (paudeo peopeu)

City

Shopping

bill	송장 (songjang)
cash register	계산대 (gyesandae)
basket	바구니 (baguni)
market	시장 (sijang)
supermarket	슈퍼마켓 (syupeomakes)
pharmacy	약국 (yaggug)
furniture store	가구점 (gagujeom)
toy shop	장난감 가게 (jangnangam gage)
shopping mall	쇼핑센터 (syopingsenteo)
sports shop	스포츠 용품점 (seupocheu yongpumjeom)
fish market	생선가게 (saengseongage)
fruit merchant	과일 상인 (gwail sang-in)
bookshop	서점 (seojeom)
pet shop	애완동물 가게 (aewandongmul gage)
second-hand shop	중고품 가게 (jung-gopum gage)
pedestrian area	보행자 구역 (bohaengja guyeog)
square	광장 (gwangjang)
shopping cart	쇼핑카트 (syopingkateu)
bar code	바코드 (bakodeu)
bargain	바겐세일 (bagenseil)
shopping basket	쇼핑바구니 (syopingbaguni)
warranty	보증서 (bojeungseo)
bar code scanner	바코드 판독기 (bakodeu pandoggi)

Buildings

house	집 (jib)
apartment	아파트 (apateu)
skyscraper	고층건물 (gocheung-geonmul)
hospital	병원 (byeong-won)
farm	농장 (nongjang)

factory	공장 (gongjang)
kindergarten	유치원 (yuchiwon)
school	학교 (haggyo)
university	대학교 (daehaggyo)
post office	우체국 (uchegug)
town hall	시청 (sicheong)
warehouse	창고 (chang-go)
church	교회 (gyohoe)
mosque	모스크 (moseukeu)
temple	절 (jeol)
synagogue	시나고그 (sinagogeu)
embassy	대사관 (daesagwan)
cathedral	성당 (seongdang)
ruin	폐허 (pyeheo)
castle	성 (seong)

Leisure

bar	술집 (suljib)
restaurant	레스토랑 (leseutolang)
gym	체육관 (cheyuggwan)
park	공원 (gong-won)
bench	벤치 (benchi)
fountain	분수대 (bunsudae)
tennis court	테니스코트 (teniseukoteu)
swimming pool (building)	수영장 (suyeongjang)
football stadium	축구 경기장 (chuggu gyeong-gijang)
golf course	골프장 (golpeujang)
ski resort	스키 지역 (seuki jiyeog)
botanic garden	식물원 (sigmul-won)
ice rink	아이스링크 (aiseulingkeu)
night club	나이트클럽 (naiteukeulleob)

Tourism

museum	박물관 (bagmulgwan)
casino	카지노 (kajino)
tourist information	관광 안내소 (gwangwang annaeso)
toilet (public)	변기 (byeongi)
map	지도 (jido)
souvenir	기념품 (ginyeompum)
promenade	산책로 (sanchaeglo)
tourist attraction	관광명소 (gwangwangmyeongso)
tourist guide	가이드 (gaideu)
monument	기념물 (ginyeommul)
national park	국립공원 (guglibgong-won)
art gallery	화랑 (hwalang)

Infrastructure

alley	골목 (golmog)
manhole cover	맨홀 뚜껑 (maenhol ttukkeong)
dam	댐 (daem)
power line	송전선 (songjeonseon)
sewage plant	폐수처리장 (pyesucheolijang)
avenue	거리 (geoli)
hydroelectric power station	수력발전소 (sulyeogbaljeonso)
nuclear power plant	원자력발전소 (wonjalyeogbaljeonso)
wind farm	풍력 발전소 (punglyeog baljeonso)

Construction

hammer	망치 (mangchi)
nail	못 (mos)
pincers	펜치 (penchi)
screwdriver	스크류 드라이버 (seukeulyu deulaibeo)
drilling machine	드릴 (deulil)
tape measure	줄자 (julja)
brick	벽돌 (byeogdol)
putty	퍼티 (peoti)

scaffolding	비계 (bigye)
spirit level	기포관수준기 (gipogwansujungi)
utility knife	다용도칼 (dayongdokal)
screw wrench	스크류 렌치 (seukeulyu lenchi)
file	줄 (jul)
smoothing plane	대패 (daepae)
safety glasses	보안경 (boangyeong)
wire	철사 (cheolsa)
handsaw	가는톱 (ganeuntob)
insulating tape	절연 테이프 (jeol-yeon teipeu)
cement	시멘트 (simenteu)
inking roller	잉크 롤러 (ingkeu lolleo)
paint	페인트 (peinteu)
pallet	파렛트 (palesteu)
cement mixer	시멘트 혼합기 (simenteu honhabgi)
steel beam	강철 빔 (gangcheol bim)
roof tile	기와 (giwa)
wooden beam	나무 빔 (namu bim)
concrete	콘크리트 (konkeuliteu)
asphalt	아스팔트 (aseupalteu)
tar	타르 (taleu)
crane	기중기 (gijung-gi)
steel	강철 (gangcheol)
varnish	래커 (laekeo)

Kids

slide	미끄럼틀 (mikkeuleomteul)
swing	그네 (geune)
playground	놀이터 (nol-iteo)
zoo	동물원 (dongmul-won)
roller coaster	롤러코스터 (lolleokoseuteo)
water slide	워터 슬라이드 (woteo seullaideu)
sandbox	모래 상자 (molae sangja)

fairground	축제마당 (chugjemadang)
theme park	놀이공원 (nol-igong-won)
water park	워터파크 (woteopakeu)
aquarium	수족관 (sujoggwan)
carousel	회전목마 (hoejeonmogma)

Ambulance

ambulance	응급차 (eung-geubcha)
police	경찰 (gyeongchal)
firefighters	소방관 (sobang-gwan)
helmet	헬멧 (helmes)
fire extinguisher	소화기 (sohwagi)
fire (emergency)	화재 (hwajae)
emergency exit (in building)	비상 출구 (bisang chulgu)
handcuff	수갑 (sugab)
gun	권총 (gwonchong)
police station	경찰서 (gyeongchalseo)
hydrant	소화전 (sohwajeon)
fire alarm	화재경보기 (hwajaegyeongbogi)
fire station	소방서 (sobangseo)
fire truck	소방차 (sobangcha)
siren	사이렌 (sailen)
warning light	경고등 (gyeong-godeung)
police car	경찰차 (gyeongchalcha)
uniform	유니폼 (yunipom)
baton	경찰봉 (gyeongchalbong)

More

village	마을 (ma-eul)
suburb	교외 (gyooe)
state	주 (ju)
colony	식민지 (sigminji)
region	지역 (jiyeog)

district	구역 (guyeog)
territory	영토 (yeongto)
province	지방 (jibang)
country	국가 (gugga)
capital	수도 (sudo)
metropolis	메트로폴리스 (meteulopolliseu)
central business district (CBD)	중앙업무지구 (jung-ang-eobmujigu)
industrial district	산업지구 (san-eobjigu)

Health

Hospital

patient	환자 (hwanja)
visitor	방문자 (bangmunja)
surgery	수술 (susul)
waiting room	대기실 (daegisil)
outpatient	외래환자 (oelaehwanja)
clinic	진료소 (jinlyoso)
visiting hours	방문시간 (bangmunsigan)
intensive care unit	중환자실 (junghwanjasil)
emergency room	응급실 (eung-geubsil)
appointment	예약 (yeyag)
operating theatre	수술실 (susulsil)
canteen	구내식당 (gunaesigdang)

Medicine

pill	알약 (al-yag)
capsule	캡슐 (kaebsyul)
infusion	수액 (suaeg)
inhaler	흡입기 (heub-ibgi)
nasal spray	비강 스프레이 (bigang seupeulei)
painkiller	진통제 (jintongje)
Chinese medicine	중의학 (jung-uihag)
antibiotics	항생제 (hangsaengje)
antiseptic	소독제 (sodogje)
vitamin	비타민 (bitamin)
powder	가루 (galu)
insulin	인슐린 (insyullin)
side effect	부작용 (bujag-yong)
cough syrup	기침약 (gichim-yag)
dosage	복용량 (bog-yonglyang)
expiry date	유효기간 (yuhyogigan)

sleeping pill	수면제 (sumyeonje)
aspirin	아스피린 (aseupilin)

Disease

virus	바이러스 (baileoseu)
bacterium	박테리아 (bagtelia)
flu	독감 (doggam)
diarrhea	설사 (seolsa)
heart attack	심장 마비 (simjang mabi)
asthma	천식 (cheonsig)
rash	두드러기 (dudeuleogi)
chickenpox	수두 (sudu)
nausea	메스꺼움 (meseukkeoum)
cancer	암 (am)
stroke	뇌졸중 (noejoljung)
diabetes	당뇨병 (dangnyobyeong)
epilepsy	간질 (ganjil)
measles	홍역 (hong-yeog)
mumps	볼거리 (bolgeoli)
migraine	편두통 (pyeondutong)

Discomfort

cough	기침 (gichim)
fever	열 (yeol)
headache	두통 (dutong)
stomach ache	복통 (bogtong)
sunburn	햇볕에 탐 (haesbyeot-e tam)
cold (sickness)	감기 (gamgi)
nosebleed	코피 (kopi)
cramp	경련 (gyeonglyeon)
eczema	습진 (seubjin)
high blood pressure	고혈압 (gohyeol-ab)
infection	감염 (gam-yeom)

allergy	알레르기 (alleleugi)
hay fever	건초열 (geonchoyeol)
sore throat	인후염 (inhuyeom)
poisoning	중독 (jungdog)
toothache	치통 (chitong)
caries	충치 (chungchi)
hemorrhoid	치질 (chijil)

Tools

needle	바늘 (baneul)
syringe (tool)	주사기 (jusagi)
bandage	붕대 (bungdae)
plaster	깁스 (gibseu)
cast	깁스 (gibseu)
crutch	목발 (mogbal)
wheelchair	휠체어 (hwilcheeo)
fever thermometer	체온계 (che-ongye)
dental brace	교정기 (gyojeong-gi)
neck brace	목 보호대 (mog bohodae)
stethoscope	청진기 (cheongjingi)
CT scanner	CT 스캐너 (CT seukaeneo)
catheter	카테터 (kateteo)
scalpel	메스 (meseu)
respiratory machine	호흡기 (hoheubgi)
blood test	혈액 검사 (hyeol-aeg geomsa)
ultrasound machine	초음파 기기 (cho-eumpa gigi)
X-ray photograph	엑스레이 사진 (egseulei sajin)
dental prostheses	의치 (uichi)
dental filling	아말감 (amalgam)
spray	스프레이 (seupeulei)
magnetic resonance imaging	자기공명영상 (jagigongmyeong-yeongsang)

Accident

injury	부상 (busang)
accident	사고 (sago)
wound	상처 (sangcheo)
pulse	맥박 (maegbag)
fracture	골절 (goljeol)
bruise	멍 (meong)
burn	화상 (hwasang)
bite	물린 상처 (mullin sangcheo)
electric shock	전기 충격 (jeongi chung-gyeog)
suture	봉합선 (bonghabseon)
concussion	뇌진탕 (noejintang)
head injury	두부 외상 (dubu oesang)
emergency	응급 (eung-geub)

Departments

cardiology	심장학 (simjanghag)
orthopaedics	정형외과 (jeonghyeong-oegwa)
gynaecology	산부인과 (sanbu-ingwa)
radiology	방사선과 (bangsaseongwa)
dermatology	피부과 (pibugwa)
paediatrics	소아과 (soagwa)
psychiatry	정신과 (jeongsingwa)
surgery	외과 (oegwa)
urology	비뇨기과 (binyogigwa)
neurology	신경과 (singyeong-gwa)
endocrinology	내분비학 (naebunbihag)
pathology	병리학 (byeonglihag)
oncology	종양학 (jong-yanghag)

Therapy

massage	마사지 (masaji)
meditation	명상 (myeongsang)
acupuncture	침술 (chimsul)

physiotherapy	물리치료 (mullichilyo)
hypnosis	최면 (choemyeon)
homoeopathy	동종요법 (dongjong-yobeob)
aromatherapy	아로마 테라피 (aloma telapi)
group therapy	집단 요법 (jibdan yobeob)
psychotherapy	심리치료 (simlichilyo)
feng shui	풍수 (pungsu)
hydrotherapy	수 치료법 (su chilyobeob)
behaviour therapy	행동 치료 (haengdong chilyo)
psychoanalysis	정신 분석 (jeongsin bunseog)
family therapy	가족 요법 (gajog yobeob)

Pregnancy

birth control pill	피임약 (piim-yag)
pregnancy test	임신 검사 (imsin geomsa)
foetus	태아 (taea)
embryo	배아 (baea)
womb	자궁 (jagung)
delivery	분만 (bunman)
miscarriage	유산 (yusan)
cesarean	제왕절개 (jewangjeolgae)
episiotomy	외음 절개술 (oeeum jeolgaesul)

Business

Company

office	사무실 (samusil)
meeting room	회의실 (hoeuisil)
business card	명함 (myeongham)
employee	직원 (jig-won)
employer	고용주 (goyongju)
colleague	동료 (donglyo)
staff	직원 (jig-won)
salary	월급 (wolgeub)
insurance	보험 (boheom)
department	부서 (buseo)
sales	영업 (yeong-eob)
marketing	마케팅 (maketing)
accounting	회계 (hoegye)
legal department	법무부 (beobmubu)
human resources	인사부 (insabu)
IT	정보기술 (jeongbogisul)
stress	스트레스 (seuteuleseu)
business dinner	회식 (hoesig)
business trip	출장 (chuljang)
tax	세금 (segeum)

Office

letter (post)	편지 (pyeonji)
envelope	봉투 (bongtu)
stamp	우표 (upyo)
address	주소 (juso)
zip code	우편번호 (upyeonbeonho)
parcel	소포 (sopo)
fax	팩스 (paegseu)
text message	문자 메시지 (munja mesiji)

voice message	음성메시지 (eumseongmesiji)
bulletin board	게시판 (gesipan)
flip chart	플립 차트 (peullib chateu)
projector	프로젝터 (peulojegteo)
rubber stamp	고무도장 (gomudojang)
clipboard	클립보드 (keullibbodeu)
folder (physical)	서류철 (seolyucheol)
lecturer	강연자 (gang-yeonja)
presentation	프레젠테이션 (peulejenteisyeon)
note (information)	필기 (pilgi)

Jobs (1)

doctor	의사 (uisa)
policeman	경찰 (gyeongchal)
firefighter	소방관 (sobang-gwan)
nurse	간호사 (ganhosa)
pilot	조종사 (jojongsa)
stewardess	승무원 (seungmuwon)
architect	건축가 (geonchugga)
manager	매니저 (maenijeo)
secretary	비서 (biseo)
general manager	총지배인 (chongjibaein)
director	이사 (isa)
chairman	회장 (hoejang)
judge	판사 (pansa)
assistant	조수 (josu)
prosecutor	검사 (geomsa)
lawyer	변호사 (byeonhosa)
consultant	컨설턴트 (keonseolteonteu)
accountant	회계사 (hoegyesa)
stockbroker	증권 중개인 (jeung-gwon jung-gaein)
librarian	사서 (saseo)
teacher	선생님 (seonsaengnim)

kindergarten teacher	유치원 선생님 (yuchiwon seonsaengnim)
scientist	과학자 (gwahagja)
professor	교수 (gyosu)
physicist	물리학자 (mullihagja)
programmer	프로그래머 (peulogeulaemeo)
politician	정치가 (jeongchiga)
intern	인턴 (inteon)
captain	선장 (seonjang)
entrepreneur	사업가 (sa-eobga)
chemist	화학자 (hwahagja)
dentist	치과의사 (chigwauisa)
chiropractor	척추지압사 (cheogchujiabsa)
detective	형사 (hyeongsa)
pharmacist	약사 (yagsa)
vet	수의사 (suuisa)
midwife	조산사 (josansa)
surgeon	외과의사 (oegwauisa)
physician	내과의사 (naegwauisa)
prime minister	국무 총리 (gugmu chongli)
minister	장관 (jang-gwan)
president (of a state)	대통령 (daetonglyeong)

Jobs (2)

cook	요리사 (yolisa)
waiter	웨이터 (weiteo)
barkeeper	바텐더 (batendeo)
farmer	농부 (nongbu)
lorry driver	트럭기사 (teuleoggisa)
train driver	기차 운전사 (gicha unjeonsa)
hairdresser	미용사 (miyongsa)
butcher	푸주한 (pujuhan)
travel agent	여행사 직원 (yeohaengsa jig-won)
real-estate agent	부동산중개인 (budongsanjung-gaein)

jeweller	보석상 (boseogsang)
tailor	재단사 (jaedansa)
cashier	출납원 (chulnab-won)
postman	집배원 (jibbaewon)
receptionist	접수담당자 (jeobsudamdangja)
construction worker	건설 노동자 (geonseol nodongja)
carpenter	목수 (mogsu)
electrician	전기기사 (jeongigisa)
plumber	배관공 (baegwangong)
mechanic	정비공 (jeongbigong)
cleaner	청소부 (cheongsobu)
gardener	정원사 (jeong-wonsa)
fisherman	어부 (eobu)
florist	플로리스트 (peulloliseuteu)
shop assistant	점원 (jeom-won)
optician	안경사 (angyeongsa)
soldier	병사 (byeongsa)
security guard	경비원 (gyeongbiwon)
bus driver	버스기사 (beoseugisa)
taxi driver	택시기사 (taegsigisa)
conductor	차장 (chajang)
apprentice	도제 (doje)
landlord	주인 (ju-in)
bodyguard	경호원 (gyeonghowon)

Jobs (3)

priest	신부 (sinbu)
nun	수녀 (sunyeo)
monk	수도승 (sudoseung)
photographer	사진작가 (sajinjagga)
coach (sport)	감독 (gamdog)
cheerleader	치어리더 (chieolideo)
referee	심판 (simpan)

reporter	기자 (gija)
actor	배우 (baeu)
musician	음악가 (eum-agga)
conductor	지휘자 (jihwija)
singer	가수 (gasu)
artist	화가 (hwaga)
designer	디자이너 (dijaineo)
model	모델 (model)
DJ	디제이 (dijei)
tour guide	가이드 (gaideu)
lifeguard	인명 구조원 (inmyeong gujowon)
physiotherapist	물리치료사 (mullichilyosa)
masseur	마사지사 (masajisa)
anchor	앵커 (aengkeo)
host	주최자 (juchoeja)
commentator	해설자 (haeseolja)
camera operator	카메라맨 (kamelamaen)
engineer	기술자 (gisulja)
thief	도둑 (dodug)
criminal	범인 (beom-in)
dancer	댄서 (daenseo)
journalist	언론인 (eonlon-in)
prostitute	매춘부 (maechunbu)
author	작가 (jagga)
air traffic controller	항공 교통 관제사 (hang-gong gyotong gwanjesa)
director	감독 (gamdog)
mufti	무프티 (mupeuti)
rabbi	랍비 (labbi)

Technology

e-mail	이메일 (imeil)
telephone	전화기 (jeonhwagi)
smartphone	스마트폰 (seumateupon)

e-mail address	이메일주소 (imeiljuso)
website	웹사이트 (websaiteu)
telephone number	전화번호 (jeonhwabeonho)
file	파일 (pail)
folder (computer)	폴더 (poldeo)
app	앱 (aeb)
laptop	노트북 (noteubug)
screen (computer)	모니터 (moniteo)
printer	프린터 (peulinteo)
scanner	스캐너 (seukaeneo)
USB stick	USB 플래시 드라이브 (USB peullaesi deulaibeu)
hard drive	하드 드라이브 (hadeu deulaibeu)
central processing unit (CPU)	CPU (CPU)
random access memory (RAM)	RAM (RAM)
keyboard (computer)	키보드 (kibodeu)
mouse (computer)	마우스 (mauseu)
earphone	이어폰 (ieopon)
mobile phone	핸드폰 (haendeupon)
webcam	웹캠 (webkaem)
server	서버 (seobeo)
network	네트워크 (neteuwokeu)
browser	브라우저 (beulaujeo)
inbox	메일함 (meilham)
url	URL (URL)
icon	아이콘 (aikon)
scrollbar	스크롤바 (seukeulolba)
recycle bin	휴지통 (hyujitong)
chat	채팅 (chaeting)
social media	소셜 미디어 (sosyeol midieo)
signal (of phone)	신호 (sinho)
database	데이터 베이스 (deiteo beiseu)

Law

law	법률 (beoblyul)
fine	벌금 (beolgeum)
prison	감옥 (gam-og)
court	법정 (beobjeong)
jury	배심 (baesim)
witness	증인 (jeung-in)
defendant	피고 (pigo)
case	사건 (sageon)
evidence	증거 (jeung-geo)
suspect	피의자 (piuija)
fingerprint	지문 (jimun)
paragraph	문단 (mundan)

Bank

money	돈 (don)
coin	동전 (dongjeon)
note (money)	지폐 (jipye)
credit card	신용카드 (sin-yongkadeu)
cash machine	현금 기계 (hyeongeum gigye)
signature	서명 (seomyeong)
dollar	달러 (dalleo)
euro	유로 (yulo)
pound	파운드 (paundeu)
bank account	은행계좌 (eunhaeng-gyejwa)
password	비밀번호 (bimilbeonho)
account number	계좌번호 (gyejwabeonho)
amount	금액 (geum-aeg)
cheque	수표 (supyo)
customer	고객 (gogaeg)
savings	저금 (jeogeum)
loan	대출 (daechul)
interest	이자 (ija)
bank transfer	계좌이체 (gyejwaiche)

yuan	위안 (wian)
yen	엔 (en)
krone	크로네 (keulone)
dividend	배당금 (baedang-geum)
share	주식 (jusig)
share price	주가 (juga)
stock exchange	증권 거래소 (jeung-gwon geolaeso)
investment	투자 (tuja)
portfolio	포트폴리오 (poteupollio)
profit	수익 (su-ig)
loss	손실 (sonsil)

Things

Sport

basketball	농구 (nong-gu)
football	축구공 (chuggugong)
goal	골대 (goldae)
tennis racket	테니스 채 (teniseu chae)
tennis ball	테니스 공 (teniseu gong)
net	네트 (neteu)
cup (trophy)	트로피 (teulopi)
medal	메달 (medal)
swimming pool (competition)	수영장 (suyeongjang)
football	미식축구공 (misigchuggugong)
bat	야구 방망이 (yagu bangmang-i)
mitt	야구 글러브 (yagu geulleobeu)
gold medal	금메달 (geummedal)
silver medal	은메달 (eunmedal)
bronze medal	동메달 (dongmedal)
shuttlecock	셔틀콕 (syeoteulkog)
golf club	골프채 (golpeuchae)
golf ball	골프공 (golpeugong)
stopwatch	초시계 (chosigye)
trampoline	트램펄린 (teulaempeollin)
boxing ring	복싱 링 (bogsing ling)
mouthguard	마우스피스 (mauseupiseu)
surfboard	서핑보드 (seopingbodeu)
ski	스키 (seuki)
ski pole	스키 스틱 (seuki seutig)
sledge	썰매 (sseolmae)
parachute	낙하산 (naghasan)
cue	당구채 (dang-guchae)
bowling ball	볼링 공 (bolling gong)
snooker table	스누커 테이블 (seunukeo teibeul)

saddle	안장 (anjang)
whip	채찍 (chaejjig)
hockey stick	하키스틱 (hakiseutig)
basket	농구 골대 (nong-gu goldae)
world record	세계 기록 (segye gilog)
table tennis table	탁구 테이블 (taggu teibeul)
puck	퍽 (peog)

Technology

robot	로봇 (lobos)
radio	라디오 (ladio)
loudspeaker	스피커 (seupikeo)
cable	케이블 (keibeul)
plug	플러그 (peulleogeu)
camera	카메라 (kamela)
MP3 player	MP3플레이어 (MP3peulleieo)
CD player	CD플레이어 (CDpeulleieo)
DVD player	DVD플레이어 (DVDpeulleieo)
record player	레코드 플레이어 (lekodeu peulleieo)
camcorder	캠코더 (kaemkodeo)
power	전원 (jeon-won)
flat screen	평면 화면 (pyeongmyeon hwamyeon)
flash	플래시 (peullaesi)
tripod	삼각대 (samgagdae)
instant camera	즉석 카메라 (jeugseog kamela)
generator	발전기 (baljeongi)
digital camera	디지털카메라 (dijiteolkamela)
walkie-talkie	무전기 (mujeongi)

Home

key	열쇠 (yeolsoe)
torch	손전등 (sonjeondeung)
candle	양초 (yangcho)

bottle	병 (byeong)
tin	통조림 (tongjolim)
vase	꽃병 (kkochbyeong)
present (gift)	선물 (seonmul)
match	성냥 (seongnyang)
lighter	라이터 (laiteo)
key chain	열쇠고리 (yeolsoegoli)
water bottle	물병 (mulbyeong)
thermos jug	보온병 (boonbyeong)
rubber band	고무줄 (gomujul)
birthday party	생일파티 (saeng-ilpati)
birthday cake	생일케익 (saeng-ilkeig)
pushchair	유모차 (yumocha)
soother	고무젖꼭지 (gomujeojkkogji)
baby bottle	젖병 (jeojbyeong)
hot-water bottle	보온병 (boonbyeong)
rattle	딸랑이 (ttallang-i)
family picture	가족사진 (gajogsajin)
jar	항아리 (hang-ali)
bag	가방 (gabang)
package	포장 (pojang)
plastic bag	비닐봉투 (binilbongtu)
picture frame	액자 (aegja)

Games

doll	인형 (inhyeong)
dollhouse	인형의 집 (inhyeong-ui jib)
puzzle	퍼즐 (peojeul)
dominoes	도미노 (domino)
Monopoly	모노폴리 (monopolli)
Tetris	테트리스 (teteuliseu)
bridge	브릿지 (beulisji)
darts	다트 (dateu)

card game	카드게임 (kadeugeim)
board game	보드게임 (bodeugeim)
backgammon	백개먼 (baeggaemeon)
draughts	체커 (chekeo)

Others

cigarette	담배 (dambae)
cigar	시가 (siga)
compass	나침판 (nachimpan)
angel	천사 (cheonsa)

Phrases

Personal

I	나 (na)
you (singular)	너 (neo)
he	그 (geu)
she	그녀 (geunyeo)
we	우리 (uli)
you (plural)	너희들 (neohuideul)
they	그들 (geudeul)
my dog	내 강아지 (nae gang-aji)
your cat	네 고양이 (ne goyang-i)
her dress	그녀의 드레스 (geunyeoui deuleseu)
his car	그의 차 (geuui cha)
our home	우리 집 (uli jib)
your team	너의 팀 (neoui tim)
their company	그들의 회사 (geudeul-ui hoesa)
everybody	모든사람 (modeunsalam)
together	함께 (hamkke)
other	다른사람 (daleunsalam)

Common

and	와 (wa)
or	또는 (ttoneun)
very	아주 (aju)
all	모두 (modu)
none	전혀 (jeonhyeo)
that	그것 (geugeos)
this	이것 (igeos)
not	아니다 (anida)
more	더 (deo)
most	가장 (gajang)
less	덜 (deol)

because	왜냐하면 (waenyahamyeon)
but	하지만 (hajiman)
already	이미 (imi)
again	다시 (dasi)
really	정말로 (jeongmallo)
if	만약 (man-yag)
although	비록 ~이지만 (bilog ~ijiman)
suddenly	갑자기 (gabjagi)
then	그때 (geuttae)
actually	실제로 (siljelo)
immediately	즉시 (jeugsi)
often	자주 (jaju)
always	항상 (hangsang)
every	모든 (modeun)

Phrases

hi	안녕 (annyeong)
hello	안녕하세요 (annyeonghaseyo)
good day	안녕하세요 (annyeonghaseyo)
bye bye	잘가 (jalga)
good bye	안녕히 가세요 (annyeonghi gaseyo)
see you later	나중에 보자 (najung-e boja)
please	제발 (jebal)
thank you	고마워 (gomawo)
sorry	미안해 (mianhae)
no worries	걱정하지마 (geogjeonghajima)
don't worry	걱정마 (geogjeongma)
take care	잘지내 (jaljinae)
ok	승인 (seung-in)
cheers	건배 (geonbae)
welcome	환영합니다 (hwan-yeonghabnida)
excuse me	실례합니다 (sillyehabnida)
of course	당연하지 (dang-yeonhaji)

I agree	동의합니다 (dong-uihabnida)
relax	진정해 (jinjeonghae)
doesn't matter	상관없어 (sang-gwan-eobs-eo)
I want this	나 이거 갖고 싶어 (na igeo gajgo sip-eo)
Come with me	나랑 같이 가자 (nalang gat-i gaja)
go straight	직진해 (jigjinhae)
turn left	좌회전해 (jwahoejeonhae)
turn right	우회전해 (uhoejeonhae)

Questions

who	누구 (nugu)
where	어디 (eodi)
what	무엇 (mueos)
why	왜 (wae)
how	어떻게 (eotteohge)
which	어느 (eoneu)
when	언제 (eonje)
how many?	몇 개? (myeochgae?)
how much?	얼마나? (eolmana?)
How much is this?	얼마에요? (eolma-eyo?)
Do you have a phone?	전화기를 가지고 있니? (jeonhwagileul gajigo issni?)
Where is the toilet?	화장실이 어디에 있어요? (hwajangsil-i eodie iss-eoyo?)
What's your name?	이름이 뭐에요? (ileum-i mwo-eyo?)
Do you love me?	나 사랑해? (na salanghae?)
How are you?	어떻게 지내? (eotteohge jinae?)
Are you ok?	괜찮아? (gwaenchanh-a?)
Can you help me?	저 좀 도와주실래요? (jeo jom dowajusillaeyo?)

Sentences

I like you	난 너가 좋아요 (nan neoga joh-ayo)
I love you	사랑해 (salanghae)
I miss you	너가 그리워. (neoga geuliwo.)

I don't like this	난 이게 싫어요 (nan ige silh-eoyo)
I have a dog	난 개를 키워요 (nan gaeleul kiwoyo)
I know	알아 (al-a)
I don't know	몰라 (molla)
I don't understand	난 이해가 안돼 (nan ihaega andwae)
I want more	난 더 원해 (nan deo wonhae)
I want a cold coke	난 차가운 콜라가 마시고 싶어 (nan chagaun kollaga masigo sip-eo)
I need this	나 이거 필요해요 (na igeo pil-yohaeyo)
I want to go to the cinema	영화관에 가고싶어요 (yeonghwagwan-e gagosip-eoyo)
I am looking forward to seeing you	난 당신을 만나기를 기대합니다. (nan dangsin-eul mannagileul gidaehabnida.)
Usually I don't eat fish	난 평소에 생선을 안 먹어 (nan pyeongso-e saengseon-eul an meog-eo)
You definitely have to come	넌 반드시 와야해 (neon bandeusi wayahae)
This is quite expensive	이거 상당히 비싸다 (igeo sangdanghi bissada)
Sorry, I'm a little late	미안, 조금 늦었네 (mian, jogeum neuj-eossne)
My name is David	내 이름은 데이비드야 (nae ileum-eun deibideuya)
I'm David, nice to meet you	난 데이비드야. 만나서 반가워. (nan deibideuya. mannaseo bangawo.)
I'm 22 years old	난 22살이야 (nan 22sal-iya)
This is my girlfriend Anna	여기는 내 여자친구 안나야 (yeogineun nae yeojachingu annaya)
Let's watch a film	영화보자 (yeonghwaboja)
Let's go home	집에가자 (jib-egaja)
My telephone number is one four three two eight seven five four three	내 전화번호는 일사삼이 팔칠오사삼 이야 (nae jeonhwabeonhoneun ilsasam-i palchil-osasam iya)
My email address is david at pinhok dot com	내 이메일 주소는 david@pinhok.com이야 (nae imeil jusoneun david@pinhok.com-iya)
Tomorrow is Saturday	내일은 토요일이다 (naeil-eun toyoil-ida)
Silver is cheaper than gold	은이 금보다 저렴해 (eun-i geumboda jeolyeomhae)
Gold is more expensive than silver	금이 은보다 더 비싸 (geum-i eunboda deo bissa)

English - Korean

A

above: 위 (wi)
acacia: 아카시아 (akasia)
accident: 사고 (sago)
accordion: 아코디언 (akodieon)
accountant: 회계사 (hoegyesa)
accounting: 회계 (hoegye)
account number: 계좌번호 (gyejwabeonho)
Achilles tendon: 아킬레스건 (akilleseugeon)
actinium: 악티늄 (agtinyum)
actor: 배우 (baeu)
actually: 실제로 (siljelo)
acupuncture: 침술 (chimsul)
addition: 덧셈 (deos-sem)
address: 주소 (juso)
adhesive tape: 테이프 (teipeu)
advertisement: 광고 (gwang-go)
aerobics: 에어로빅 (eeolobig)
Afghanistan: 아프가니스탄 (apeuganiseutan)
afternoon: 오후 (ohu)
aftershave: 애프터셰이브 (aepeuteosyeibeu)
again: 다시 (dasi)
airbag: 에어백 (eeobaeg)
air conditioner: 에어컨 (eeokeon)
aircraft carrier: 항공모함 (hang-gongmoham)
airline: 항공사 (hang-gongsa)
air mattress: 에어메트리스 (eeometeuliseu)
airport: 공항 (gonghang)
air pressure: 기압 (giab)
air pump: 공기 펌프 (gong-gi peompeu)
air traffic controller: 항공 교통 관제사 (hang-gong gyotong gwanjesa)
aisle: 복도 (bogdo)
alarm clock: 알람시계 (allamsigye)
Albania: 알바니아 (albania)
Algeria: 알제리 (aljeli)
all: 모두 (modu)
allergy: 알레르기 (alleleugi)
alley: 골목 (golmog)
almond: 아몬드 (amondeu)
alphabet: 알파벳 (alpabes)
already: 이미 (imi)
although: 비록 ~이지만 (bilog ~ijiman)
aluminium: 알루미늄 (alluminyum)
always: 항상 (hangsang)
Amazon: 아마존 (amajon)
ambulance: 응급차 (eung-geubcha)
American football: 미식 축구 (misig chuggu)
American Samoa: 아메리칸 사모아 (amelikan samoa)
americium: 아메리슘 (amelisyum)
amount: 금액 (geum-aeg)
ampere: 암페어 (ampeeo)
anchor: 닻 (dach), 앵커 (aengkeo)
and: 와 (wa)
Andes: 안데스 산맥 (andeseu sanmaeg)
Andorra: 안도라 (andola)
angel: 천사 (cheonsa)
angle: 각도 (gagdo)
Angola: 앙골라 (ang-golla)

angry: 화난 (hwanan)
ankle: 발목 (balmog)
anorak: 아노락 (anolag)
answer: 답변하다 (dabbyeonhada)
ant: 개미 (gaemi)
ant-eater: 개미핥기 (gaemihaltgi)
antibiotics: 항생제 (hangsaengje)
antifreeze fluid: 부동액 (budong-aeg)
Antigua and Barbuda: 앤티가 바부다 (aentiga babuda)
antimony: 안티모니 (antimoni)
antiseptic: 소독제 (sodogje)
antiwrinkle cream: 노화방지 크림 (nohwabangji keulim)
anus: 항문 (hangmun)
apartment: 아파트 (apateu)
apostrophe: 아포스트로피 (aposeuteulopi)
app: 앱 (aeb)
appendix: 맹장 (maengjang)
apple: 사과 (sagwa)
apple juice: 사과 주스 (sagwa juseu)
apple pie: 애플파이 (aepeulpai)
appointment: 예약 (yeyag)
apprentice: 도제 (doje)
apricot: 살구 (salgu)
April: 4월 (4wol)
aquarium: 수족관 (sujoggwan)
Arabic: 아랍어 (alab-eo)
archery: 양궁 (yang-gung)
architect: 건축가 (geonchugga)
area: 면적 (myeonjeog)
Are you ok?: 괜찮아? (gwaenchanh-a?)
Argentina: 아르헨티나 (aleuhentina)
argon: 아르곤 (aleugon)
argue: 언쟁하다 (eonjaenghada)
arithmetic: 산수 (sansu)
arm: 팔 (pal)
Armenia: 아르메니아 (aleumenia)
aromatherapy: 아로마 테라피 (aloma telapi)
arrival: 도착 (dochag)
arsenic: 비소 (biso)
art: 미술 (misul)
artery: 동맥 (dongmaeg)
art gallery: 화랑 (hwalang)
artichoke: 아티초크 (atichokeu)
article: 기사 (gisa)
artist: 화가 (hwaga)
Aruba: 아루바 (aluba)
ash: 재 (jae)
ask: 질문하다 (jilmunhada)
asphalt: 아스팔트 (aseupalteu)
aspirin: 아스피린 (aseupilin)
assistant: 조수 (josu)
astatine: 아스타틴 (aseutatin)
asteroid: 소행성 (sohaengseong)
asthma: 천식 (cheonsig)
Atlantic Ocean: 대서양 (daeseoyang)
atmosphere: 대기 (daegi)
atom: 원자 (wonja)
atomic number: 원자 번호 (wonja beonho)
attack: 공격하다 (gong-gyeoghada)
attic: 다락 (dalag)
aubergine: 가지 (gaji)
audience: 관객 (gwangaeg)

August: 8월 (8wol)
aunt: 이모 (imo)
aurora: 오로라 (olola)
Australia: 호주 (hoju)
Australian football: 호주식 축구 (hojusig chuggu)
Austria: 오스트리아 (oseuteulia)
author: 작가 (jagga)
automatic: 자동 (jadong)
autumn: 가을 (ga-eul)
avenue: 거리 (geoli)
avocado: 아보카도 (abokado)
axe: 도끼 (dokki)
Azerbaijan: 아제르바이잔 (ajeleubaijan)

B

baby: 아기 (agi)
baby bottle: 젖병 (jeojbyeong)
baby monitor: 아기 감시용 모니터 (agi gamsiyong moniteo)
bachelor: 학사 학위 (hagsa hag-wi)
back: 등 (deung), 뒤 (dwi)
backgammon: 백개먼 (baeggaemeon)
backpack: 배낭 (baenang)
back seat: 뒷좌석 (dwisjwaseog)
bacon: 베이컨 (beikeon)
bacterium: 박테리아 (bagtelia)
bad: 나쁜 (nappeun)
badminton: 배드민턴 (baedeuminteon)
bag: 가방 (gabang)
Bahrain: 바레인 (balein)
bake: 굽다 (gubda)
baked beans: 구운 콩 (guun kong)
baking powder: 베이킹파우더 (beikingpaudeo)
balcony: 발코니 (balkoni)
bald head: 대머리 (daemeoli)
ballet: 발레 (balle)
ballet shoes: 발레화 (ballehwa)
ball pen: 볼펜 (bolpen)
Ballroom dance: 사교 댄스 (sagyo daenseu)
bamboo: 대나무 (daenamu)
banana: 바나나 (banana)
bandage: 붕대 (bungdae)
Bangladesh: 방글라데시 (bang-geulladesi)
bank account: 은행계좌 (eunhaeng-gyejwa)
bank transfer: 계좌이체 (gyejwaiche)
bar: 술집 (suljib)
Barbados: 바베이도스 (babeidoseu)
barbecue: 바비큐 (babikyu)
barbell: 역기 (yeoggi)
bar code: 바코드 (bakodeu)
bar code scanner: 바코드 판독기 (bakodeu pandoggi)
bargain: 바겐세일 (bagenseil)
barium: 바륨 (balyum)
barkeeper: 바텐더 (batendeo)
barrette: 머리핀 (meolipin)
baseball: 야구 (yagu)
baseball cap: 야구 모자 (yagu moja)
basement: 지하 (jiha)
basil: 바질 (bajil)
basin: 세면기 (semyeongi)
basket: 바구니 (baguni), 농구 골대 (nong-gu goldae)

basketball: 농구 (nong-gu)
bass guitar: 베이스 기타 (beiseu gita)
bassoon: 바순 (basun)
bat: 박쥐 (bagjwi), 야구 방망이 (yagu bangmang-i)
bathrobe: 목욕가운 (mog-yoggaun)
bathroom: 욕실 (yogsil)
bathroom slippers: 화장실슬리퍼 (hwajangsilseullipeo)
bath towel: 목욕수건 (mog-yogsugeon)
bathtub: 욕조 (yogjo)
baton: 경찰봉 (gyeongchalbong)
battery: 배터리 (baeteoli)
beach: 해변 (haebyeon)
beach volleyball: 비치 발리볼 (bichi ballibol)
bean: 콩 (kong)
bear: 곰 (gom)
beard: 턱수염 (teogsuyeom)
beautiful: 아름다운 (aleumdaun)
because: 왜냐하면 (waenyahamyeon)
bed: 침대 (chimdae)
bedroom: 침실 (chimsil)
bedside lamp: 침실등 (chimsildeung)
bee: 꿀벌 (kkulbeol)
beech: 너도밤나무 (neodobamnamu)
beef: 쇠고기 (soegogi)
beer: 맥주 (maegju)
behaviour therapy: 행동 치료 (haengdong chilyo)
beige: 베이지 (beiji)
Beijing duck: 북경오리 (buggyeong-oli)
Belarus: 벨라루스 (bellaluseu)
Belgium: 벨기에 (belgie)
Belize: 벨리즈 (bellijeu)
bell: 초인종 (choinjong)
belly: 배 (bae)
belly button: 배꼽 (baekkob)
below: 아래 (alae)
belt: 벨트 (belteu)
bench: 벤치 (benchi)
bench press: 벤치 프레스 (benchi peuleseu)
Benin: 베냉 (benaeng)
berkelium: 버클륨 (beokeullyum)
beryllium: 베릴륨 (belillyum)
beside: 옆 (yeop)
bet: 내기하다 (naegihada)
Bhutan: 부탄 (butan)
biathlon: 바이애슬론 (baiaeseullon)
bib: 턱받이 (teogbad-i)
bicycle: 자전거 (jajeongeo)
big: 큰 (keun)
big brother: 형/오빠 (hyeong/oppa)
big sister: 누나/언니 (nuna/eonni)
bikini: 비키니 (bikini)
bill: 송장 (songjang)
billiards: 당구 (dang-gu)
biology: 생물학 (saengmulhag)
birch: 자작나무 (jajagnamu)
birth: 탄생 (tansaeng)
birth certificate: 출생증명서 (chulsaengjeungmyeongseo)
birth control pill: 피임약 (piim-yag)
birthday: 생일 (saeng-il)
birthday cake: 생일케익 (saeng-ilkeig)
birthday party: 생일파티 (saeng-ilpati)
biscuit: 비스킷 (biseukis)

bismuth: 비스무트 (biseumuteu)
bison: 들소 (deulso)
bite: 깨물다 (kkaemulda), 물린 상처 (mullin sangcheo)
black: 검정색 (geomjeongsaeg)
blackberry: 블랙베리 (beullaegbeli)
blackboard: 칠판 (chilpan)
black hole: 블랙홀 (beullaeghol)
Black Sea: 흑해 (heughae)
black tea: 홍차 (hongcha)
bladder: 방광 (bang-gwang)
blanket: 담요 (dam-yo)
blazer: 블레이저 (beulleijeo)
blind: 맹인 (maeng-in), 블라인드 (beullaindeu)
blond: 금발의 (geumbal-ui)
blood test: 혈액 검사 (hyeol-aeg geomsa)
bloody: 피투성이의 (pituseong-iui)
blossom: 꽃 (kkoch)
blue: 파랑색 (palangsaeg)
blueberry: 블루베리 (beullubeli)
blues: 블루스 (beulluseu)
board game: 보드게임 (bodeugeim)
bobsleigh: 봅슬레이 (bobseullei)
bodybuilding: 보디빌딩 (bodibilding)
bodyguard: 경호원 (gyeonghowon)
body lotion: 바디로션 (badilosyeon)
bohrium: 보륨 (bolyum)
boil: 끓이다 (kkeulh-ida)
boiled: 삶은 (salm-eun)
boiled egg: 삶은계란 (salm-eungyelan)
Bolivia: 볼리비아 (bollibia)
bone: 뼈 (ppyeo)
bone marrow: 골수 (golsu)
bonnet: 보닛 (bonis)
book: 책 (chaeg)
booking: 예약 (yeyag)
bookshelf: 책장 (chaegjang)
bookshop: 서점 (seojeom)
boring: 지루한 (jiluhan)
boron: 붕소 (bungso)
Bosnia: 보스니아 (boseunia)
bosom: 유방 (yubang)
botanic garden: 식물원 (sigmul-won)
Botswana: 보츠와나 (bocheuwana)
bottle: 병 (byeong)
bottom: 엉덩이 (eongdeong-i)
bowl: 그릇 (geuleus)
bowling: 볼링 (bolling)
bowling ball: 볼링 공 (bolling gong)
bow tie: 나비넥타이 (nabinegtai)
boxing: 권투 (gwontu)
boxing glove: 권투장갑 (gwontujang-gab)
boxing ring: 복싱 링 (bogsing ling)
boy: 소년 (sonyeon)
boyfriend: 남자친구 (namjachingu)
bra: 브라 (beula)
bracelet: 팔찌 (paljji)
brain: 뇌 (noe)
brake: 브레이크 (beuleikeu)
brake light: 브레이크 등 (beuleikeu deung)
branch: 나뭇가지 (namusgaji)
brandy: 브랜디 (beulaendi)
brave: 용감한 (yong-gamhan)

Brazil: 브라질 (beulajil)
bread: 빵 (ppang)
breakdance: 브레이크댄싱 (beuleikeudaensing)
breakfast: 아침식사 (achimsigsa)
breastbone: 흉골 (hyung-gol)
breathe: 숨을 쉬다 (sum-eul swida)
brick: 벽돌 (byeogdol)
bride: 신부 (sinbu)
bridge: 다리 (dali), 브릿지 (beulisji)
briefcase: 서류가방 (seolyugabang)
broad: 넓은 (neolb-eun)
broccoli: 브로콜리 (beulokolli)
bromine: 브로민 (beulomin)
bronze medal: 동메달 (dongmedal)
brooch: 브로치 (beulochi)
broom: 빗자루 (bisjalu)
brother-in-law: 매형 (maehyeong)
brown: 갈색 (galsaeg)
brownie: 브라우니 (beulauni)
browser: 브라우저 (beulaujeo)
bruise: 멍 (meong)
Brunei: 브루나이 (beulunai)
brunette: 갈색머리의 (galsaegmeoliui)
brush: 붓 (bus), 빗 (bis)
Brussels sprouts: 방울양배추 (bang-ul-yangbaechu)
bucket: 양동이 (yangdong-i)
buffalo: 물소 (mulso)
buffet: 뷔페 (bwipe)
bug: 벌레 (beolle)
Bulgaria: 불가리아 (bulgalia)
bull: 황소 (hwangso)
bulletin board: 게시판 (gesipan)
bumblebee: 호박벌 (hobagbeol)
bumper: 범퍼 (beompeo)
bungee jumping: 번지 점프 (beonji jeompeu)
bunk bed: 이층침대 (icheungchimdae)
burger: 버거 (beogeo)
Burkina Faso: 부르키나파소 (buleukinapaso)
Burma: 버마 (beoma)
burn: 태우다 (taeuda), 화상 (hwasang)
Burundi: 부룬디 (bulundi)
bus: 버스 (beoseu)
bus driver: 버스기사 (beoseugisa)
bush: 관목 (gwanmog)
business card: 명함 (myeongham)
business class: 비즈니스석 (bijeuniseuseog)
business dinner: 회식 (hoesig)
business school: 경영대학 (gyeong-yeongdaehag)
business trip: 출장 (chuljang)
bus stop: 버스정류장 (beoseujeonglyujang)
busy: 바쁜 (bappeun)
but: 하지만 (hajiman)
butcher: 푸주한 (pujuhan)
butter: 버터 (beoteo)
buttercup: 미나리아재비 (minaliajaebi)
butterfly: 나비 (nabi)
buttermilk: 버터밀크 (beoteomilkeu)
button: 단추 (danchu)
buy: 구매하다 (gumaehada)
bye bye: 잘가 (jalga)

C

cabbage: 배추 (baechu)
cabin: 객실 (gaegsil)
cable: 케이블 (keibeul)
cable car: 케이블카 (keibeulka)
cactus: 선인장 (seon-injang)
cadmium: 카드뮴 (kadeumyum)
caesium: 세슘 (sesyum)
cake: 케이크 (keikeu)
calcite: 방해석 (banghaeseog)
calcium: 칼슘 (kalsyum)
calculate: 계산하다 (gyesanhada)
calendar: 달력 (dallyeog)
californium: 칼리포르늄 (kallipoleunyum)
call: 전화하다 (jeonhwahada)
Cambodia: 캄보디아 (kambodia)
camcorder: 캠코더 (kaemkodeo)
camel: 낙타 (nagta)
camera: 카메라 (kamela)
camera operator: 카메라맨 (kamelamaen)
Cameroon: 카메룬 (kamelun)
campfire: 캠프파이어 (kaempeupaieo)
camping: 캠핑 (kaemping)
camping site: 캠프장 (kaempeujang)
Canada: 캐나다 (kaenada)
cancer: 암 (am)
candle: 양초 (yangcho)
candy: 사탕 (satang)
candy floss: 솜사탕 (somsatang)
canoe: 카누 (kanu)
canoeing: 카누 타기 (kanu tagi)
canteen: 구내식당 (gunaesigdang)
canyon: 협곡 (hyeobgog)
Can you help me?: 저 좀 도와주실래요? (jeo jom dowajusillaeyo?)
Cape Verde: 카보베르데 (kabobeleude)
capital: 수도 (sudo)
cappuccino: 카푸치노 (kapuchino)
capsule: 캡슐 (kaebsyul)
captain: 선장 (seonjang)
car: 승용차 (seung-yongcha)
caramel: 카라멜 (kalamel)
caravan: 여행 트레일러 (yeohaeng teuleilleo)
carbon: 탄소 (tanso)
carbon dioxide: 이산화탄소 (isanhwatanso)
carbon monoxide: 일산화탄소 (ilsanhwatanso)
card game: 카드게임 (kadeugeim)
cardigan: 가디건 (gadigeon)
cardiology: 심장학 (simjanghag)
cargo aircraft: 화물수송기 (hwamulsusong-gi)
caricature: 캐리커쳐 (kaelikeochyeo)
caries: 충치 (chungchi)
carousel: 회전목마 (hoejeonmogma)
car park: 주차장 (juchajang)
carpenter: 목수 (mogsu)
carpet: 카페트 (kapeteu)
car racing: 자동차 경주 (jadongcha gyeongju)
carrot: 당근 (dang-geun)
carry: 들다 (deulda)
carry-on luggage: 기내 휴대 수하물 (ginae hyudae suhamul)
cartilage: 연골 (yeongol)
cartoon: 만화 (manhwa)

car wash: 세차 (secha)
case: 사건 (sageon)
cashew: 캐슈 (kaesyu)
cashier: 출납원 (chulnab-won)
cash machine: 현금 기계 (hyeongeum gigye)
cash register: 계산대 (gyesandae)
casino: 카지노 (kajino)
cast: 출연진 (chul-yeonjin), 깁스 (gibseu)
castle: 성 (seong)
cat: 고양이 (goyang-i)
catch: 잡다 (jabda)
caterpillar: 애벌레 (aebeolle)
cathedral: 성당 (seongdang)
catheter: 카테터 (kateteo)
cauliflower: 콜리플라워 (kollipeullawo)
cave: 동굴 (dong-gul)
Cayman Islands: 케이맨 제도 (keimaen jedo)
CD player: CD플레이어 (CDpeulleieo)
ceiling: 천장 (cheonjang)
celebrate: 기념하다 (ginyeomhada)
celery: 셀러리 (selleoli)
cello: 첼로 (chello)
cement: 시멘트 (simenteu)
cement mixer: 시멘트 혼합기 (simenteu honhabgi)
cemetery: 묘지 (myoji)
centigrade: 섭씨 (seobssi)
centimeter: 센티미터 (sentimiteo)
Central African Republic: 중앙아프리카 공화국 (jung-ang-apeulika gonghwagug)
central business district (CBD): 중앙업무지구 (jung-ang-eobmujigu)
central processing unit (CPU): CPU (CPU)
century: 백년 (baegnyeon)
cereal: 씨리얼 (ssilieol)
cerium: 세륨 (selyum)
cesarean: 제왕절개 (jewangjeolgae)
cha-cha: 차차차 (chachacha)
Chad: 차드 (chadeu)
chain: 체인 (chein)
chainsaw: 전기톱 (jeongitob)
chair: 의자 (uija)
chairman: 회장 (hoejang)
chalk: 분필 (bunpil)
chameleon: 카멜레온 (kamelle-on)
champagne: 샴페인 (syampein)
changing room: 탈의실 (tal-uisil)
channel: 채널 (chaeneol)
character: 글자 (geulja)
chat: 채팅 (chaeting)
cheap: 싼 (ssan)
check-in desk: 체크인 데스크 (chekeu-in deseukeu)
cheek: 빰 (ppyam)
cheerleader: 치어리더 (chieolideo)
cheers: 건배 (geonbae)
cheese: 치즈 (chijeu)
cheeseburger: 치즈버거 (chijeubeogeo)
cheesecake: 치즈케이크 (chijeukeikeu)
cheetah: 치타 (chita)
chemical compound: 화합물 (hwahabmul)
chemical reaction: 화학 반응 (hwahag ban-eung)
chemical structure: 화학 구조 (hwahag gujo)
chemist: 화학자 (hwahagja)
chemistry: 화학 (hwahag)
cheque: 수표 (supyo)

cherry: 체리 (cheli)
chess: 체스 (cheseu)
chest: 가슴 (gaseum)
chewing gum: 껌 (kkeom)
chick: 병아리 (byeong-ali)
chicken: 닭 (dalg), 닭고기 (dalg-gogi)
chicken nugget: 치킨너겟 (chikinneoges)
chickenpox: 수두 (sudu)
chicken wings: 치킨 윙 (chikin wing)
child: 아이 (ai)
child seat: 유아용 안전시트 (yuayong anjeonsiteu)
Chile: 칠레 (chille)
chili: 고추 (gochu)
chimney: 굴뚝 (gulttug)
chin: 턱 (teog)
China: 중국 (jung-gug)
Chinese medicine: 중의학 (jung-uihag)
chips: 감자칩 (gamjachib)
chiropractor: 척추지압사 (cheogchujiabsa)
chive: 골파 (golpa)
chlorine: 염소 (yeomso)
chocolate: 초콜릿 (chokollis)
chocolate cream: 초콜릿 크림 (chokollis keulim)
choose: 선택하다 (seontaeghada)
chopping board: 도마 (doma)
chopstick: 젓가락 (jeosgalag)
Christmas: 크리스마스 (keuliseumaseu)
chromium: 크로뮴 (keulomyum)
chubby: 통통한 (tongtonghan)
church: 교회 (gyohoe)
cider: 사이다 (saida)
cigar: 시가 (siga)
cigarette: 담배 (dambae)
cinema: 영화관 (yeonghwagwan)
cinnamon: 시나몬 (sinamon)
circle: 원 (won)
circuit training: 서킷 트레이닝 (seokis teuleining)
clarinet: 클라리넷 (keullalines)
classical music: 클래식 음악 (keullaesig eum-ag)
classic car: 고전차 (gojeoncha)
clay: 찰흙 (chalheulg)
clean: 깨끗한 (kkaekkeushan), 청소하다 (cheongsohada)
cleaner: 청소부 (cheongsobu)
clef: 음자리표 (eumjalipyo)
clever: 영리한 (yeonglihan)
cliff: 절벽 (jeolbyeog)
cliff diving: 암벽 다이빙 (ambyeog daibing)
climb: 오르다 (oleuda)
climbing: 등반 (deungban)
clinic: 진료소 (jinlyoso)
clipboard: 클립보드 (keullibbodeu)
clitoris: 음핵 (eumhaeg)
clock: 시계 (sigye)
close: 가까운 (gakkaun), 닫다 (dadda)
cloud: 구름 (guleum)
cloudy: 구름 낀 (guleum kkin)
clover: 클로버 (keullobeo)
clutch: 클러치 (keulleochi)
coach: 감독 (gamdog)
coal: 석탄 (seogtan)
coast: 해안가 (haeanga)
coat: 코트 (koteu)

cobalt: 코발트 (kobalteu)
cockerel: 어린 수탉 (eolin sutalg)
cockpit: 조종석 (jojongseog)
cocktail: 칵테일 (kagteil)
coconut: 코코넛 (kokoneos)
coffee: 커피 (keopi)
coffee machine: 커피머신 (keopimeosin)
coffee table: 탁자 (tagja)
coffin: 관 (gwan)
coin: 동전 (dongjeon)
coke: 콜라 (kolla)
cold: 추운 (chuun), 감기 (gamgi)
collar: 깃 (gis)
collarbone: 쇄골 (swaegol)
colleague: 동료 (donglyo)
Colombia: 콜롬비아 (kollombia)
colon: 결장 (gyeoljang), 콜론 (kollon)
colony: 식민지 (sigminji)
coloured pencil: 색연필 (saeg-yeonpil)
comb: 빗 (bis)
combine harvester: 콤바인 수확기 (kombain suhwaggi)
come: 오다 (oda)
comedy: 코미디 (komidi)
comet: 혜성 (hyeseong)
Come with me: 나랑 같이 가자 (nalang gat-i gaja)
comic book: 만화책 (manhwachaeg)
comma: 쉼표 (swimpyo)
commentator: 해설자 (haeseolja)
Comoros: 코모로 (komolo)
compass: 나침판 (nachimpan)
concealer: 컨실러 (keonsilleo)
concert: 콘서트 (konseoteu)
concrete: 콘크리트 (konkeuliteu)
concrete mixer: 콘크리트 혼합기 (konkeuliteu honhabgi)
concussion: 뇌진탕 (noejintang)
condom: 콘돔 (kondom)
conductor: 차장 (chajang), 지휘자 (jihwija)
cone: 원뿔 (wonppul)
construction site: 공사현장 (gongsahyeonjang)
construction worker: 건설 노동자 (geonseol nodongja)
consultant: 컨설턴트 (keonseolteonteu)
contact lens: 콘택트 렌즈 (kontaegteu lenjeu)
container: 컨테이너 (keonteineo)
container ship: 컨테이너선 (keonteineoseon)
content: 내용 (naeyong)
continent: 대륙 (daelyug)
control tower: 관제탑 (gwanjetab)
cook: 요리하다 (yolihada), 요리사 (yolisa)
cooker: 가스레인지 (gaseuleinji)
cooker hood: 가스레인지 후드 (gaseuleinji hudeu)
cookie: 쿠키 (kuki)
Cook Islands: 쿡 제도 (kug jedo)
cool: 멋진 (meosjin)
copernicium: 코페르니슘 (kopeleunisyum)
copper: 구리 (guli)
copy: 복사하다 (bogsahada)
coral reef: 산호초 (sanhocho)
coriander: 고수 (gosu)
corkscrew: 타래 송곳 (talae song-gos)
corn: 옥수수 (ogsusu)
corn oil: 옥수수기름 (ogsusugileum)
corpse: 시체 (siche)

correct: 옳은 (olh-eun)
corridor: 복도 (bogdo)
Costa Rica: 코스타리카 (koseutalika)
cotton: 솜 (som)
cough: 기침 (gichim)
cough syrup: 기침약 (gichim-yag)
count: 세다 (seda)
country: 국가 (gugga)
courgette: 애호박 (aehobag)
court: 법정 (beobjeong)
cousin: 사촌 (sachon)
cow: 암소 (amso)
crab: 게 (ge)
cramp: 경련 (gyeonglyeon)
cranberry: 크랜베리 (keulaenbeli)
crane: 기중기 (gijung-gi)
crane truck: 기중기 트럭 (gijung-gi teuleog)
crater: 분화구 (bunhwagu)
crawl: 포복 (pobog)
crazy: 미친 (michin)
cream: 크림 (keulim)
credit card: 신용카드 (sin-yongkadeu)
cricket: 귀뚜라미 (gwittulami), 크리켓 (keulikes)
criminal: 범인 (beom-in)
Croatia: 크로아티아 (keuloatia)
crocodile: 악어 (ag-eo)
croissant: 크루아상 (keuluasang)
cross-country skiing: 크로스컨트리 스키 (keuloseukeonteuli seuki)
cross trainer: 크로스 트레이너 (keuloseu teuleineo)
crosswords: 십자말풀이 (sibjamalpul-i)
crow: 까마귀 (kkamagwi)
crown: 왕관 (wang-gwan)
cruise ship: 유람선 (yulamseon)
crutch: 목발 (mogbal)
cry: 울다 (ulda)
crêpe: 크레페 (keulepe)
CT scanner: CT 스캐너 (CT seukaeneo)
Cuba: 쿠바 (kuba)
cube: 정육면체 (jeong-yugmyeonche)
cubic meter: 세제곱미터 (sejegobmiteo)
cucumber: 오이 (oi)
cuddly toy: 봉제 인형 (bongje inhyeong)
cue: 당구채 (dang-guchae)
cup: 컵 (keob), 머그컵 (meogeukeob), 트로피 (teulopi)
cupboard: 찬장 (chanjang)
curium: 퀴륨 (kwilyum)
curling: 컬링 (keolling)
curling iron: 컬 고데기 (keol godegi)
curly: 곱슬곱슬한 (gobseulgobseulhan)
currant: 까막까치밥나무 열매 (kkamagkkachibabnamu yeolmae)
curry: 커리 (keoli)
curtain: 커튼 (keoteun)
curve: 곡선 (gogseon)
custard: 커스터드 (keoseuteodeu)
customer: 고객 (gogaeg)
customs: 관세 (gwanse)
cut: 자르다 (jaleuda)
cute: 귀여운 (gwiyeoun)
cutlery: 식기도구 (siggidogu)
cycling: 사이클링 (saikeulling)
cylinder: 원기둥 (wongidung)
cymbals: 심벌즈 (simbeoljeu)

Cyprus: 키프로스 (kipeuloseu)
Czech Republic: 체코 (cheko)

D

dad: 아빠 (appa)
daffodil: 수선화 (suseonhwa)
daisy: 데이지 (deiji)
dam: 댐 (daem)
dancer: 댄서 (daenseo)
dancing: 춤 (chum)
dancing shoes: 댄스화 (daenseuhwa)
dandelion: 민들레 (mindeulle)
dandruff: 비듬 (bideum)
dark: 어두운 (eoduun)
darmstadtium: 다름스타튬 (daleumseutatyum)
darts: 다트 (dateu)
dashboard: 계기판 (gyegipan)
database: 데이터 베이스 (deiteo beiseu)
date: 대추 (daechu)
daughter: 딸 (ttal)
daughter-in-law: 며느리 (myeoneuli)
day: 일 (il)
deaf: 귀머거리의 (gwimeogeoliui)
death: 죽음 (jug-eum)
decade: 십 년 (sibnyeon)
December: 12월 (12wol)
decimeter: 데시미터 (desimiteo)
deck: 갑판 (gabpan)
deck chair: 갑판 의자 (gabpan uija)
deep: 깊은 (gip-eun)
deer: 사슴 (saseum)
defend: 방어하다 (bang-eohada)
defendant: 피고 (pigo)
degree: 학위 (hag-wi)
deliver: 전달하다 (jeondalhada)
delivery: 분만 (bunman)
Democratic Republic of the Congo: 콩고 민주 공화국 (kong-go minju gonghwagug)
Denmark: 덴마크 (denmakeu)
denominator: 분모 (bunmo)
dental brace: 교정기 (gyojeong-gi)
dental filling: 아말감 (amalgam)
dental prostheses: 의치 (uichi)
dentist: 치과의사 (chigwauisa)
department: 부서 (buseo)
departure: 출발 (chulbal)
dermatology: 피부과 (pibugwa)
desert: 사막 (samag)
designer: 디자이너 (dijaineo)
desk: 책상 (chaegsang)
dessert: 디저트 (dijeoteu)
detective: 형사 (hyeongsa)
diabetes: 당뇨병 (dangnyobyeong)
diagonal: 대각선 (daegagseon)
diamond: 다이아몬드 (daiamondeu)
diaper: 기저귀 (gijeogwi)
diaphragm: 횡경막 (hoeng-gyeongmag)
diarrhea: 설사 (seolsa)
diary: 일기 (ilgi)
dictionary: 사전 (sajeon)
die: 죽다 (jugda)

diesel: 디젤 (dijel)
difficult: 어려운 (eolyeoun)
dig: 파다 (pada)
digital camera: 디지털카메라 (dijiteolkamela)
dill: 딜 (dil)
dimple: 보조개 (bojogae)
dim sum: 딤섬 (dimseom)
dinner: 저녁식사 (jeonyeogsigsa)
dinosaur: 공룡 (gonglyong)
diploma: 졸업장 (jol-eobjang)
director: 이사 (isa), 감독 (gamdog)
dirty: 더러운 (deoleoun)
discus throw: 원반 던지기 (wonban deonjigi)
dishwasher: 식기세척기 (siggisecheoggi)
district: 구역 (guyeog)
dividend: 배당금 (baedang-geum)
diving: 다이빙 (daibing)
diving mask: 다이빙 마스크 (daibing maseukeu)
division: 나눗셈 (nanus-sem)
divorce: 이혼 (ihon)
DJ: 디제이 (dijei)
Djibouti: 지부티 (jibuti)
doctor: 의사 (uisa)
doesn't matter: 상관없어 (sang-gwan-eobs-eo)
dog: 개 (gae)
doll: 인형 (inhyeong)
dollar: 달러 (dalleo)
dollhouse: 인형의 집 (inhyeong-ui jib)
dolphin: 돌고래 (dolgolae)
Dominica: 도미니카 (dominika)
Dominican Republic: 도미니카 공화국 (dominika gonghwagug)
dominoes: 도미노 (domino)
don't worry: 걱정마 (geogjeongma)
donkey: 당나귀 (dangnagwi)
door: 문 (mun)
door handle: 문손잡이 (munsonjab-i)
dorm room: 도미토리 룸 (domitoli lum)
dosage: 복용량 (bog-yonglyang)
double bass: 더블베이스 (deobeulbeiseu)
double room: 2인실 (2insil)
doughnut: 도넛 (doneos)
Do you love me?: 나 사랑해? (na salanghae?)
dragonfly: 잠자리 (jamjali)
draughts: 체커 (chekeo)
drawer: 서랍 (seolab)
drawing: 그림 (geulim)
dreadlocks: 레게머리 (legemeoli)
dream: 꿈을 꾸다 (kkum-eul kkuda)
dress: 드레스 (deuleseu)
dress size: 드레스 사이즈 (deuleseu saijeu)
dried fruit: 말린과일 (mallingwail)
drill: 드릴질하다 (deuliljilhada)
drilling machine: 드릴 (deulil)
drink: 마시다 (masida)
drums: 드럼 (deuleom)
drunk: 술취한 (sulchwihan)
dry: 건조한 (geonjohan), 말리다 (mallida)
dubnium: 더브늄 (deobeunyum)
duck: 오리 (oli)
dumbbell: 아령 (alyeong)
dumpling: 만두 (mandu)
duodenum: 십이지장 (sib-ijijang)

DVD player: DVD플레이어 (DVDpeulleieo)
dyed: 염색머리 (yeomsaegmeoli)
dysprosium: 디스프로슘 (diseupeulosyum)

E

e-mail: 이메일 (imeil)
e-mail address: 이메일주소 (imeiljuso)
eagle: 독수리 (dogsuli)
ear: 귀 (gwi)
earn: 돈을 벌다 (don-eul beolda)
earphone: 이어폰 (ieopon)
earplug: 귀마개 (gwimagae)
earring: 귀걸이 (gwigeol-i)
earth: 지구 (jigu)
earth's core: 지구핵 (jiguhaeg)
earth's crust: 지각 (jigag)
earthquake: 지진 (jijin)
east: 동 (dong)
Easter: 부활절 (buhwaljeol)
East Timor: 동티모르 (dongtimoleu)
easy: 쉬운 (swiun)
eat: 먹다 (meogda)
economics: 경제학 (gyeongjehag)
economy class: 이코노미석 (ikonomiseog)
Ecuador: 에콰도르 (ekwadoleu)
eczema: 습진 (seubjin)
egg: 계란 (gyelan)
egg white: 달걀 흰자 (dalgyal huinja)
Egypt: 이집트 (ijibteu)
einsteinium: 아인슈타이늄 (ainsyutainyum)
elbow: 팔꿈치 (palkkumchi)
electric guitar: 일렉트릭 기타 (illegteulig gita)
electrician: 전기기사 (jeongigisa)
electric iron: 전기다리미 (jeongidalimi)
electric shock: 전기 충격 (jeongi chung-gyeog)
electron: 전자 (jeonja)
elephant: 코끼리 (kokkili)
elevator: 엘리베이터 (ellibeiteo)
elk: 엘크 (elkeu)
ellipse: 타원 (tawon)
El Salvador: 엘살바도르 (elsalbadoleu)
embassy: 대사관 (daesagwan)
embryo: 배아 (baea)
emergency: 응급 (eung-geub)
emergency exit: 비상출구 (bisangchulgu), 비상 출구 (bisang chulgu)
emergency room: 응급실 (eung-geubsil)
employee: 직원 (jig-won)
employer: 고용주 (goyongju)
empty: 빈 (bin)
endocrinology: 내분비학 (naebunbihag)
energy drink: 에너지 드링크 (eneoji deulingkeu)
engagement: 약혼 (yaghon)
engagement ring: 약혼반지 (yaghonbanji)
engine: 엔진 (enjin)
engineer: 기술자 (gisulja)
engine room: 기관실 (gigwansil)
English: 영어 (yeong-eo)
enjoy: 즐기다 (jeulgida)
entrepreneur: 사업가 (sa-eobga)
envelope: 봉투 (bongtu)

epilepsy: 간질 (ganjil)
episiotomy: 외음 절개술 (oeeum jeolgaesul)
equation: 방정식 (bangjeongsig)
equator: 적도 (jeogdo)
Equatorial Guinea: 적도 기니 (jeogdo gini)
erbium: 어븀 (eobyum)
Eritrea: 에리트레아 (eliteulea)
espresso: 에스프레소 (eseupeuleso)
essay: 수필 (supil)
Estonia: 에스토니아 (eseutonia)
Ethiopia: 에티오피아 (etiopia)
eucalyptus: 유칼립투스 (yukallibtuseu)
euro: 유로 (yulo)
europium: 유로퓸 (yulopyum)
evening: 저녁 (jeonyeog)
evening dress: 이브닝 드레스 (ibeuning deuleseu)
every: 모든 (modeun)
everybody: 모든사람 (modeunsalam)
evidence: 증거 (jeung-geo)
evil: 악한 (aghan)
exam: 시험 (siheom)
excavator: 굴착기 (gulchaggi)
exclamation mark: 느낌표 (neukkimpyo)
excuse me: 실례합니다 (sillyehabnida)
exercise bike: 실내 운동용 자전거 (silnae undong-yong jajeongeo)
exhaust pipe: 배기관 (baegigwan)
expensive: 비싼 (bissan)
expiry date: 유효기간 (yuhyogigan)
eye: 눈 (nun)
eyebrow: 눈썹 (nunsseob)
eyebrow pencil: 브로우 펜슬 (beulou penseul)
eyelashes: 속눈썹 (sognunsseob)
eyeliner: 아이라이너 (ailaineo)
eye shadow: 아이섀도우 (aisyaedou)

F

fabric: 천 (cheon)
face cream: 얼굴로션 (eolgullosyeon)
face mask: 얼굴 마스크 (eolgul maseukeu)
face powder: 얼굴 파우더 (eolgul paudeo)
facial toner: 토너 (toneo)
factory: 공장 (gongjang)
Fahrenheit: 화씨 (hwassi)
fail: 실패하다 (silpaehada)
faint: 기절하다 (gijeolhada)
fair: 공평한 (gongpyeonghan)
fairground: 축제마당 (chugjemadang)
falcon: 매 (mae)
Falkland Islands: 포클랜드 제도 (pokeullaendeu jedo)
fall: 떨어지다 (tteol-eojida)
family picture: 가족사진 (gajogsajin)
family therapy: 가족 요법 (gajog yobeob)
fan: 선풍기 (seonpung-gi)
far: 먼 (meon)
fare: 요금 (yogeum)
farm: 농장 (nongjang)
farmer: 농부 (nongbu)
Faroe Islands: 페로 제도 (pelo jedo)
father: 아버지 (abeoji)
father-in-law: 장인어른 (jang-in-eoleun)

fat meat: 지방이 많은 고기 (jibang-i manh-eun gogi)
fax: 팩스 (paegseu)
February: 2월 (2wol)
feed: 먹이를 주다 (meog-ileul juda)
fence: 울타리 (ultali)
fencing: 펜싱 (pensing)
feng shui: 풍수 (pungsu)
fennel: 회향 (hoehyang)
fermium: 페르뮴 (peleumyum)
fern: 양치식물 (yangchisigmul)
ferry: 연락선 (yeonlagseon)
feta: 페타 (peta)
fever: 열 (yeol)
fever thermometer: 체온계 (che-ongye)
few: 적은 (jeog-eun)
fiancé: 약혼자 (yaghonja)
fiancée: 약혼녀 (yaghonnyeo)
field hockey: 필드하키 (pildeuhaki)
fifth floor: 5층 (5cheung)
fig: 무화과 (muhwagwa)
fight: 싸우다 (ssauda)
figure skating: 피겨 스케이팅 (pigyeo seukeiting)
Fiji: 피지 (piji)
file: 줄 (jul), 파일 (pail)
filter: 필터 (pilteo)
fin: 오리발 (olibal)
find: 찾다 (chajda)
fine: 벌금 (beolgeum)
finger: 손가락 (songalag)
fingernail: 손톱 (sontob)
fingerprint: 지문 (jimun)
Finland: 핀란드 (pinlandeu)
fire: 불 (bul), 화재 (hwajae)
fire alarm: 화재경보기 (hwajaegyeongbogi)
fire extinguisher: 소화기 (sohwagi)
firefighter: 소방관 (sobang-gwan)
firefighters: 소방관 (sobang-gwan)
fire station: 소방서 (sobangseo)
fire truck: 소방차 (sobangcha)
first: 첫째 (cheosjjae)
first basement floor: 지하1층 (jiha1cheung)
first class: 일등석 (ildeungseog)
first floor: 1층 (1cheung)
fish: 물고기 (mulgogi), 낚시를 하다 (nakksileul hada), 생선 (saengseon)
fish and chips: 피시 앤 칩스 (pisi aen chibseu)
fishbone: 생선 가시 (saengseon gasi)
fisherman: 어부 (eobu)
fishing boat: 어선 (eoseon)
fish market: 생선가게 (saengseongage)
fist: 주먹 (jumeog)
fix: 수리하다 (sulihada)
flamingo: 홍학 (honghag)
flash: 플래시 (peullaesi)
flat: 평평한 (pyeongpyeonghan)
flat screen: 평면 화면 (pyeongmyeon hwamyeon)
flerovium: 플레로븀 (peullelobyum)
flip-flops: 조리 (jjoli)
flip chart: 플립 차트 (peullib chateu)
flood: 홍수 (hongsu)
floor: 바닥 (badag)
florist: 플로리스트 (peulloliseuteu)
flour: 밀가루 (milgalu)

flower: 꽃 (kkoch)
flower bed: 화단 (hwadan)
flower pot: 화분 (hwabun)
flu: 독감 (doggam)
fluid: 액체 (aegche)
fluorine: 플루오르 (peulluoleu)
flute: 플루트 (peulluteu)
fly: 파리 (pali), 날다 (nalda)
flyer: 광고지 (gwang-goji)
foetus: 태아 (taea)
fog: 안개 (angae)
foggy: 안개 낀 (angae kkin)
folder: 서류철 (seolyucheol), 폴더 (poldeo)
folk music: 민요 (min-yo)
follow: 따르다 (ttaleuda)
foot: 발 (bal), 풋 (pus)
football: 축구 (chuggu), 축구공 (chuggugong), 미식축구공 (misigchuggugong)
football boots: 축구화 (chugguhwa)
football stadium: 축구 경기장 (chuggu gyeong-gijang)
force: 힘 (him)
forehead: 이마 (ima)
forest: 숲 (sup)
fork: 포크 (pokeu)
forklift truck: 지게차 (jigecha)
Formula 1: 포뮬러 원 (pomyulleo won)
foundation: 파운데이션 (paundeisyeon)
fountain: 분수대 (bunsudae)
fourth: 넷째 (nesjjae)
fox: 여우 (yeou)
fraction: 분수 (bunsu)
fracture: 골절 (goljeol)
France: 프랑스 (peulangseu)
francium: 프란슘 (peulansyum)
freckles: 주근깨 (jugeunkkae)
freestyle skiing: 프리스타일 스키 (peuliseutail seuki)
freezer: 냉동실 (naengdongsil)
freight train: 화물 기차 (hwamul gicha)
French: 불어 (bul-eo)
French fries: 프렌치 프라이 (peulenchi peulai)
French horn: 프렌치 호른 (peulenchi holeun)
French Polynesia: 프랑스령 폴리네시아 (peulangseulyeong pollinesia)
Friday: 금요일 (geum-yoil)
fridge: 냉장고 (naengjang-go)
fried noodles: 볶음면 (bokk-eummyeon)
fried rice: 볶음밥 (bokk-eumbab)
fried sausage: 튀긴소시지 (twiginsosiji)
friend: 친구 (chingu)
friendly: 친절한 (chinjeolhan)
frog: 개구리 (gaeguli)
front: 앞 (ap)
front door: 현관문 (hyeongwanmun)
front light: 전방라이트 (jeonbanglaiteu)
front seat: 앞좌석 (apjwaseog)
fruit gum: 과일 껌 (gwail kkeom)
fruit merchant: 과일 상인 (gwail sang-in)
fruit salad: 과일 샐러드 (gwail saelleodeu)
fry: 튀기다 (twigida)
full: 배부른 (baebuleun), 가득찬 (gadeugchan)
full stop: 마침표 (machimpyo)
funeral: 장례식 (janglyesig)
funnel: 깔때기 (kkalttaegi)
funny: 재미있는 (jaemiissneun)

furniture store: 가구점 (gagujeom)

G

Gabon: 가봉 (gabong)
gadolinium: 가돌리늄 (gadollinyum)
gain weight: 체중을 늘리다 (chejung-eul neullida)
galaxy: 은하계 (eunhagye)
gall bladder: 쓸개 (sseulgae)
gallium: 갈륨 (gallyum)
gamble: 도박을 하다 (dobag-eul hada)
game: 사슴고기 (saseumgogi)
garage: 차고 (chago)
garage door: 차고 문 (chago mun)
garbage bin: 쓰레기통 (sseulegitong)
garden: 정원 (jeong-won)
gardener: 정원사 (jeong-wonsa)
garlic: 마늘 (maneul)
gas: 기체 (giche)
gear lever: 변속 레버 (byeonsog lebeo)
gear shift: 변속 기어 (byeonsog gieo)
gecko: 도마뱀붙이 (domabaembut-i)
gender: 성별 (seongbyeol)
general manager: 총지배인 (chongjibaein)
generator: 발전기 (baljeongi)
generous: 관대한 (gwandaehan)
geography: 지리 (jili)
geometry: 기하학 (gihahag)
Georgia: 그루지아 (geulujia)
German: 독일어 (dog-il-eo)
germanium: 게르마늄 (geleumanyum)
Germany: 독일 (dog-il)
geyser: 간헐 온천 (ganheol oncheon)
Ghana: 가나 (gana)
Gibraltar: 지브롤터 (jibeulolteo)
gin: 진 (jin)
ginger: 생강 (saeng-gang), 붉은머리의 (bulg-eunmeoliui)
giraffe: 기린 (gilin)
girl: 소녀 (sonyeo)
girlfriend: 여자친구 (yeojachingu)
give: 주다 (juda)
give a massage: 마사지를 해주다 (masajileul haejuda)
glacier: 빙하 (bingha)
gladiolus: 글라디올러스 (geulladiolleoseu)
glass: 유리컵 (yulikeob)
glasses: 안경 (angyeong)
glider: 글라이더 (geullaideo)
glove: 장갑 (jang-gab)
glue: 풀 (pul)
gluten: 글루텐 (geulluten)
goal: 골대 (goldae)
goat: 염소 (yeomso)
gold: 금 (geum)
Gold is more expensive than silver: 금이 은보다 더 비싸 (geum-i eunboda deo bissa)
gold medal: 금메달 (geummedal)
golf: 골프 (golpeu)
golf ball: 골프공 (golpeugong)
golf club: 골프채 (golpeuchae)
golf course: 골프장 (golpeujang)
good: 좋은 (joh-eun)
good bye: 안녕히 가세요 (annyeonghi gaseyo)

good day: 안녕하세요 (annyeonghaseyo)
goose: 거위 (geowi)
go straight: 직진해 (jigjinhae)
goulash: 굴라시 (gullasi)
GPS: GPS (GPS)
graduation: 졸업 (jol-eob)
graduation ceremony: 졸업식 (jol-eobsig)
gram: 그램 (geulaem)
grandchild: 손주 (sonju)
granddaughter: 손녀 (sonnyeo)
grandfather: 친할아버지 (chinhal-abeoji), 외할아버지 (oehal-abeoji)
grandmother: 친할머니 (chinhalmeoni), 외할머니 (oehalmeoni)
grandson: 손자 (sonja)
granite: 화강암 (hwagang-am)
granulated sugar: 입자가 굵은 설탕 (ibjaga gulg-eun seoltang)
grape: 포도 (podo)
grapefruit: 자몽 (jamong)
graphite: 흑연 (heug-yeon)
grass: 잔디 (jandi)
grasshopper: 메뚜기 (mettugi)
grater: 강판 (gangpan)
grave: 무덤 (mudeom)
gravity: 중력 (junglyeog)
Greece: 그리스 (geuliseu)
greedy: 탐욕스러운 (tam-yogseuleoun)
green: 초록색 (chologsaeg)
greenhouse: 온실 (onsil)
Greenland: 그린란드 (geulinlandeu)
green tea: 녹차 (nogcha)
Grenada: 그레나다 (geulenada)
grey: 회색 (hoesaeg)
groom: 신랑 (sinlang)
ground floor: 지상층 (jisangcheung)
group therapy: 집단 요법 (jibdan yobeob)
grow: 자라다 (jalada)
Guatemala: 과테말라 (gwatemalla)
guest: 손님 (sonnim)
guilty: 유죄의 (yujoeui)
Guinea: 기니 (gini)
Guinea-Bissau: 기니비사우 (ginibisau)
guinea pig: 기니피그 (ginipigeu)
guitar: 기타 (gita)
gun: 권총 (gwonchong)
Guyana: 가이아나 (gaiana)
gym: 체육관 (cheyuggwan)
gymnastics: 체조 (chejo)
gynaecology: 산부인과 (sanbu-ingwa)

H

hafnium: 하프늄 (hapeunyum)
hair: 머리카락 (meolikalag)
hairdresser: 미용사 (miyongsa)
hairdryer: 헤어 드라이어 (heeo deulaieo)
hair gel: 헤어 젤 (heeo jel)
hair straightener: 고데기 (godegi)
Haiti: 아이티 (aiti)
half an hour: 삼십분 (samsibbun)
Halloween: 할로윈 (hallowin)
ham: 햄 (haem)
hamburger: 햄버거 (haembeogeo)

hammer: 망치질하다 (mangchijilhada), 망치 (mangchi)
hammer throw: 해머 던지기 (haemeo deonjigi)
hamster: 햄스터 (haemseuteo)
hand: 손 (son)
handbag: 핸드백 (haendeubaeg)
handball: 핸드볼 (haendeubol)
hand brake: 핸드 브레이크 (haendeu beuleikeu)
handcuff: 수갑 (sugab)
handsaw: 가는톱 (ganeuntob)
handsome: 잘생긴 (jalsaeng-gin)
happy: 행복한 (haengboghan)
harbour: 항구 (hang-gu)
hard: 딱딱한 (ttagttaghan)
hard drive: 하드 드라이브 (hadeu deulaibeu)
harmonica: 하모니카 (hamonika)
harp: 하프 (hapeu)
hassium: 하슘 (hasyum)
hat: 모자 (moja)
hay fever: 건초열 (geonchoyeol)
hazelnut: 헤이즐넛 (heijeulneos)
he: 그 (geu)
head: 머리 (meoli)
headache: 두통 (dutong)
heading: 머리말 (meolimal)
head injury: 두부 외상 (dubu oesang)
healthy: 건강한 (geonganghan)
heart: 심장 (simjang)
heart attack: 심장 마비 (simjang mabi)
heating: 난방 (nanbang)
heavy: 무거운 (mugeoun)
heavy metal: 헤비메탈 (hebimetal)
hedge: 산울타리 (san-ultali)
hedgehog: 고슴도치 (goseumdochi)
heel: 발꿈치 (balkkumchi), 굽 (gub)
height: 높이 (nop-i)
heir: 상속인 (sangsog-in)
helicopter: 헬리콥터 (hellikobteo)
helium: 헬륨 (hellyum)
hello: 안녕하세요 (annyeonghaseyo)
helmet: 헬멧 (helmes)
help: 돕다 (dobda)
hemorrhoid: 치질 (chijil)
her dress: 그녀의 드레스 (geunyeoui deuleseu)
here: 여기 (yeogi)
heritage: 유산 (yusan)
hexagon: 육각형 (yuggaghyeong)
hi: 안녕 (annyeong)
hide: 숨다 (sumda)
high: 높은 (nop-eun)
high-speed train: 고속열차 (gosog-yeolcha)
high blood pressure: 고혈압 (gohyeol-ab)
high heels: 하이힐 (haihil)
high jump: 높이뛰기 (nop-ittwigi)
high school: 고등학교 (godeunghaggyo)
hiking: 하이킹 (haiking)
hiking boots: 등산화 (deungsanhwa)
hill: 언덕 (eondeog)
Himalayas: 히말라야 (himallaya)
hippo: 하마 (hama)
his car: 그의 차 (geuui cha)
history: 역사 (yeogsa)
hit: 때리다 (ttaelida)

hockey stick: 하키스틱 (hakiseutig)
hoe: 괭이 (gwaeng-i)
hole puncher: 펀치 (peonchi)
holmium: 홀뮴 (holmyum)
holy: 신성한 (sinseonghan)
homework: 숙제 (sugje)
homoeopathy: 동종요법 (dongjong-yobeob)
Honduras: 온두라스 (ondulaseu)
honey: 꿀 (kkul)
honeymoon: 신혼여행 (sinhon-yeohaeng)
Hong Kong: 홍콩 (hongkong)
horn: 경적 (gyeongjeog)
horror movie: 공포 영화 (gongpo yeonghwa)
horse: 말 (mal)
hose: 호스 (hoseu)
hospital: 병원 (byeong-won)
host: 주최자 (juchoeja)
hostel: 호스텔 (hoseutel)
hot: 매운 (maeun), 더운 (deoun)
hot-air balloon: 열기구 (yeolgigu)
hot-water bottle: 보온병 (boonbyeong)
hot chocolate: 핫초콜릿 (haschokollis)
hot dog: 핫도그 (hasdogeu)
hotel: 호텔 (hotel)
hot pot: 전골 (jeongol)
hour: 시 (si)
house: 집 (jib)
houseplant: 화초 (hwacho)
how: 어떻게 (eotteohge)
How are you?: 어떻게 지내? (eotteohge jinae?)
how many?: 몇 개? (myeochgae?)
how much?: 얼마나? (eolmana?)
How much is this?: 얼마에요? (eolma-eyo?)
huge: 큰 (keun)
human resources: 인사부 (insabu)
humidity: 습도 (seubdo)
Hungary: 헝가리 (heong-gali)
hungry: 배고픈 (baegopeun)
hurdles: 허들 경기 (heodeul gyeong-gi)
hurricane: 허리케인 (heolikein)
husband: 남편 (nampyeon)
hydrant: 소화전 (sohwajeon)
hydroelectric power station: 수력발전소 (sulyeogbaljeonso)
hydrogen: 수소 (suso)
hydrotherapy: 수 치료법 (su chilyobeob)
hyphen: 하이픈 (haipeun)
hypnosis: 최면 (choemyeon)

I

I: 나 (na)
I agree: 동의합니다 (dong-uihabnida)
ice: 얼음 (eol-eum)
ice climbing: 빙벽 등반 (bingbyeog deungban)
ice cream: 아이스크림 (aiseukeulim)
iced coffee: 아이스커피 (aiseukeopi)
ice hockey: 아이스하키 (aiseuhaki)
Iceland: 아이스랜드 (aiseulaendeu)
ice rink: 아이스링크 (aiseulingkeu)
ice skating: 아이스 스케이팅 (aiseu seukeiting)
icing sugar: 가루 설탕 (galu seoltang)

icon: 아이콘 (aikon)
I don't know: 몰라 (molla)
I don't like this: 난 이게 싫어요 (nan ige silh-eoyo)
I don't understand: 난 이해가 안돼 (nan ihaega andwae)
if: 만약 (man-yag)
I have a dog: 난 개를 키워요 (nan gaeleul kiwoyo)
I know: 알아 (al-a)
I like you: 난 너가 좋아요 (nan neoga joh-ayo)
I love you: 사랑해 (salanghae)
I miss you: 너가 그리워. (neoga geuliwo.)
immediately: 즉시 (jeugsi)
inbox: 메일함 (meilham)
inch: 인치 (inchi)
index finger: 집게 손가락 (jibge songalag)
India: 인도 (indo)
Indian Ocean: 인도양 (indoyang)
indium: 인듐 (indyum)
Indonesia: 인도네시아 (indonesia)
industrial district: 산업지구 (san-eobjigu)
I need this: 나 이거 필요해요 (na igeo pil-yohaeyo)
infant: 유아 (yua)
infection: 감염 (gam-yeom)
infusion: 수액 (suaeg)
inhaler: 흡입기 (heub-ibgi)
injure: 다치다 (dachida)
injury: 부상 (busang)
ink: 잉크 (ingkeu)
inking roller: 잉크 롤러 (ingkeu lolleo)
insect repellent: 방충제 (bangchungje)
inside: 안 (an)
instant camera: 즉석 카메라 (jeugseog kamela)
instant noodles: 인스턴트 면류 (inseuteonteu myeonlyu)
insulating tape: 절연 테이프 (jeol-yeon teipeu)
insulin: 인슐린 (insyullin)
insurance: 보험 (boheom)
intensive care unit: 중환자실 (junghwanjasil)
interest: 이자 (ija)
intern: 인턴 (inteon)
intersection: 교차로 (gyochalo)
intestine: 장 (jang)
investment: 투자 (tuja)
iodine: 요오드 (yoodeu)
ion: 이온 (ion)
Iran: 이란 (ilan)
Iraq: 이라크 (ilakeu)
Ireland: 아일랜드 (aillaendeu)
iridium: 이리듐 (ilidyum)
iris: 붓꽃 (buskkoch)
iron: 다림질 하다 (dalimjil hada), 철 (cheol)
ironing table: 다리미판 (dalimipan)
island: 섬 (seom)
isotope: 동위 원소 (dong-wi wonso)
Israel: 이스라엘 (iseula-el)
IT: 정보기술 (jeongbogisul)
Italy: 이탈리아 (itallia)
Ivory Coast: 코트디부아르 (koteudibualeu)
I want more: 난 더 원해 (nan deo wonhae)
I want this: 나 이거 갖고 싶어 (na igeo gajgo sip-eo)

J

jack: 잭 (jaeg)
jacket: 자켓 (jakes)
jackfruit: 잭푸르트 (jaegpuleuteu)
jade: 옥 (og)
jam: 잼 (jaem)
Jamaica: 자메이카 (jameika)
January: 1월 (1wol)
Japan: 일본 (ilbon)
Japanese: 일본어 (ilbon-eo)
jar: 항아리 (hang-ali)
javelin throw: 창던지기 (changdeonjigi)
jawbone: 턱뼈 (teogppyeo)
jazz: 재즈 (jaejeu)
jeans: 청바지 (cheongbaji)
jellyfish: 해파리 (haepali)
jersey: 저지 (jeoji)
jet ski: 제트 스키 (jeteu seuki)
jeweller: 보석상 (boseogsang)
jive: 자이브 (jaibeu)
job: 직업 (jig-eob)
jogging bra: 스포츠브라 (seupocheubeula)
joke: 농담 (nongdam)
Jordan: 요르단 (yoleudan)
journalist: 언론인 (eonlon-in)
judge: 판사 (pansa)
judo: 유도 (yudo)
juicy: 즙이 많은 (jeub-i manh-eun)
July: 7월 (7wol)
jump: 점프하다 (jeompeuhada)
June: 6월 (6wol)
junior school: 중학교 (junghaggyo)
Jupiter: 목성 (mogseong)
jury: 배심 (baesim)

K

kangaroo: 캥거루 (kaeng-geolu)
karate: 가라데 (galade)
kart: 레이싱 카트 (leising kateu)
Kazakhstan: 카자흐스탄 (kajaheuseutan)
kebab: 케밥 (kebab)
kennel: 개집 (gaejib)
Kenya: 케냐 (kenya)
kettle: 주전자 (jujeonja)
kettledrum: 케틀 드럼 (keteul deuleom)
key: 열쇠 (yeolsoe)
keyboard: 건반 (geonban), 키보드 (kibodeu)
key chain: 열쇠고리 (yeolsoegoli)
keyhole: 열쇠구멍 (yeolsoegumeong)
kick: 발로 차다 (ballo chada)
kidney: 신장 (sinjang)
kill: 죽이다 (jug-ida)
killer whale: 범고래 (beomgolae)
kilogram: 킬로그램 (killogeulaem)
kindergarten: 유치원 (yuchiwon)
kindergarten teacher: 유치원 선생님 (yuchiwon seonsaengnim)
Kiribati: 키리바시 (kilibasi)
kiss: 키스하다 (kiseuhada), 키스 (kiseu)
kitchen: 부엌 (bueok)
kiwi: 키위 (kiwi)
knee: 무릎 (muleup)

kneecap: 슬개골 (seulgaegol)
knife: 칼 (kal)
knit cap: 비니 (bini)
know: 알다 (alda)
koala: 코알라 (koalla)
Kosovo: 코소보 (kosobo)
krone: 크로네 (keulone)
krypton: 크립톤 (keulibton)
Kuwait: 쿠웨이트 (kuweiteu)
Kyrgyzstan: 키르기스스탄 (kileugiseuseutan)

L

laboratory: 실험실 (silheomsil)
lace: 신발 끈 (sinbal kkeun)
lacrosse: 라크로스 (lakeuloseu)
ladder: 사다리 (sadali)
ladle: 국자 (gugja)
ladybird: 무당벌레 (mudangbeolle)
lake: 호수 (hosu)
lamb: 양고기 (yang-gogi)
lamp: 램프 (laempeu)
landlord: 주인 (ju-in)
lanthanum: 란타넘 (lantaneom)
Laos: 라오스 (laoseu)
laptop: 노트북 (noteubug)
larch: 낙엽송 (nag-yeobsong)
lasagne: 라자냐 (lajanya)
last month: 지난달 (jinandal)
last week: 지난주 (jinanju)
last year: 작년 (jagnyeon)
Latin: 라틴어 (latin-eo)
Latin dance: 라틴 댄스 (latin daenseu)
latitude: 위도 (wido)
Latvia: 라트비아 (lateubia)
laugh: 웃다 (usda)
laundry: 빨래 (ppallae)
laundry basket: 빨래통 (ppallaetong)
lava: 용암 (yong-am)
law: 법률 (beoblyul)
lawn mower: 잔디깎이 (jandikkakk-i)
lawrencium: 로렌슘 (lolensyum)
lawyer: 변호사 (byeonhosa)
lazy: 게으른 (geeuleun)
lead: 납 (nab)
leaf: 잎 (ip)
leaflet: 전단지 (jeondanji)
lean meat: 지방이 적은 고기 (jibang-i jeog-eun gogi)
leather shoes: 가죽신발 (gajugsinbal)
Lebanon: 레바논 (lebanon)
lecture: 강의 (gang-ui)
lecturer: 강연자 (gang-yeonja)
lecture theatre: 계단식 강의실 (gyedansig gang-uisil)
leek: 골파 (golpa)
left: 왼쪽 (oenjjog)
leg: 다리 (dali)
legal department: 법무부 (beobmubu)
leggings: 레깅스 (legingseu)
leg press: 레그 프레스 (legeu peuleseu)
lemon: 레몬 (lemon)
lemonade: 레모네이드 (lemoneideu)

lemongrass: 레몬그라스 (lemongeulaseu)
lemur: 여우원숭이 (yeouwonsung-i)
leopard: 표범 (pyobeom)
Lesotho: 레소토 (lesoto)
less: 덜 (deol)
lesson: 수업 (sueob)
Let's go home: 집에가자 (jib-egaja)
letter: 글자 (geulja), 편지 (pyeonji)
lettuce: 상추 (sangchu)
Liberia: 라이베리아 (laibelia)
librarian: 사서 (saseo)
library: 도서관 (doseogwan)
Libya: 리비아 (libia)
lie: 눕다 (nubda)
Liechtenstein: 리히텐슈타인 (lihitensyutain)
lifeboat: 구명보트 (gumyeongboteu)
life buoy: 구명 부표 (gumyeong bupyo)
lifeguard: 인명 구조원 (inmyeong gujowon)
life jacket: 구명조끼 (gumyeongjokki)
lift: 들어올리다 (deul-eoollida)
light: 가벼운 (gabyeoun), 밝은 (balg-eun)
light bulb: 전구 (jeongu)
lighter: 라이터 (laiteo)
lighthouse: 등대 (deungdae)
lightning: 번개 (beongae)
light switch: 스위치 (seuwichi)
like: 좋아하다 (joh-ahada)
lime: 라임 (laim)
limestone: 석회석 (seoghoeseog)
limousine: 리무진 (limujin)
lingerie: 란제리 (lanjeli)
lion: 사자 (saja)
lip: 입술 (ibsul)
lip balm: 립밤 (libbam)
lip gloss: 립글로스 (libgeulloseu)
lipstick: 립스틱 (libseutig)
liqueur: 리큐어 (likyueo)
liquorice: 감초사탕 (gamchosatang)
listen: 듣다 (deudda)
liter: 리터 (liteo)
literature: 문학 (munhag)
lithium: 리튬 (lityum)
Lithuania: 리투아니아 (lituania)
little black dress: 리틀 블랙 드레스 (liteul beullaeg deuleseu)
little brother: 남동생 (namdongsaeng)
little finger: 새끼 손가락 (saekki songalag)
little sister: 여동생 (yeodongsaeng)
live: 살다 (salda)
liver: 간 (gan)
livermorium: 리버모륨 (libeomolyum)
living room: 거실 (geosil)
lizard: 도마뱀 (domabaem)
llama: 라마 (lama)
loan: 대출 (daechul)
lobby: 로비 (lobi)
lobster: 바닷가재 (badasgajae)
lock: 잠그다 (jamgeuda)
locomotive: 기관차 (gigwancha)
lonely: 외로운 (oeloun)
long: 긴 (gin)
longitude: 경도 (gyeongdo)
long jump: 멀리뛰기 (meollittwigi)

look for: 찾다 (chajda)
loppers: 절단기 (jeoldangi)
lorry: 대형 트럭 (daehyeong teuleog)
lorry driver: 트럭기사 (teuleoggisa)
lose: 지다 (jida)
lose weight: 체중을 빼다 (chejung-eul ppaeda)
loss: 손실 (sonsil)
lotus root: 연근 (yeongeun)
loud: 시끄러운 (sikkeuleoun)
loudspeaker: 스피커 (seupikeo)
love: 사랑하다 (salanghada), 사랑 (salang)
lovesickness: 상사병 (sangsabyeong)
low: 낮은 (naj-eun)
lubricant: 윤활제 (yunhwalje)
luge: 루지 (luji)
luggage: 짐 (jim)
lunar eclipse: 월식 (wolsig)
lunch: 점심식사 (jeomsimsigsa)
lung: 허파 (heopa)
lutetium: 루테튬 (lutetyum)
Luxembourg: 룩셈부르크 (lugsembuleukeu)
lychee: 리치 (lichi)
lyrics: 가사 (gasa)

M

Macao: 마카오 (makao)
Macedonia: 마케도니아 (makedonia)
Madagascar: 마다가스카르 (madagaseukaleu)
magazine: 잡지 (jabji)
magma: 마그마 (mageuma)
magnesium: 마그네슘 (mageunesyum)
magnet: 자석 (jaseog)
magnetic resonance imaging: 자기공명영상 (jagigongmyeong-yeongsang)
magpie: 까치 (kkachi)
mailbox: 우편함 (upyeonham)
Malawi: 말라위 (mallawi)
Malaysia: 말레이시아 (malleisia)
Maldives: 몰디브 (moldibeu)
Mali: 말리 (malli)
Malta: 몰타 (molta)
man: 남자 (namja)
manager: 매니저 (maenijeo)
Mandarin: 북경어 (buggyeong-eo)
manganese: 망간 (mang-gan)
mango: 망고 (mang-go)
manhole cover: 맨홀 뚜껑 (maenhol ttukkeong)
manicure: 매니큐어 (maenikyueo)
mannequin: 마네킹 (maneking)
many: 많은 (manh-eun)
map: 지도 (jido)
maple: 단풍나무 (danpungnamu)
maple syrup: 메이플 시럽 (meipeul sileob)
marathon: 마라톤 (malaton)
March: 3월 (3wol)
marjoram: 마저럼 (majeoleom)
market: 시장 (sijang)
marketing: 마케팅 (maketing)
marry: 결혼하다 (gyeolhonhada)
Mars: 화성 (hwaseong)
marsh: 습지 (seubji)

Marshall Islands: 마셜 제도 (masyeol jedo)
marshmallow: 마시멜로 (masimello)
martini: 마티니 (matini)
mascara: 마스카라 (maseukala)
mashed potatoes: 으깬 감자 (eukkaen gamja)
massage: 마사지 (masaji)
masseur: 마사지사 (masajisa)
mast: 돛대 (dochdae)
master: 석사 학위 (seogsa hag-wi)
match: 성냥 (seongnyang)
mathematics: 수학 (suhag)
mattress: 메트리스 (meteuliseu)
Mauritania: 모리타니 (molitani)
Mauritius: 모리셔스 (molisyeoseu)
May: 5월 (5wol)
mayonnaise: 마요네즈 (mayonejeu)
measles: 홍역 (hong-yeog)
measure: 재다 (jaeda)
meat: 고기 (gogi)
meatball: 미트볼 (miteubol)
mechanic: 정비공 (jeongbigong)
medal: 훈장 (hunjang), 메달 (medal)
meditation: 명상 (myeongsang)
Mediterranean Sea: 지중해 (jijunghae)
meerkat: 미어캣 (mieokaes)
meet: 만나다 (mannada)
meeting room: 회의실 (hoeuisil)
meitnerium: 마이트너륨 (maiteuneolyum)
melody: 멜로디 (mellodi)
member: 회원 (hoewon)
membership: 회원권 (hoewongwon)
mendelevium: 멘델레븀 (mendellebyum)
menu: 메뉴판 (menyupan)
Mercury: 수성 (suseong)
mercury: 수은 (sueun)
metal: 금속 (geumsog)
metalloid: 반금속 (bangeumsog)
meteorite: 운석 (unseog)
meter: 미터 (miteo)
methane: 메탄 (metan)
metropolis: 메트로폴리스 (meteulopolliseu)
Mexico: 멕시코 (megsiko)
Micronesia: 미크로네시아 (mikeulonesia)
microscope: 현미경 (hyeonmigyeong)
microwave: 전자레인지 (jeonjaleinji)
middle finger: 가운데 손가락 (gaunde songalag)
midnight: 자정 (jajeong)
midwife: 조산사 (josansa)
migraine: 편두통 (pyeondutong)
mile: 마일 (mail)
milk: 우유 (uyu)
milk powder: 분유 (bun-yu)
milkshake: 밀크쉐이크 (milkeusweikeu)
milk tea: 밀크티 (milkeuti)
Milky Way: 우리은하 (ulieunha)
millennium: 천년 (cheonnyeon)
milliliter: 밀리리터 (milliliteo)
millimeter: 밀리미터 (millimiteo)
minced meat: 다진고기 (dajingogi)
minibar: 미니바 (miniba)
minibus: 소형 버스 (sohyeong beoseu)
minister: 장관 (jang-gwan)

mint: 민트 (minteu)
minute: 분 (bun)
mirror: 거울 (geoul)
miscarriage: 유산 (yusan)
mitt: 야구 글러브 (yagu geulleobeu)
mixer: 믹서기 (migseogi)
mobile phone: 핸드폰 (haendeupon)
mocha: 모카 (moka)
model: 모델 (model)
modern pentathlon: 근대 5종 경기 (geundae 5jong gyeong-gi)
Moldova: 몰도바 (moldoba)
molecule: 분자 (bunja)
molybdenum: 몰리브데넘 (mollibeudeneom)
Monaco: 모나코 (monako)
Monday: 월요일 (wol-yoil)
money: 돈 (don)
Mongolia: 몽골 (mong-gol)
monk: 수도승 (sudoseung)
monkey: 원숭이 (wonsung-i)
Monopoly: 모노폴리 (monopolli)
monorail: 모노레일 (monoleil)
monsoon: 우기 (ugi)
Montenegro: 몬테네그로 (montenegeulo)
month: 달 (dal)
Montserrat: 몬세라트 (monselateu)
monument: 기념물 (ginyeommul)
moon: 달 (dal)
more: 더 (deo)
morning: 아침 (achim), 오전 (ojeon)
Morocco: 모로코 (moloko)
mosque: 모스크 (moseukeu)
mosquito: 모기 (mogi)
most: 가장 (gajang)
moth: 나방 (nabang)
mother: 어머니 (eomeoni)
mother-in-law: 장모 (jangmo)
motocross: 모터크로스 (moteokeuloseu)
motor: 모터 (moteo)
motorcycle: 오토바이 (otobai)
motorcycle racing: 오토바이 경주 (otobai gyeongju)
motor scooter: 스쿠터 (seukuteo)
motorway: 고속도로 (gosogdolo)
mountain: 산 (san)
mountain biking: 산악 자전거 타기 (san-ag jajeongeo tagi)
mountaineering: 등산 (deungsan)
mountain range: 산맥 (sanmaeg)
mouse: 생쥐 (saengjwi), 마우스 (mauseu)
mouth: 입 (ib)
mouthguard: 마우스피스 (mauseupiseu)
Mozambique: 모잠비크 (mojambikeu)
mozzarella: 모차렐라 (mochalella)
MP3 player: MP3플레이어 (MP3peulleieo)
muesli: 뮤즐리 (myujeulli)
muffin: 머핀 (meopin)
mufti: 무프티 (mupeuti)
multiplication: 곱셈 (gobsem)
mum: 엄마 (eomma)
mumps: 볼거리 (bolgeoli)
muscle: 근육 (geun-yug)
museum: 박물관 (bagmulgwan)
mushroom: 버섯 (beoseos)
musician: 음악가 (eum-agga)

mustard: 머스타드 (meoseutadeu)
mute: 농아자 (nong-aja)
my dog: 내 강아지 (nae gang-aji)

N

nachos: 나쵸 (nachyo)
nail: 못 (mos)
nail clipper: 손톱깎이 (sontobkkakk-i)
nail file: 손톱 다듬는 줄 (sontob dadeumneun jul)
nail polish: 매니큐어 (maenikyueo)
nail scissors: 손톱가위 (sontobgawi)
nail varnish remover: 매니큐어 리무버 (maenikyueo limubeo)
Namibia: 나미비아 (namibia)
nape: 목덜미 (mogdeolmi)
narrow: 좁은 (job-eun)
nasal bone: 코뼈 (koppyeo)
nasal spray: 비강 스프레이 (bigang seupeulei)
national park: 국립공원 (guglibgong-won)
Nauru: 나우루 (naulu)
nausea: 메스꺼움 (meseukkeoum)
neck: 목 (mog)
neck brace: 목 보호대 (mog bohodae)
necklace: 목걸이 (moggeol-i)
nectar: 꽃꿀 (kkochkkul)
needle: 바늘 (baneul)
negligee: 네글리제 (negeullije)
neighbour: 이웃 (ius)
neodymium: 네오디뮴 (ne-odimyum)
neon: 네온 (ne-on)
Nepal: 네팔 (nepal)
nephew: 조카 (joka)
Neptune: 해왕성 (haewangseong)
neptunium: 넵투늄 (nebtunyum)
nerve: 신경 (singyeong)
net: 네트 (neteu)
Netherlands: 네덜란드 (nedeollandeu)
network: 네트워크 (neteuwokeu)
neurology: 신경과 (singyeong-gwa)
neutron: 중성자 (jungseongja)
new: 새로운 (saeloun)
New Caledonia: 뉴칼레도니아 (nyukalledonia)
news: 뉴스 (nyuseu)
newsletter: 뉴스레터 (nyuseuleteo)
newspaper: 신문 (sinmun)
New Year: 새해 (saehae)
New Zealand: 뉴질랜드 (nyujillaendeu)
next month: 다음달 (da-eumdal)
next week: 다음주 (da-eumju)
next year: 내년 (naenyeon)
Nicaragua: 니카라과 (nikalagwa)
nickel: 니켈 (nikel)
niece: 조카딸 (jokattal)
Niger: 니제르 (nijeleu)
Nigeria: 나이지리아 (naijilia)
night: 밤 (bam)
night club: 나이트클럽 (naiteukeulleob)
nightie: 잠옷 (jam-os)
night table: 침실용 탁자 (chimsil-yong tagja)
niobium: 나이오븀 (naiobyum)
nipple: 유두 (yudu)

nitrogen: 질소 (jilso)
Niue: 니우에 (niue)
nobelium: 노벨륨 (nobellyum)
non-metal: 비금속 (bigeumsog)
none: 전혀 (jeonhyeo)
noodle: 국수 (gugsu)
noon: 정오 (jeong-o)
Nordic combined: 노르딕 복합 (noleudig boghab)
north: 북 (bug)
northern hemisphere: 북반구 (bugbangu)
North Korea: 북한 (bughan)
North Pole: 북극 (buggeug)
Norway: 노르웨이 (noleuwei)
nose: 코 (ko)
nosebleed: 코피 (kopi)
nostril: 콧구멍 (kosgumeong)
not: 아니다 (anida)
note: 음표 (eumpyo), 필기 (pilgi), 지폐 (jipye)
notebook: 공책 (gongchaeg)
nougat: 누가 (nuga)
novel: 소설 (soseol)
November: 11월 (11wol)
now: 지금 (jigeum)
no worries: 걱정하지마 (geogjeonghajima)
nuclear power plant: 원자력발전소 (wonjalyeogbaljeonso)
numerator: 분자 (bunja)
nun: 수녀 (sunyeo)
nurse: 간호사 (ganhosa)
nursery: 아기 방 (agi bang), 보육원 (boyug-won)
nut: 견과 (gyeongwa)
nutmeg: 육두구 (yugdugu)
nylon: 나일론 (naillon)

O

oak: 오크 (okeu)
oat: 귀리 (gwili)
oatmeal: 오트밀 (oteumil)
oboe: 오보에 (obo-e)
ocean: 해양 (haeyang)
octagon: 팔각형 (palgaghyeong)
October: 10월 (10wol)
octopus: 문어 (mun-eo)
oesophagus: 식도 (sigdo)
of course: 당연하지 (dang-yeonhaji)
office: 사무실 (samusil)
often: 자주 (jaju)
oil: 기름 (gileum)
oil paint: 오일 페인트 (oil peinteu)
oil pastel: 오일 파스텔 (oil paseutel)
ok: 승인 (seung-in)
okra: 오크라 (okeula)
old: 오래된 (olaedoen), 늙은 (neulg-eun)
olive: 올리브 (ollibeu)
olive oil: 올리브유 (ollibeuyu)
Oman: 오만 (oman)
oncology: 종양학 (jong-yanghag)
one-way street: 일방통행 (ilbangtonghaeng)
one o'clock in the morning: 새벽 한시 (saebyeog hansi)
onion: 양파 (yangpa)
onion ring: 어니언링 (eonieonling)

opal: 오팔 (opal)
open: 열다 (yeolda)
opera: 오페라 (opela)
operating theatre: 수술실 (susulsil)
optician: 안경사 (angyeongsa)
or: 또는 (ttoneun)
orange: 주황색 (juhwangsaeg), 오렌지 (olenji)
orange juice: 오렌지 주스 (olenji juseu)
orchestra: 오케스트라 (okeseuteula)
oregano: 오레가노 (olegano)
organ: 오르간 (oleugan)
origami: 종이접기 (jong-ijeobgi)
orphan: 고아 (goa)
orthopaedics: 정형외과 (jeonghyeong-oegwa)
osmium: 오스뮴 (oseumyum)
ostrich: 타조 (tajo)
other: 다른사람 (daleunsalam)
otter: 수달 (sudal)
ounce: 온스 (onseu)
our home: 우리 집 (uli jib)
outpatient: 외래환자 (oelaehwanja)
outside: 밖 (bakk)
ovary: 난소 (nanso)
oven: 오븐 (obeun)
overpass: 고가 도로 (goga dolo)
oviduct: 나팔관 (napalgwan)
ovum: 난자 (nanja)
owl: 부엉이 (bueong-i)
oxygen: 산소 (sanso)

P

Pacific Ocean: 태평양 (taepyeong-yang)
package: 포장 (pojang)
paediatrics: 소아과 (soagwa)
painkiller: 진통제 (jintongje)
paint: 그리다 (geulida), 페인트 (peinteu)
painting: 그림 (geulim)
Pakistan: 파키스탄 (pakiseutan)
Palau: 팔라우 (pallau)
pale: 창백한 (changbaeghan)
Palestine: 팔레스타인 (palleseutain)
palette: 팔레트 (palleteu)
palladium: 팔라듐 (palladyum)
pallet: 파렛트 (palesteu)
palm: 손바닥 (sonbadag)
palm tree: 야자수 (yajasu)
pan: 후라이팬 (hulaipaen)
Panama: 파나마 (panama)
pancake: 팬케익 (paenkeig)
pancreas: 췌장 (chwejang)
panda: 판다 (panda)
panties: 팬티 (paenti)
pantyhose: 팬티스타킹 (paentiseutaking)
panty liner: 팬티라이너 (paentilaineo)
papaya: 파파야 (papaya)
paperclip: 클립 (keullib)
paprika: 파프리카 (papeulika)
Papua New Guinea: 파푸아뉴기니 (papuanyugini)
parachute: 낙하산 (naghasan)
parachuting: 낙하산 (naghasan)

paragraph: 문단 (mundan)
Paraguay: 파라과이 (palagwai)
parasol: 파라솔 (palasol)
parcel: 소포 (sopo)
parents: 부모님 (bumonim)
parents-in-law: 시부모 (sibumo)
park: 공원 (gong-won)
parking meter: 주차 요금 미터기 (jucha yogeum miteogi)
parmesan: 파르메산 치즈 (paleumesan chijeu)
parrot: 앵무새 (aengmusae)
passport: 여권 (yeogwon)
password: 비밀번호 (bimilbeonho)
pathology: 병리학 (byeonglihag)
patient: 환자 (hwanja)
pavement: 보도 (bodo)
pay: 지불하다 (jibulhada)
pea: 완두콩 (wandukong)
peach: 복숭아 (bogsung-a)
peacock: 공작새 (gongjagsae)
peanut: 땅콩 (ttangkong)
peanut butter: 땅콩버터 (ttangkongbeoteo)
peanut oil: 땅콩기름 (ttangkong-gileum)
pear: 배 (bae)
pearl necklace: 진주목걸이 (jinjumoggeol-i)
pedestrian area: 보행자 구역 (bohaengja guyeog)
pedestrian crossing: 횡단보도 (hoengdanbodo)
pedicure: 페디큐어 (pedikyueo)
peel: 껍질을 까다 (kkeobjil-eul kkada)
peg: 빨래집게 (ppallaejibge)
pelican: 펠리컨 (pellikeon)
pelvis: 골반 (golban)
pen: 펜 (pen)
pencil: 연필 (yeonpil)
pencil case: 필통 (piltong)
pencil sharpener: 연필깎이 (yeonpilkkakk-i)
penguin: 펭귄 (peng-gwin)
peninsula: 반도 (bando)
penis: 음경 (eumgyeong)
pepper: 고추류 (gochulyu), 후추 (huchu)
perfume: 향수 (hyangsu)
periodic table: 주기율표 (jugiyulpyo)
Peru: 페루 (pelu)
petal: 꽃잎 (kkoch-ip)
Petri dish: 페트리 접시 (peteuli jeobsi)
petrol: 휘발유 (hwibal-yu)
petrol station: 주유소 (juyuso)
pet shop: 애완동물 가게 (aewandongmul gage)
pharmacist: 약사 (yagsa)
pharmacy: 약국 (yaggug)
PhD: 박사 학위 (bagsa hag-wi)
Philippines: 필리핀 (pillipin)
philosophy: 철학 (cheolhag)
phoalbum: 사진첩 (sajincheob)
phosphorus: 인 (in)
photographer: 사진작가 (sajinjagga)
physical education: 체육 (cheyug)
physician: 내과의사 (naegwauisa)
physicist: 물리학자 (mullihagja)
physics: 물리학 (mullihag)
physiotherapist: 물리치료사 (mullichilyosa)
physiotherapy: 물리치료 (mullichilyo)
piano: 피아노 (piano)

picnic: 피크닉 (pikeunig)
picture: 그림 (geulim)
picture frame: 액자 (aegja)
pie: 파이 (pai)
pier: 부두 (budu)
pig: 돼지 (dwaeji)
pigeon: 비둘기 (bidulgi)
piglet: 새끼돼지 (saekkidwaeji)
Pilates: 필라테스 (pillateseu)
pill: 알약 (al-yag)
pillow: 베개 (begae)
pilot: 조종사 (jojongsa)
pincers: 펜치 (penchi)
pine: 소나무 (sonamu)
pineapple: 파인애플 (pain-aepeul)
pink: 분홍색 (bunhongsaeg)
pipette: 피펫 (pipes)
pistachio: 피스타치오 (piseutachio)
pit: 심지 (simji)
pitchfork: 쇠스랑 (soeseulang)
pizza: 피자 (pija)
plane: 비행기 (bihaeng-gi)
planet: 행성 (haengseong)
plaster: 깁스 (gibseu)
plastic: 플라스틱 (peullaseutig)
plastic bag: 비닐봉투 (binilbongtu)
plate: 접시 (jeobsi)
platform: 승강장 (seung-gangjang)
platinum: 백금 (baeggeum)
play: 놀다 (nolda), 연극 (yeongeug)
playground: 놀이터 (nol-iteo)
please: 제발 (jebal)
plug: 플러그 (peulleogeu)
plum: 자두 (jadu)
plumber: 배관공 (baegwangong)
plump: 통통한 (tongtonghan)
Pluto: 명왕성 (myeong-wangseong)
plutonium: 플루토늄 (peullutonyum)
pocket: 주머니 (jumeoni)
poisoning: 중독 (jungdog)
poker: 포커 (pokeo)
Poland: 폴란드 (pollandeu)
polar bear: 북극곰 (buggeuggom)
pole: 극 (geug)
pole vault: 장대높이뛰기 (jangdaenop-ittwigi)
police: 경찰 (gyeongchal)
police car: 경찰차 (gyeongchalcha)
policeman: 경찰 (gyeongchal)
police station: 경찰서 (gyeongchalseo)
politician: 정치가 (jeongchiga)
politics: 정치학 (jeongchihag)
polo: 폴로 (pollo)
polonium: 폴로늄 (pollonyum)
polo shirt: 폴로셔츠 (pollosyeocheu)
polyester: 폴리에스테르 (pollieseuteleu)
pond: 연못 (yeonmos)
ponytail: 포니테일 (poniteil)
poor: 가난한 (gananhan)
pop: 팝 (pab)
popcorn: 팝콘 (pabkon)
pork: 돼지고기 (dwaejigogi)
porridge: 죽 (jug)

portfolio: 포트폴리오 (poteupollio)
portrait: 초상화 (chosanghwa)
Portugal: 포르투갈 (poleutugal)
postcard: 엽서 (yeobseo)
postman: 집배원 (jibbaewon)
post office: 우체국 (uchegug)
pot: 냄비 (naembi)
potasalad: 감자샐러드 (gamjasaelleodeu)
potassium: 칼륨 (kallyum)
potato: 감자 (gamja)
potawedges: 웨지감자 (wejigamja)
pottery: 도기류 (dogilyu)
pound: 파운드 (paundeu)
powder: 가루 (galu)
powder puff: 파우더 퍼프 (paudeo peopeu)
power: 전원 (jeon-won)
power line: 송전선 (songjeonseon)
power outlet: 콘센트 (konsenteu)
practice: 연습하다 (yeonseubhada)
praseodymium: 프라세오디뮴 (peulase-odimyum)
pray: 기도하다 (gidohada)
praying mantis: 사마귀 (samagwi)
preface: 서문 (seomun)
pregnancy test: 임신 검사 (imsin geomsa)
present: 선물 (seonmul)
presentation: 프레젠테이션 (peulejenteisyeon)
president: 대통령 (daetonglyeong)
press: 누르다 (nuleuda)
priest: 신부 (sinbu)
primary school: 초등학교 (chodeunghaggyo)
prime minister: 국무 총리 (gugmu chongli)
print: 출력하다 (chullyeoghada)
printer: 프린터 (peulinteo)
prison: 감옥 (gam-og)
professor: 교수 (gyosu)
profit: 수익 (su-ig)
programmer: 프로그래머 (peulogeulaemeo)
projector: 프로젝터 (peulojegteo)
promenade: 산책로 (sanchaeglo)
promethium: 프로메튬 (peulometyum)
prosecutor: 검사 (geomsa)
prostate: 전립샘 (jeonlibsaem)
prostitute: 매춘부 (maechunbu)
protactinium: 프로트악티늄 (peuloteuagtinyum)
proton: 양성자 (yangseongja)
proud: 자랑스러운 (jalangseuleoun)
province: 지방 (jibang)
psychiatry: 정신과 (jeongsingwa)
psychoanalysis: 정신 분석 (jeongsin bunseog)
psychotherapy: 심리치료 (simlichilyo)
publisher: 출판사 (chulpansa)
puck: 퍽 (peog)
pudding: 푸딩 (puding)
PuerRico: 푸에르토리코 (pueleutoliko)
pull: 당기다 (dang-gida)
pulse: 맥박 (maegbag)
pumpkin: 호박 (hobag)
punk: 펑크 (peongkeu)
pupil: 동공 (dong-gong)
purple: 보라색 (bolasaeg)
purse: 여성용 지갑 (yeoseong-yong jigab)
push: 밀다 (milda)

push-up: 팔굽혀 펴기 (palgubhyeo pyeogi)
pushchair: 유모차 (yumocha)
put: 놓다 (nohda)
putty: 퍼티 (peoti)
puzzle: 퍼즐 (peojeul)
pyjamas: 잠옷 (jam-os)
pyramid: 피라미드 (pilamideu)

Q

Qatar: 카타르 (kataleu)
quarter of an hour: 십오분 (sib-obun)
quartz: 석영 (seog-yeong)
question mark: 물음표 (mul-eumpyo)
quick: 빠른 (ppaleun)
quickstep: 퀵스텝 (kwigseuteb)
quiet: 조용한 (joyonghan)
quote: 인용하다 (in-yonghada)

R

rabbi: 랍비 (labbi)
rabbit: 토끼 (tokki)
raccoon: 미국너구리 (migugneoguli)
racing bicycle: 경주용 자전거 (gyeongjuyong jajeongeo)
radar: 레이더 (leideo)
radiator: 라디에이터 (ladieiteo)
radio: 라디오 (ladio)
radiology: 방사선과 (bangsaseongwa)
radish: 무 (mu)
radium: 라듐 (ladyum)
radius: 반지름 (banjileum)
radon: 라돈 (ladon)
rafting: 래프팅 (laepeuting)
railtrack: 선로 (seonlo)
rain: 비 (bi)
rainbow: 무지개 (mujigae)
raincoat: 우비 (ubi)
rainforest: 우림 (ulim)
rainy: 비가 오는 (biga oneun)
raisin: 건포도 (geonpodo)
rake: 갈퀴 (galkwi)
rally racing: 랠리 경주 (laelli gyeongju)
Ramadan: 라마단 (lamadan)
ramen: 라멘 (lamen)
random access memory (RAM): RAM (RAM)
rap: 랩 (laeb)
rapeseed oil: 유채씨유 (yuchaessiyu)
rash: 두드러기 (dudeuleogi)
raspberry: 라즈베리 (lajeubeli)
rat: 쥐 (jwi)
rattle: 딸랑이 (ttallang-i)
raven: 큰까마귀 (keunkkamagwi)
raw: 날것의 (nalgeos-ui)
razor: 면도기 (myeondogi)
razor blade: 면도날 (myeondonal)
read: 읽다 (ilgda)
reading room: 독서실 (dogseosil)
real-estate agent: 부동산중개인 (budongsanjung-gaein)
really: 정말로 (jeongmallo)
rear light: 후미등 (humideung)

rear mirror: 백미러 (baegmileo)
rear trunk: 트렁크 (teuleongkeu)
receptionist: 접수담당자 (jeobsudamdangja)
record player: 레코드 플레이어 (lekodeu peulleieo)
rectangle: 직사각형 (jigsagaghyeong)
recycle bin: 휴지통 (hyujitong)
red: 빨간색 (ppalgansaeg)
red panda: 레서판다 (leseopanda)
Red Sea: 홍해 (honghae)
red wine: 적포도주 (jeogpodoju)
reed: 갈대 (galdae)
referee: 심판 (simpan)
reggae: 레게 (lege)
region: 지역 (jiyeog)
relax: 진정해 (jinjeonghae)
remote control: 리모컨 (limokeon)
reporter: 기자 (gija)
Republic of the Congo: 콩고 공화국 (kong-go gonghwagug)
rescue: 구조하다 (gujohada)
research: 연구 (yeongu)
reservation: 예약 (yeyag)
respiratory machine: 호흡기 (hoheubgi)
rest: 쉬다 (swida)
restaurant: 레스토랑 (leseutolang)
result: 결과 (gyeolgwa)
retirement: 은퇴 (euntoe)
rhenium: 레늄 (lenyum)
rhino: 코뿔소 (koppulso)
rhodium: 로듐 (lodyum)
rhomboid: 평행사변형 (pyeonghaengsabyeonhyeong)
rhombus: 마름모 (maleummo)
rhythmic gymnastics: 리듬 체조 (lideum chejo)
rib: 늑골 (neuggol)
rice: 쌀 (ssal)
rice cooker: 전기 밥솥 (jeongi babsot)
rich: 부유한 (buyuhan)
right: 오른쪽 (oleunjjog)
right angle: 직각 (jiggag)
ring: 반지 (banji)
ring finger: 약손가락 (yagsongalag)
river: 강 (gang)
road: 도로 (dolo)
road roller: 로드 롤러 (lodeu lolleo)
roast chicken: 로스트치킨 (loseuteuchikin)
roast pork: 구운 돼지고기 (guun dwaejigogi)
robot: 로봇 (lobos)
rock: 록 (log), 바위 (bawi)
rock 'n' roll: 록큰롤 (logkeunlol)
rocket: 로켓 (lokes)
rocking chair: 흔들의자 (heundeul-uija)
roentgenium: 뢴트게늄 (loenteugenyum)
roll: 구르다 (guleuda)
roller coaster: 롤러코스터 (lolleokoseuteo)
roller skating: 롤러 스케이팅 (lolleo seukeiting)
Romania: 루마니아 (lumania)
roof: 지붕 (jibung)
roof tile: 기와 (giwa)
room key: 방열쇠 (bang-yeolsoe)
room number: 방번호 (bangbeonho)
room service: 룸서비스 (lumseobiseu)
root: 뿌리 (ppuli)
rose: 장미 (jangmi)

rosemary: 로즈마리 (lojeumali)
round: 둥근 (dung-geun)
roundabout: 로터리 (loteoli)
router: 공유기 (gong-yugi)
row: 열 (yeol)
rowing: 조정 (jojeong)
rowing boat: 노 젓는 배 (no jeosneun bae)
rubber: 지우개 (jiugae)
rubber band: 고무줄 (gomujul)
rubber boat: 고무보트 (gomuboteu)
rubber stamp: 고무도장 (gomudojang)
rubidium: 루비듐 (lubidyum)
ruby: 루비 (lubi)
rugby: 럭비 (leogbi)
ruin: 폐허 (pyeheo)
ruler: 자 (ja)
rum: 럼 (leom)
rumba: 룸바 (lumba)
run: 달리다 (dallida)
running: 달리기 (dalligi)
runway: 활주로 (hwaljulo)
rush hour: 러시아워 (leosiawo)
Russia: 러시아 (leosia)
ruthenium: 루테늄 (lutenyum)
rutherfordium: 러더포듐 (leodeopodyum)
Rwanda: 르완다 (leuwanda)

S

sad: 슬픈 (seulpeun)
saddle: 안장 (anjang)
safe: 안전한 (anjeonhan), 금고 (geumgo)
safety glasses: 보안경 (boangyeong)
Sahara: 사하라 (sahala)
sail: 항해하다 (hanghaehada)
sailing: 세일링 (seilling)
sailing boat: 돛단배 (dochdanbae)
Saint Kitts and Nevis: 세인트키츠 네비스 (seinteukicheu nebiseu)
Saint Lucia: 세인트루시아 (seinteulusia)
Saint Vincent and the Grenadines: 세인트빈센트 그레나딘 (seinteubinsenteu geulenadin)
sake: 사케 (sake)
salad: 샐러드 (saelleodeu)
salami: 살라미 (sallami)
salary: 월급 (wolgeub)
sales: 영업 (yeong-eob)
salmon: 연어 (yeon-eo)
salsa: 살사 (salsa)
salt: 소금 (sogeum)
salty: 짠 (jjan)
samarium: 사마륨 (samalyum)
samba: 삼바 (samba)
Samoa: 사모아 (samoa)
sand: 모래 (molae)
sandals: 샌들 (saendeul)
sandbox: 모래 상자 (molae sangja)
sandwich: 샌드위치 (saendeuwichi)
sanitary towel: 생리대 (saenglidae)
San Marino: 산마리노 (sanmalino)
sapphire: 사파이어 (sapaieo)
sardine: 정어리 (jeong-eoli)
satellite: 위성 (wiseong)

satellite dish: 위성방송 수신 안테나 (wiseongbangsong susin antena)
Saturday: 토요일 (toyoil)
Saturn: 토성 (toseong)
Saudi Arabia: 사우디아라비아 (saudialabia)
sauna: 사우나 (sauna)
sausage: 소시지 (sosiji)
savings: 저금 (jeogeum)
saw: 톱질하다 (tobjilhada), 톱 (tob)
saxophone: 색소폰 (saegsopon)
scaffolding: 비계 (bigye)
scale: 체중계 (chejung-gye)
scalpel: 메스 (meseu)
scan: 스캔하다 (seukaenhada)
scandium: 스칸듐 (seukandyum)
scanner: 스캐너 (seukaeneo)
scarf: 스카프 (seukapeu)
scholarship: 장학금 (janghaggeum)
school: 학교 (haggyo)
schoolbag: 책가방 (chaeggabang)
school bus: 스쿨버스 (seukulbeoseu)
school uniform: 교복 (gyobog)
schoolyard: 학교 운동장 (haggyo undongjang)
science: 과학 (gwahag)
science fiction: 공상 과학 (gongsang gwahag)
scientist: 과학자 (gwahagja)
scissors: 가위 (gawi)
scorpion: 전갈 (jeongal)
scrambled eggs: 스크램블드 에그 (seukeulaembeuldeu egeu)
screen: 스크린 (seukeulin), 모니터 (moniteo)
screwdriver: 스크류 드라이버 (seukeulyu deulaibeo)
screw wrench: 스크류 렌치 (seukeulyu lenchi)
script: 대본 (daebon)
scrollbar: 스크롤바 (seukeulolba)
scrotum: 음낭 (eumnang)
scrunchy: 헤어밴드 (heeobaendeu)
sculpting: 조각하다 (jogaghada)
sea: 바다 (bada)
seaborgium: 시보귬 (sibogyum)
seafood: 해산물 요리 (haesanmul yoli)
seagull: 갈매기 (galmaegi)
sea horse: 해마 (haema)
seal: 바다표범 (badapyobeom)
sea lion: 바다사자 (badasaja)
seat: 자리 (jali)
seatbelt: 안전벨트 (anjeonbelteu)
seaweed: 미역 (miyeog)
second: 초 (cho), 둘째 (duljjae)
second-hand shop: 중고품 가게 (jung-gopum gage)
second basement floor: 지하2층 (jiha2cheung)
secretary: 비서 (biseo)
security camera: 보안카메라 (boankamela)
security guard: 경비원 (gyeongbiwon)
seed: 씨앗 (ssias)
see you later: 나중에 보자 (najung-e boja)
selenium: 셀레늄 (sellenyum)
sell: 판매하다 (panmaehada)
semicolon: 세미콜론 (semikollon)
Senegal: 세네갈 (senegal)
September: 9월 (9wol)
Serbia: 세르비아 (seleubia)
server: 서버 (seobeo)
sewage plant: 폐수처리장 (pyesucheolijang)

sewing machine: 재봉틀 (jaebongteul)
sex: 섹스 (segseu)
sexy: 섹시한 (segsihan)
Seychelles: 세이셸 (seisyel)
shallow: 얕은 (yat-eun)
shampoo: 샴푸 (syampu)
share: 나누다 (nanuda), 주식 (jusig)
share price: 주가 (juga)
shark: 상어 (sang-eo)
shaver: 전기 면도기 (jeongi myeondogi)
shaving foam: 면도용 거품 (myeondoyong geopum)
she: 그녀 (geunyeo)
shed: 오두막 (odumag)
sheep: 양 (yang)
shelf: 선반 (seonban)
shell: 조개 (jogae)
shinpad: 신 패드 (sin paedeu)
ship: 선박 (seonbag)
shirt: 셔츠 (syeocheu)
shiver: 몸을 떨다 (mom-eul tteolda)
shock absorber: 완충기 (wanchung-gi)
shoe cabinet: 신발장 (sinbaljang)
shoot: 쏘다 (ssoda)
shooting: 사격 (sagyeog)
shop assistant: 점원 (jeom-won)
shopping basket: 쇼핑바구니 (syopingbaguni)
shopping cart: 쇼핑카트 (syopingkateu)
shopping mall: 쇼핑센터 (syopingsenteo)
shore: 해안 (haean)
short: 짧은 (jjalb-eun), 키가 작은 (kiga jag-eun)
shorts: 반바지 (banbaji)
short track: 쇼트트랙 (syoteuteulaeg)
shot put: 포환던지기 (pohwandeonjigi)
shoulder: 어깨 (eokkae)
shoulder blade: 어깨뼈 (eokkaeppyeo)
shout: 소리지르다 (solijileuda)
shovel: 삽 (sab)
shower: 샤워기 (syawogi)
shower cap: 샤워캡 (syawokaeb)
shower curtain: 샤워커튼 (syawokeoteun)
shower gel: 샤워젤 (syawojel)
show jumping: 장애물 경주 (jang-aemul gyeongju)
shrink: 줄어들다 (jul-eodeulda)
shuttlecock: 셔틀콕 (syeoteulkog)
shy: 수줍은 (sujub-eun)
siblings: 형제 (hyeongje)
sick: 아픈 (apeun)
side dish: 사이드 디쉬 (saideu diswi)
side door: 옆문 (yeopmun)
side effect: 부작용 (bujag-yong)
Sierra Leone: 시에라리온 (sielalion)
signal: 신호 (sinho)
signature: 서명 (seomyeong)
silent: 고요한 (goyohan)
silicon: 규소 (gyuso)
silk: 비단 (bidan)
silly: 바보 같은 (babo gat-eun)
silver: 은 (eun)
silver medal: 은메달 (eunmedal)
sing: 노래하다 (nolaehada)
Singapore: 싱가포르 (sing-gapoleu)
singer: 가수 (gasu)

single room: 1인실 (1insil)
sink: 싱크대 (singkeudae)
siren: 사이렌 (sailen)
sister-in-law: 시누이 (sinu-i)
sit: 앉다 (anjda)
sit-ups: 윗몸 일으키기 (wismom il-eukigi)
skateboarding: 스케이트보드 타기 (seukeiteubodeu tagi)
skates: 스케이트 (seukeiteu)
skeleton: 스켈레톤 (seukelleton), 골격 (golgyeog)
skewer: 꼬치 (kkochi)
ski: 스키 (seuki)
skiing: 스키 (seuki)
ski jumping: 스키 점프 (seuki jeompeu)
skinny: 마른 (maleun)
ski pole: 스키 스틱 (seuki seutig)
ski resort: 스키 지역 (seuki jiyeog)
skirt: 치마 (chima)
ski suit: 스키복 (seukibog)
skull: 두개골 (dugaegol)
skyscraper: 고층건물 (gocheung-geonmul)
sledge: 썰매 (sseolmae)
sleep: 잠을 자다 (jam-eul jada)
sleeping bag: 침낭 (chimnang)
sleeping mask: 수면 마스크 (sumyeon maseukeu)
sleeping pill: 수면제 (sumyeonje)
sleeve: 소매 (somae)
slide: 미끄럼틀 (mikkeuleomteul)
slim: 날씬한 (nalssinhan)
slippers: 슬리퍼 (seullipeo)
slope: 경사면 (gyeongsamyeon)
Slovakia: 슬로바키아 (seullobakia)
Slovenia: 슬로베니아 (seullobenia)
slow: 느린 (neulin)
small: 작은 (jag-eun)
small intestine: 소장 (sojang)
smartphone: 스마트폰 (seumateupon)
smell: 냄새 맡다 (naemsae matda)
smile: 미소를 짓다 (misoleul jisda)
smoke: 피우다 (piuda)
smoke detector: 연기감지기 (yeongigamjigi)
smoothie: 스무디 (seumudi)
smoothing plane: 대패 (daepae)
snack: 간식 (gansig)
snail: 달팽이 (dalpaeng-i)
snake: 뱀 (baem)
snare drum: 스네어 드럼 (seuneeo deuleom)
snooker: 스누커 (seunukeo)
snooker table: 스누커 테이블 (seunukeo teibeul)
snow: 눈 (nun)
snowboarding: 스노보드 (seunobodeu)
snowmobile: 설상차 (seolsangcha)
soap: 비누 (binu)
sober: 냉정한 (naengjeonghan)
social media: 소셜 미디어 (sosyeol midieo)
sock: 양말 (yangmal)
soda: 탄산수 (tansansu)
sodium: 나트륨 (nateulyum)
sofa: 소파 (sopa)
soft: 부드러운 (budeuleoun)
soil: 흙 (heulg)
solar eclipse: 일식 (ilsig)
solar panel: 태양 전지판 (taeyang jeonjipan)

soldier: 병사 (byeongsa)
sole: 구두밑창 (gudumitchang)
solid: 고체 (goche)
Solomon Islands: 솔로몬 제도 (sollomon jedo)
Somalia: 소말리아 (somallia)
son: 아들 (adeul)
son-in-law: 사위 (sawi)
soother: 고무젖꼭지 (gomujeojkkogji)
sore throat: 인후염 (inhuyeom)
sorry: 미안해 (mianhae)
soup: 수프 (supeu)
sour: 사워 (sawo)
sour cream: 사워크림 (sawokeulim)
south: 남 (nam)
South Africa: 남아프리카 공화국 (nam-apeulika gonghwagug)
southern hemisphere: 남반구 (nambangu)
South Korea: 대한민국 (daehanmingug)
South Pole: 남극 (namgeug)
South Sudan: 남수단 (namsudan)
souvenir: 기념품 (ginyeompum)
soy: 콩 (kong)
soy milk: 두유 (duyu)
space: 공간 (gong-gan)
space shuttle: 우주 왕복선 (uju wangbogseon)
space station: 우주 정거장 (uju jeong-geojang)
space suit: 우주복 (ujubog)
spaghetti: 스파게티 (seupageti)
Spain: 스페인 (seupein)
Spanish: 스페인어 (seupein-eo)
sparkling wine: 스파클링 와인 (seupakeulling wain)
speed limit: 속도제한 (sogdojehan)
speedometer: 속도계 (sogdogye)
speed skating: 스피드 스케이팅 (seupideu seukeiting)
sperm: 정액 (jeong-aeg)
sphere: 구 (gu)
spider: 거미 (geomi)
spinach: 시금치 (sigeumchi)
spinal cord: 척수 (cheogsu)
spine: 척추 (cheogchu)
spirit level: 기포관수준기 (gipogwansujungi)
spit: 침을 뱉다 (chim-eul baetda)
spleen: 비장 (bijang)
sponge: 스폰지 (seuponji)
spoon: 숟가락 (sudgalag)
sports ground: 체육관 (cheyuggwan)
sports shop: 스포츠 용품점 (seupocheu yongpumjeom)
spray: 스프레이 (seupeulei)
spring: 봄 (bom)
spring onion: 파 (pa)
spring roll: 춘권 (chungwon)
sprint: 단거리 달리기 (dangeoli dalligi)
square: 각진 (gagjin), 정사각형 (jeongsagaghyeong), 광장 (gwangjang)
square meter: 제곱미터 (jegobmiteo)
squat: 스쿼트 (seukwoteu)
squid: 오징어 (ojing-eo)
squirrel: 다람쥐 (dalamjwi)
Sri Lanka: 스리랑카 (seulilangka)
staff: 직원 (jig-won)
stage: 무대 (mudae)
stairs: 계단 (gyedan)
stalk: 줄기 (julgi)
stamp: 우표 (upyo)

stand: 서다 (seoda)
stapler: 호치키스 (hochikiseu)
star: 별 (byeol)
stare: 쳐다보다 (chyeodaboda)
starfish: 불가사리 (bulgasali)
starter: 전채 요리 (jeonchae yoli)
state: 주 (ju)
steak: 스테이크 (seuteikeu)
steal: 훔치다 (humchida)
steam train: 증기 기관차 (jeung-gi gigwancha)
steel: 강철 (gangcheol)
steel beam: 강철 빔 (gangcheol bim)
steep: 가파른 (gapaleun)
steering wheel: 핸들 (haendeul)
stepdaughter: 의붓딸 (uibusttal)
stepfather: 새아버지 (saeabeoji)
stepmother: 새어머니 (saeeomeoni)
stepson: 의붓아들 (uibus-adeul)
stethoscope: 청진기 (cheongjingi)
stewardess: 승무원 (seungmuwon)
stockbroker: 증권 중개인 (jeung-gwon jung-gaein)
stock exchange: 증권 거래소 (jeung-gwon geolaeso)
stocking: 스타킹 (seutaking)
stomach: 위 (wi)
stomach ache: 복통 (bogtong)
stool: 스툴 (seutul)
stopwatch: 초시계 (chosigye)
stork: 황새 (hwangsae)
storm: 폭풍 (pogpung)
straight: 직진 (jigjin), 직모의 (jigmoui)
straight line: 직선 (jigseon)
strange: 이상한 (isanghan)
strawberry: 딸기 (ttalgi)
stream: 시내 (sinae)
street food: 길거리 음식 (gilgeoli eumsig)
street light: 가로등 (galodeung)
stress: 스트레스 (seuteuleseu)
stretching: 스트레칭 (seuteuleching)
strict: 엄격한 (eomgyeoghan)
stroke: 뇌졸중 (noejoljung)
strong: 강한 (ganghan)
strontium: 스트론튬 (seuteulontyum)
study: 공부하다 (gongbuhada)
stupid: 바보 (babo)
submarine: 잠수함 (jamsuham)
subtraction: 뺄셈 (ppaelsem)
suburb: 교외 (gyooe)
subway: 지하철 (jihacheol)
Sudan: 수단 (sudan)
suddenly: 갑자기 (gabjagi)
Sudoku: 스도쿠 (seudoku)
sugar: 설탕 (seoltang)
sugar beet: 사탕무 (satangmu)
sugar cane: 사탕수수 (satangsusu)
sugar melon: 멜론 (mellon)
suit: 양복 (yangbog)
sulphur: 황 (hwang)
summer: 여름 (yeoleum)
sun: 태양 (taeyang)
sunburn: 햇볕에 탐 (haesbyeot-e tam)
Sunday: 일요일 (il-yoil)
sunflower: 해바라기 (haebalagi)

sunflower oil: 해바라기유 (haebalagiyu)
sunglasses: 선글라스 (seongeullaseu)
sun hat: 모자 (moja)
sunny: 화창한 (hwachanghan)
sunscreen: 자외선 차단제 (jaoeseon chadanje)
sunshine: 햇빛 (haesbich)
supermarket: 슈퍼마켓 (syupeomakes)
surfboard: 서핑보드 (seopingbodeu)
surfing: 서핑 (seoping)
surgeon: 외과의사 (oegwauisa)
surgery: 수술 (susul), 외과 (oegwa)
Suriname: 수리남 (sulinam)
surprised: 놀란 (nollan)
sushi: 스시 (seusi)
suspect: 피의자 (piuija)
suture: 봉합선 (bonghabseon)
swallow: 삼키다 (samkida)
swan: 백조 (baegjo)
Swaziland: 스와질란드 (seuwajillandeu)
sweatband: 땀흡수밴드 (ttamheubsubaendeu)
sweater: 스웨터 (seuweteo)
sweatpants: 트레이닝바지 (teuleiningbaji)
Sweden: 스웨덴 (seuweden)
sweet: 단 (dan)
sweet potato: 고구마 (goguma)
swim: 수영하다 (suyeonghada)
swim cap: 수영모 (suyeongmo)
swim goggles: 고글 (gogeul)
swimming: 수영 (suyeong)
swimming pool: 수영장 (suyeongjang)
swimsuit: 수영복 (suyeongbog)
swim trunks: 남성용 사각 수영복 (namseong-yong sagag suyeongbog)
swing: 그네 (geune)
Switzerland: 스위스 (seuwiseu)
symphony: 심포니 (simponi)
synagogue: 시나고그 (sinagogeu)
synchronized swimming: 수중 발레 (sujung balle)
Syria: 시리아 (silia)
syringe: 주사기 (jusagi)
São Tomé and Príncipe: 상투메 프린시페 (sangtume peulinsipe)

T

T-shirt: 티셔츠 (tisyeocheu)
table: 식탁 (sigtag)
tablecloth: 식탁보 (sigtagbo)
table of contents: 목차 (mogcha)
table tennis: 탁구 (taggu)
table tennis table: 탁구 테이블 (taggu teibeul)
taekwondo: 태권도 (taegwondo)
tailor: 재단사 (jaedansa)
Taiwan: 대만 (daeman)
Tajikistan: 타지키스탄 (tajikiseutan)
take: 가지고 가다 (gajigo gada)
take a shower: 샤워를 하다 (syawoleul hada)
take care: 잘지내 (jaljinae)
talk: 말하다 (malhada)
tall: 키가 큰 (kiga keun)
tambourine: 탬버린 (taembeolin)
tampon: 탐폰 (tampon)
tandem: 2인용 자전거 (2in-yong jajeongeo)

tangent: 접선 (jeobseon)
tango: 탱고 (taeng-go)
tank: 탱크 (taengkeu)
tantalum: 탄탈럼 (tantalleom)
Tanzania: 탄자니아 (tanjania)
tap: 수도꼭지 (sudokkogji)
tape measure: 줄자 (julja)
tapir: 맥 (maeg)
tap water: 수돗물 (sudosmul)
tar: 타르 (taleu)
tarantula: 타란튤라 (talantyulla)
tattoo: 타투 (tatu)
tax: 세금 (segeum)
taxi: 택시 (taegsi)
taxi driver: 택시기사 (taegsigisa)
tea: 차 (cha)
teacher: 선생님 (seonsaengnim)
teapot: 차주전자 (chajujeonja)
technetium: 테크네튬 (tekeunetyum)
telephone: 전화기 (jeonhwagi)
telephone number: 전화번호 (jeonhwabeonho)
telescope: 망원경 (mang-wongyeong)
tellurium: 텔루륨 (tellulyum)
temperature: 온도 (ondo)
temple: 관자놀이 (gwanjanol-i), 절 (jeol)
tendon: 힘줄 (himjul)
tennis: 테니스 (teniseu)
tennis ball: 테니스 공 (teniseu gong)
tennis court: 테니스코트 (teniseukoteu)
tennis racket: 테니스 채 (teniseu chae)
tent: 텐트 (tenteu)
tequila: 테킬라 (tekilla)
terbium: 터븀 (teobyum)
term: 학기 (haggi)
termite: 흰개미 (huingaemi)
terrace: 테라스 (telaseu)
territory: 영토 (yeongto)
testament: 유언 (yueon)
testicle: 고환 (gohwan)
Tetris: 테트리스 (teteuliseu)
text: 본문 (bonmun)
textbook: 교과서 (gyogwaseo)
text message: 문자 메시지 (munja mesiji)
Thailand: 태국 (taegug)
thallium: 탈륨 (tallyum)
Thanksgiving: 추수감사절 (chusugamsajeol)
thank you: 고마워 (gomawo)
that: 그것 (geugeos)
theatre: 극장 (geugjang)
The Bahamas: 바하마 (bahama)
the day after tomorrow: 모레 (mole)
the day before yesterday: 그저께 (geujeokke)
The Gambia: 감비아 (gambia)
their company: 그들의 회사 (geudeul-ui hoesa)
theme park: 놀이공원 (nol-igong-won)
then: 그때 (geuttae)
theory of relativity: 상대성 이론 (sangdaeseong ilon)
there: 저기 (jeogi)
thermal underwear: 내복 (naebog)
thermos jug: 보온병 (boonbyeong)
thesis: 논문 (nonmun)
The United States of America: 미국 (migug)

they: 그들 (geudeul)
thief: 도둑 (dodug)
think: 생각하다 (saeng-gaghada)
third: 셋째 (sesjjae)
thirsty: 목마른 (mogmaleun)
this: 이것 (igeos)
this month: 이번달 (ibeondal)
this week: 이번주 (ibeonju)
this year: 올해 (olhae)
thong: 티팬티 (tipaenti)
thorium: 토륨 (tolyum)
threaten: 협박하다 (hyeobbaghada)
three quarters of an hour: 사십오분 (sasib-obun)
thriller: 스릴러 (seulilleo)
throttle: 조절판 (jojeolpan)
throw: 던지다 (deonjida)
thulium: 툴륨 (tullyum)
thumb: 엄지 (eomji)
thunder: 천둥 (cheondung)
thunderstorm: 뇌우 (noeu)
Thursday: 목요일 (mog-yoil)
thyme: 백리향 (baeglihyang)
ticket: 표 (pyo)
ticket office: 매표소 (maepyoso)
ticket vending machine: 매표기기 (maepyogigi)
tidal wave: 해일 (haeil)
tie: 넥타이 (negtai)
tiger: 호랑이 (holang-i)
tile: 타일 (tail)
timetable: 시간표 (siganpyo)
tin: 주석 (juseog), 통조림 (tongjolim)
tip: 팁 (tib)
tired: 피곤한 (pigonhan)
tissue: 휴지 (hyuji)
titanium: 타이타늄 (taitanyum)
toaster: 토스터 (toseuteo)
tobacco: 담배 (dambae)
today: 오늘 (oneul)
toe: 발가락 (balgalag)
tofu: 두부 (dubu)
together: 함께 (hamkke)
Togo: 토고 (togo)
toilet: 화장실 (hwajangsil), 변기 (byeongi)
toilet brush: 변기청소솔 (byeongicheongsosol)
toilet paper: 화장지 (hwajangji)
toll: 통행료 (tonghaenglyo)
tomasauce: 토마토소스 (tomatososeu)
tomato: 토마토 (tomato)
tomorrow: 내일 (naeil)
ton: 톤 (ton)
Tonga: 통가 (tong-ga)
tongue: 혀 (hyeo)
tooth: 치아 (chia)
toothache: 치통 (chitong)
toothbrush: 칫솔 (chis-sol)
toothpaste: 치약 (chiyag)
torch: 손전등 (sonjeondeung)
tornado: 토네이도 (toneido)
tortoise: 거북이 (geobug-i)
touch: 만지다 (manjida)
tour guide: 가이드 (gaideu)
tourist attraction: 관광명소 (gwangwangmyeongso)

tourist guide: 가이드 (gaideu)
tourist information: 관광 안내소 (gwangwang annaeso)
towel: 수건 (sugeon)
town hall: 시청 (sicheong)
toy shop: 장난감 가게 (jangnangam gage)
track cycling: 트랙 사이클링 (teulaeg saikeulling)
tracksuit: 운동복 (undongbog)
tractor: 트랙터 (teulaegteo)
traffic jam: 교통체증 (gyotongchejeung)
traffic light: 신호등 (sinhodeung)
trailer: 트레일러 (teuleilleo)
train: 기차 (gicha)
train driver: 기차 운전사 (gicha unjeonsa)
trainers: 운동화 (undonghwa)
train station: 기차역 (gichayeog)
tram: 트램 (teulaem)
trampoline: 트램펄린 (teulaempeollin)
trapezoid: 사다리꼴 (sadalikkol)
travel: 여행을 하다 (yeohaeng-eul hada)
travel agent: 여행사 직원 (yeohaengsa jig-won)
treadmill: 밟아 돌리는 바퀴 (balb-a dollineun bakwi)
tree: 나무 (namu)
tree house: 트리하우스 (teulihauseu)
triangle: 트라이앵글 (teulaiaeng-geul), 삼각형 (samgaghyeong)
triathlon: 철인3종경기 (cheol-in3jong-gyeong-gi)
Trinidad and Tobago: 트리니다드 토바고 (teulinidadeu tobago)
triple jump: 3단뛰기 (3danttwigi)
triplets: 세쌍둥이 (sessangdung-i)
tripod: 삼각대 (samgagdae)
trombone: 트럼본 (teuleombon)
tropics: 열대 (yeoldae)
trousers: 바지 (baji)
truffle: 트러플 (teuleopeul)
trumpet: 트럼펫 (teuleompes)
trunk: 줄기 (julgi)
tuba: 튜바 (tyuba)
Tuesday: 화요일 (hwayoil)
tulip: 튤립 (tyullib)
tuna: 참치 (chamchi)
tungsten: 텅스텐 (teongseuten)
Tunisia: 튀니지 (twiniji)
Turkey: 터키 (teoki)
turkey: 칠면조 (chilmyeonjo), 칠면조 고기 (chilmyeonjo gogi)
Turkmenistan: 투르크메니스탄 (tuleukeumeniseutan)
turnip cabbage: 콜라비 (kollabi)
turn left: 좌회전해 (jwahoejeonhae)
turn off: 끄다 (kkeuda)
turn on: 켜다 (kyeoda)
turn right: 우회전해 (uhoejeonhae)
turtle: 바다 거북 (bada geobug)
Tuvalu: 투발루 (tuballu)
TV: 텔레비전 (tellebijeon)
TV series: 티비 시리즈 (tibi silijeu)
TV set: 텔레비전 (tellebijeon)
tweezers: 족집게 (jogjibge)
twins: 쌍둥이 (ssangdung-i)
twisting: 비틀림 (biteullim)
two o'clock in the afternoon: 오후 두시 (ohu dusi)
typhoon: 태풍 (taepung)
tyre: 타이어 (taieo)

U

Uganda: 우간다 (uganda)
ugly: 못생긴 (mos-saeng-gin)
Ukraine: 우크라이나 (ukeulaina)
ukulele: 우쿨렐레 (ukullelle)
ultrasound machine: 초음파 기기 (cho-eumpa gigi)
umbrella: 우산 (usan)
uncle: 삼촌 (samchon)
underpants: 팬티 (paenti)
underpass: 지하도 (jihado)
underscore: 밑줄 (mitjul)
undershirt: 속셔츠 (sogsyeocheu)
unfair: 불공평한 (bulgongpyeonghan)
uniform: 유니폼 (yunipom)
United Arab Emirates: 아랍에미리트 (alab-emiliteu)
United Kingdom: 영국 (yeong-gug)
university: 대학교 (daehaggyo)
uranium: 우라늄 (ulanyum)
Uranus: 천왕성 (cheon-wangseong)
url: URL (URL)
urn: 유골 단지 (yugol danji)
urology: 비뇨기과 (binyogigwa)
Uruguay: 우루과이 (ulugwai)
USB stick: USB 플래시 드라이브 (USB peullaesi deulaibeu)
uterus: 자궁 (jagung)
utility knife: 다용도칼 (dayongdokal)
Uzbekistan: 우즈베키스탄 (ujeubekiseutan)

V

vacuum: 청소기를 돌리다 (cheongsogileul dollida)
vacuum cleaner: 진공청소기 (jingongcheongsogi)
vagina: 질 (jil)
valley: 계곡 (gyegog)
vanadium: 바나듐 (banadyum)
vanilla: 바닐라 (banilla)
vanilla sugar: 바닐라 설탕 (banilla seoltang)
Vanuatu: 바누아투 (banuatu)
varnish: 래커 (laekeo)
vase: 꽃병 (kkochbyeong)
Vatican City: 바티칸 시국 (batikan sigug)
veal: 송아지고기 (song-ajigogi)
vector: 벡터 (begteo)
vein: 정맥 (jeongmaeg)
Venezuela: 베네수엘라 (benesuella)
Venus: 금성 (geumseong)
vertebra: 척추뼈 (cheogchuppyeo)
very: 아주 (aju)
vet: 수의사 (suuisa)
Viennese waltz: 비엔나 왈츠 (bienna walcheu)
Vietnam: 베트남 (beteunam)
village: 마을 (ma-eul)
vinegar: 식초 (sigcho)
viola: 비올라 (biolla)
violin: 바이올린 (baiollin)
virus: 바이러스 (baileoseu)
visa: 비자 (bija)
visiting hours: 방문시간 (bangmunsigan)
visitor: 방문자 (bangmunja)
vitamin: 비타민 (bitamin)

vocational training: 직업학교 (jig-eobhaggyo)
vodka: 보드카 (bodeuka)
voice message: 음성메시지 (eumseongmesiji)
volcano: 화산 (hwasan)
volleyball: 배구 (baegu)
volt: 볼트 (bolteu)
volume: 부피 (bupi)
vomit: 구토하다 (gutohada)
vote: 투표를 하다 (tupyoleul hada)

W

waffle: 와플 (wapeul)
waist: 허리 (heoli)
wait: 기다리다 (gidalida)
waiter: 웨이터 (weiteo)
waiting room: 대기실 (daegisil)
walk: 걷다 (geodda)
walkie-talkie: 무전기 (mujeongi)
wall: 벽 (byeog)
wallet: 지갑 (jigab)
walnut: 호두 (hodu)
walrus: 바다코끼리 (badakokkili)
waltz: 왈츠 (walcheu)
wardrobe: 옷장 (osjang)
warehouse: 창고 (chang-go)
warm: 따뜻한 (ttatteushan)
warm-up: 준비운동 (junbiundong)
warn: 경고하다 (gyeong-gohada)
warning light: 경고등 (gyeong-godeung)
warranty: 보증서 (bojeungseo)
wash: 씻다 (ssisda)
washing machine: 세탁기 (setaggi)
washing powder: 가루비누 (galubinu)
wasp: 말벌 (malbeol)
watch: 지켜보다 (jikyeoboda), 손목시계 (sonmogsigye)
water: 물 (mul)
water bottle: 물병 (mulbyeong)
water can: 물뿌리개 (mulppuligae)
waterfall: 폭포 (pogpo)
water melon: 수박 (subag)
water park: 워터파크 (woteopakeu)
water polo: 수구 (sugu)
waterskiing: 수상스키 (susangseuki)
water slide: 워터 슬라이드 (woteo seullaideu)
watt: 와트 (wateu)
we: 우리 (uli)
weak: 약한 (yaghan)
webcam: 웹캠 (webkaem)
website: 웹사이트 (websaiteu)
wedding: 결혼식 (gyeolhonsig)
wedding cake: 웨딩 케이크 (weding keikeu)
wedding dress: 웨딩드레스 (wedingdeuleseu)
wedding ring: 결혼반지 (gyeolhonbanji)
Wednesday: 수요일 (suyoil)
weed: 잡초 (jabcho)
week: 주 (ju)
weightlifting: 역도 (yeogdo)
welcome: 환영합니다 (hwan-yeonghabnida)
well-behaved: 행실이 바른 (haengsil-i baleun)
wellington boots: 장화 (janghwa)

west: 서 (seo)
western film: 서부 (seobu)
wet: 젖은 (jeoj-eun)
wetsuit: 잠수복 (jamsubog)
whale: 고래 (golae)
what: 무엇 (mueos)
What's your name?: 이름이 뭐에요? (ileum-i mwo-eyo?)
wheat: 밀 (mil)
wheelbarrow: 외바퀴 손수레 (oebakwi sonsule)
wheelchair: 휠체어 (hwilcheeo)
when: 언제 (eonje)
where: 어디 (eodi)
Where is the toilet?: 화장실이 어디에 있어요? (hwajangsil-i eodie iss-eoyo?)
which: 어느 (eoneu)
whip: 채찍 (chaejjig)
whipped cream: 생크림 (saengkeulim)
whiskey: 위스키 (wiseuki)
whisper: 속삭이다 (sogsag-ida)
white: 하얀색 (hayansaeg)
white wine: 백포도주 (baegpodoju)
who: 누구 (nugu)
why: 왜 (wae)
widow: 과부 (gwabu)
widower: 홀아비 (hol-abi)
width: 폭 (pog)
wife: 아내 (anae)
wig: 가발 (gabal)
willow: 버드나무 (beodeunamu)
win: 이기다 (igida)
wind: 바람 (balam)
wind farm: 풍력 발전소 (punglyeog baljeonso)
window: 창문 (changmun)
windpipe: 기관 (gigwan)
windscreen: 앞유리 (ap-yuli)
windscreen wiper: 와이퍼 (waipeo)
windsurfing: 윈드 서핑 (windeu seoping)
windy: 바람이 부는 (balam-i buneun)
wine: 와인 (wain)
wing: 날개 (nalgae)
wing mirror: 사이드미러 (saideumileo)
winter: 겨울 (gyeoul)
wire: 철사 (cheolsa)
witness: 증인 (jeung-in)
wolf: 늑대 (neugdae)
woman: 여자 (yeoja)
womb: 자궁 (jagung)
wooden beam: 나무 빔 (namu bim)
wooden spoon: 나무 숟가락 (namu sudgalag)
woodwork: 목세공 (mogsegong)
wool: 양모 (yangmo)
work: 일하다 (ilhada)
workroom: 작업실 (jag-eobsil)
world record: 세계 기록 (segye gilog)
worried: 걱정하는 (geogjeonghaneun)
wound: 상처 (sangcheo)
wrestling: 레슬링 (leseulling)
wrinkle: 주름 (juleum)
wrist: 손목 (sonmog)
write: 쓰다 (sseuda)
wrong: 틀린 (teullin)

X

X-ray photograph: 엑스레이 사진 (egseulei sajin)
xenon: 제논 (jenon)
xylophone: 실로폰 (sillopon)

Y

yacht: 요트 (yoteu)
yard: 야드 (yadeu)
year: 년 (nyeon)
yeast: 효모 (hyomo)
yellow: 노랑색 (nolangsaeg)
Yemen: 예멘 (yemen)
yen: 엔 (en)
yesterday: 어제 (eoje)
yoga: 요가 (yoga)
yoghurt: 요구르트 (yoguleuteu)
yolk: 달걀 노른자 (dalgyal noleunja)
you: 너 (neo), 너희들 (neohuideul)
young: 젊은 (jeolm-eun)
your cat: 네 고양이 (ne goyang-i)
your team: 너의 팀 (neoui tim)
ytterbium: 이터븀 (iteobyum)
yttrium: 이트륨 (iteulyum)
yuan: 위안 (wian)

Z

Zambia: 잠비아 (jambia)
zebra: 얼룩말 (eollugmal)
Zimbabwe: 짐바브웨 (jimbabeuwe)
zinc: 아연 (ayeon)
zip code: 우편번호 (upyeonbeonho)
zipper: 지퍼 (jipeo)
zirconium: 지르코늄 (jileukonyum)
zoo: 동물원 (dongmul-won)

Korean - English

@

1cheung (1층): first floor
1insil (1인실): single room
1wol (1월): January
2in-yong jajeongeo (2인용 자전거): tandem
2insil (2인실): double room
2wol (2월): February
3danttwigi (3단뛰기): triple jump
3wol (3월): March
4wol (4월): April
5cheung (5층): fifth floor
5wol (5월): May
6wol (6월): June
7wol (7월): July
8wol (8월): August
9wol (9월): September
10wol (10월): October
11wol (11월): November
12wol (12월): December

A

abeoji (아버지): father
abokado (아보카도): avocado
achim (아침): morning
achimsigsa (아침식사): breakfast
adeul (아들): son
aeb (앱): app
aebeolle (애벌레): caterpillar
aegche (액체): fluid
aegja (액자): picture frame
aehobag (애호박): courgette
aengkeo (앵커): anchor
aengmusae (앵무새): parrot
aentiga babuda (앤티가 바부다): Antigua and Barbuda
aepeulpai (애플파이): apple pie
aepeuteosyeibeu (애프터셰이브): aftershave
aewandongmul gage (애완동물 가게): pet shop
ag-eo (악어): crocodile
aghan (악한): evil
agi (아기): baby
agi bang (아기 방): nursery
agi gamsiyong moniteo (아기 감시용 모니터): baby monitor
agtinyum (악티늄): actinium
ai (아이): child
aikon (아이콘): icon
ailaineo (아이라이너): eyeliner
aillaendeu (아일랜드): Ireland
ainsyutainyum (아인슈타이늄): einsteinium
aiseuhaki (아이스하키): ice hockey
aiseukeopi (아이스커피): iced coffee
aiseukeulim (아이스크림): ice cream
aiseulaendeu (아이스랜드): Iceland
aiseulingkeu (아이스링크): ice rink
aiseu seukeiting (아이스 스케이팅): ice skating
aisyaedou (아이섀도우): eye shadow
aiti (아이티): Haiti

ajeleubaijan (아제르바이잔): Azerbaijan
aju (아주): very
akasia (아카시아): acacia
akilleseugeon (아킬레스건): Achilles tendon
akodieon (아코디언): accordion
al-a (알아): I know
al-yag (알약): pill
alab-emiliteu (아랍에미리트): United Arab Emirates
alab-eo (아랍어): Arabic
alae (아래): below
albania (알바니아): Albania
alda (알다): to know
aleugon (아르곤): argon
aleuhentina (아르헨티나): Argentina
aleumdaun (아름다운): beautiful
aleumenia (아르메니아): Armenia
aljeli (알제리): Algeria
allamsigye (알람시계): alarm clock
alleleugi (알레르기): allergy
alluminyum (알루미늄): aluminium
aloma telapi (아로마 테라피): aromatherapy
alpabes (알파벳): alphabet
aluba (아루바): Aruba
alyeong (아령): dumbbell
am (암): cancer
amajon (아마존): Amazon
amalgam (아말감): dental filling
ambyeog daibing (암벽 다이빙): cliff diving
amelikan samoa (아메리칸 사모아): American Samoa
amelisyum (아메리슘): americium
amondeu (아몬드): almond
ampeeo (암페어): ampere
amso (암소): cow
an (안): inside
anae (아내): wife
andeseu sanmaeg (안데스 산맥): Andes
andola (안도라): Andorra
ang-golla (앙골라): Angola
angae (안개): fog
angae kkin (안개 낀): foggy
angyeong (안경): glasses
angyeongsa (안경사): optician
anida (아니다): not
anjang (안장): saddle
anjda (앉다): to sit
anjeonbelteu (안전벨트): seatbelt
anjeonhan (안전한): safe
annyeong (안녕): hi
annyeonghaseyo (안녕하세요): hello, good day
annyeonghi gaseyo (안녕히 가세요): good bye
anolag (아노락): anorak
antimoni (안티모니): antimony
ap (앞): front
ap-yuli (앞유리): windscreen
apateu (아파트): apartment
apeuganiseutan (아프가니스탄): Afghanistan
apeun (아픈): sick
apjwaseog (앞좌석): front seat
aposeuteulopi (아포스트로피): apostrophe
appa (아빠): dad
aseupalteu (아스팔트): asphalt
aseupilin (아스피린): aspirin

aseutatin (아스타틴): astatine
atichokeu (아티초크): artichoke
ayeon (아연): zinc

B

babeidoseu (바베이도스): Barbados
babikyu (바비큐): barbecue
babo (바보): stupid
babo gat-eun (바보 같은): silly
bada (바다): sea
badag (바닥): floor
bada geobug (바다 거북): turtle
badakokkili (바다코끼리): walrus
badapyobeom (바다표범): seal
badasaja (바다사자): sea lion
badasgajae (바닷가재): lobster
badilosyeon (바디로션): body lotion
bae (배): belly, pear
baea (배아): embryo
baebuleun (배부른): full
baechu (배추): cabbage
baedang-geum (배당금): dividend
baedeuminteon (배드민턴): badminton
baeggaemeon (백개먼): backgammon
baeggeum (백금): platinum
baegigwan (배기관): exhaust pipe
baegjo (백조): swan
baeglihyang (백리향): thyme
baegmileo (백미러): rear mirror
baegnyeon (백년): century
baegopeun (배고픈): hungry
baegpodoju (백포도주): white wine
baegu (배구): volleyball
baegwangong (배관공): plumber
baekkob (배꼽): belly button
baem (뱀): snake
baenang (배낭): backpack
baesim (배심): jury
baeteoli (배터리): battery
baeu (배우): actor
bagenseil (바겐세일): bargain
bagjwi (박쥐): bat
bagmulgwan (박물관): museum
bagsa hag-wi (박사 학위): PhD
bagtelia (박테리아): bacterium
baguni (바구니): basket
bahama (바하마): The Bahamas
baiaeseullon (바이애슬론): biathlon
baileoseu (바이러스): virus
baiollin (바이올린): violin
baji (바지): trousers
bajil (바질): basil
bakk (밖): outside
bakodeu (바코드): bar code
bakodeu pandoggi (바코드 판독기): bar code scanner
bal (발): foot
balam (바람): wind
balam-i buneun (바람이 부는): windy
balb-a dollineun bakwi (밟아 돌리는 바퀴): treadmill
balein (바레인): Bahrain

balg-eun (밝은): light
balgalag (발가락): toe
baljeongi (발전기): generator
balkkumchi (발꿈치): heel
balkoni (발코니): balcony
balle (발레): ballet
ballehwa (발레화): ballet shoes
ballo chada (발로 차다): to kick
balmog (발목): ankle
balyum (바륨): barium
bam (밤): night
banadyum (바나듐): vanadium
banana (바나나): banana
banbaji (반바지): shorts
bando (반도): peninsula
baneul (바늘): needle
bang-eohada (방어하다): to defend
bang-geulladesi (방글라데시): Bangladesh
bang-gwang (방광): bladder
bang-ul-yangbaechu (방울양배추): Brussels sprouts
bang-yeolsoe (방열쇠): room key
bangbeonho (방번호): room number
bangchungje (방충제): insect repellent
bangeumsog (반금속): metalloid
banghaeseog (방해석): calcite
bangjeongsig (방정식): equation
bangmunja (방문자): visitor
bangmunsigan (방문시간): visiting hours
bangsaseongwa (방사선과): radiology
banilla (바닐라): vanilla
banilla seoltang (바닐라 설탕): vanilla sugar
banji (반지): ring
banjileum (반지름): radius
banuatu (바누아투): Vanuatu
bappeun (바쁜): busy
basun (바순): bassoon
batendeo (바텐더): barkeeper
batikan sigug (바티칸 시국): Vatican City
bawi (바위): rock
begae (베개): pillow
begteo (벡터): vector
beiji (베이지): beige
beikeon (베이컨): bacon
beikingpaudeo (베이킹파우더): baking powder
beiseu gita (베이스 기타): bass guitar
belgie (벨기에): Belgium
belillyum (베릴륨): beryllium
bellaluseu (벨라루스): Belarus
bellijeu (벨리즈): Belize
belteu (벨트): belt
benaeng (베냉): Benin
benchi (벤치): bench
benchi peuleseu (벤치 프레스): bench press
benesuella (베네수엘라): Venezuela
beobjeong (법정): court
beoblyul (법률): law
beobmubu (법무부): legal department
beodeunamu (버드나무): willow
beogeo (버거): burger
beokeullyum (버클륨): berkelium
beolgeum (벌금): fine
beolle (벌레): bug

beom-in (범인): criminal
beoma (버마): Burma
beomgolae (범고래): killer whale
beompeo (범퍼): bumper
beongae (번개): lightning
beonji jeompeu (번지 점프): bungee jumping
beoseos (버섯): mushroom
beoseu (버스): bus
beoseugisa (버스기사): bus driver
beoseujeonglyujang (버스정류장): bus stop
beoteo (버터): butter
beoteomilkeu (버터밀크): buttermilk
beteunam (베트남): Vietnam
beula (브라): bra
beulaendi (브랜디): brandy
beulajil (브라질): Brazil
beulaujeo (브라우저): browser
beulauni (브라우니): brownie
beuleikeu (브레이크): brake
beuleikeudaensing (브레이크댄싱): breakdance
beuleikeu deung (브레이크 등): brake light
beulisji (브릿지): bridge
beullaegbeli (블랙베리): blackberry
beullaeghol (블랙홀): black hole
beullaindeu (블라인드): blind
beulleijeo (블레이저): blazer
beullubeli (블루베리): blueberry
beulluseu (블루스): blues
beulochi (브로치): brooch
beulokolli (브로콜리): broccoli
beulomin (브로민): bromine
beulou penseul (브로우 펜슬): eyebrow pencil
beulunai (브루나이): Brunei
bi (비): rain
bichi ballibol (비치 발리볼): beach volleyball
bidan (비단): silk
bideum (비듬): dandruff
bidulgi (비둘기): pigeon
bienna walcheu (비엔나 왈츠): Viennese waltz
bigang seupeulei (비강 스프레이): nasal spray
biga oneun (비가 오는): rainy
bigeumsog (비금속): non-metal
bigye (비계): scaffolding
bihaeng-gi (비행기): plane
bija (비자): visa
bijang (비장): spleen
bijeuniseuseog (비즈니스석): business class
bikini (비키니): bikini
bilog ~ijiman (비록 ~이지만): although
bimilbeonho (비밀번호): password
bin (빈): empty
bingbyeog deungban (빙벽 등반): ice climbing
bingha (빙하): glacier
bini (비니): knit cap
binilbongtu (비닐봉투): plastic bag
binu (비누): soap
binyogigwa (비뇨기과): urology
biolla (비올라): viola
bis (빗): comb, brush
bisang chulgu (비상 출구): emergency exit
bisangchulgu (비상출구): emergency exit
biseo (비서): secretary

biseukis (비스킷): biscuit
biseumuteu (비스무트): bismuth
bisjalu (빗자루): broom
biso (비소): arsenic
bissan (비싼): expensive
bitamin (비타민): vitamin
biteullim (비틀림): twisting
boangyeong (보안경): safety glasses
boankamela (보안카메라): security camera
bobseullei (봅슬레이): bobsleigh
bocheuwana (보츠와나): Botswana
bodeugeim (보드게임): board game
bodeuka (보드카): vodka
bodibilding (보디빌딩): bodybuilding
bodo (보도): pavement
bog-yonglyang (복용량): dosage
bogdo (복도): corridor, aisle
bogsahada (복사하다): to copy
bogsing ling (복싱 링): boxing ring
bogsung-a (복숭아): peach
bogtong (복통): stomach ache
bohaengja guyeog (보행자 구역): pedestrian area
boheom (보험): insurance
bojeungseo (보증서): warranty
bojogae (보조개): dimple
bokk-eumbab (볶음밥): fried rice
bokk-eummyeon (볶음면): fried noodles
bolasaeg (보라색): purple
bolgeoli (볼거리): mumps
bollibia (볼리비아): Bolivia
bolling (볼링): bowling
bolling gong (볼링 공): bowling ball
bolpen (볼펜): ball pen
bolteu (볼트): volt
bolyum (보륨): bohrium
bom (봄): spring
bonghabseon (봉합선): suture
bongje inhyeong (봉제 인형): cuddly toy
bongtu (봉투): envelope
bonis (보닛): bonnet
bonmun (본문): text
boonbyeong (보온병): thermos jug, hot-water bottle
boseogsang (보석상): jeweller
boseunia (보스니아): Bosnia
boyug-won (보육원): nursery
budeuleoun (부드러운): soft
budong-aeg (부동액): antifreeze fluid
budongsanjung-gaein (부동산중개인): real-estate agent
budu (부두): pier
bueok (부엌): kitchen
bueong-i (부엉이): owl
bug (북): north
bugbangu (북반구): northern hemisphere
buggeug (북극): North Pole
buggeuggom (북극곰): polar bear
buggyeong-eo (북경어): Mandarin
buggyeong-oli (북경오리): Beijing duck
bughan (북한); North Korea
buhwaljeol (부활절): Easter
bujag-yong (부작용): side effect
bul (불): fire
bul-eo (불어): French

buleukinapaso (부르키나파소): Burkina Faso
bulg-eunmeoliui (붉은머리의): ginger
bulgalia (불가리아): Bulgaria
bulgasali (불가사리): starfish
bulgongpyeonghan (불공평한): unfair
bulundi (부룬디): Burundi
bumonim (부모님): parents
bun (분): minute
bun-yu (분유): milk powder
bungdae (붕대): bandage
bungso (붕소): boron
bunhongsaeg (분홍색): pink
bunhwagu (분화구): crater
bunja (분자): numerator, molecule
bunman (분만): delivery
bunmo (분모): denominator
bunpil (분필): chalk
bunsu (분수): fraction
bunsudae (분수대): fountain
bupi (부피): volume
bus (붓): brush
busang (부상): injury
buseo (부서): department
buskkoch (붓꽃): iris
butan (부탄): Bhutan
buyuhan (부유한): rich
bwipe (뷔페): buffet
byeog (벽): wall
byeogdol (벽돌): brick
byeol (별): star
byeong (병): bottle
byeong-ali (병아리): chick
byeong-won (병원): hospital
byeongi (변기): toilet
byeongicheongsosol (변기청소솔): toilet brush
byeonglihag (병리학): pathology
byeongsa (병사): soldier
byeonhosa (변호사): lawyer
byeonsog gieo (변속 기어): gear shift
byeonsog lebeo (변속 레버): gear lever

C

CDpeulleieo (CD플레이어): CD player
cha (차): tea
chachacha (차차차): cha-cha
chadeu (차드): Chad
chaeg (책): book
chaeggabang (책가방): schoolbag
chaegjang (책장): bookshelf
chaegsang (책상): desk
chaejjig (채찍): whip
chaeneol (채널): channel
chaeting (채팅): chat
chago (차고): garage
chago mun (차고 문): garage door
chajang (차장): conductor
chajda (찾다): to find, to look for
chajujeonja (차주전자): teapot
chalheulg (찰흙): clay
chamchi (참치): tuna

chang-go (창고): warehouse
changbaeghan (창백한): pale
changdeonjigi (창던지기): javelin throw
changmun (창문): window
chanjang (찬장): cupboard
che-ongye (체온계): fever thermometer
chein (체인): chain
chejo (체조): gymnastics
chejung-eul neullida (체중을 늘리다): to gain weight
chejung-eul ppaeda (체중을 빼다): to lose weight
chejung-gye (체중계): scale
chekeo (체커): draughts
chekeu-in deseukeu (체크인 데스크): check-in desk
cheko (체코): Czech Republic
cheli (체리): cherry
chello (첼로): cello
cheogchu (척추): spine
cheogchujiabsa (척추지압사): chiropractor
cheogchuppyeo (척추뼈): vertebra
cheogsu (척수): spinal cord
cheol (철): iron
cheol-in3jong-gyeong-gi (철인3종경기): triathlon
cheolhag (철학): philosophy
cheolsa (철사): wire
cheon (천): fabric
cheon-wangseong (천왕성): Uranus
cheondung (천둥): thunder
cheongbaji (청바지): jeans
cheongjingi (청진기): stethoscope
cheongsobu (청소부): cleaner
cheongsogileul dollida (청소기를 돌리다): to vacuum
cheongsohada (청소하다): to clean
cheonjang (천장): ceiling
cheonnyeon (천년): millennium
cheonsa (천사): angel
cheonsig (천식): asthma
cheosjjae (첫째): first
cheseu (체스): chess
cheyug (체육): physical education
cheyuggwan (체육관): sports ground, gym
chia (치아): tooth
chieolideo (치어리더): cheerleader
chigwauisa (치과의사): dentist
chijeu (치즈): cheese
chijeubeogeo (치즈버거): cheeseburger
chijeukeikeu (치즈케이크): cheesecake
chijil (치질): hemorrhoid
chikinneoges (치킨너겟): chicken nugget
chikin wing (치킨 윙): chicken wings
chille (칠레): Chile
chilmyeonjo (칠면조): turkey
chilmyeonjo gogi (칠면조 고기): turkey
chilpan (칠판): blackboard
chim-eul baetda (침을 뱉다): to spit
chima (치마): skirt
chimdae (침대): bed
chimnang (침낭): sleeping bag
chimsil (침실): bedroom
chimsil-yong tagja (침실용 탁자): night table
chimsildeung (침실등): bedside lamp
chimsul (침술): acupuncture
chingu (친구): friend

chinhal-abeoji (친할아버지): grandfather
chinhalmeoni (친할머니): grandmother
chinjeolhan (친절한): friendly
chis-sol (칫솔): toothbrush
chita (치타): cheetah
chitong (치통): toothache
chiyag (치약): toothpaste
cho (초): second
cho-eumpa gigi (초음파 기기): ultrasound machine
chodeunghaggyo (초등학교): primary school
choemyeon (최면): hypnosis
choinjong (초인종): bell
chokollis (초콜릿): chocolate
chokollis keulim (초콜릿 크림): chocolate cream
chologsaeg (초록색): green
chongjibaein (총지배인): general manager
chosanghwa (초상화): portrait
chosigye (초시계): stopwatch
chuggu (축구): football
chuggugong (축구공): football
chuggu gyeong-gijang (축구 경기장): football stadium
chugguhwa (축구화): football boots
chugjemadang (축제마당): fairground
chul-yeonjin (출연진): cast
chulbal (출발): departure
chuljang (출장): business trip
chullyeoghada (출력하다): to print
chulnab-won (출납원): cashier
chulpansa (출판사): publisher
chulsaengjeungmyeongseo (출생증명서): birth certificate
chum (춤): dancing
chungchi (충치): caries
chungwon (춘권): spring roll
chusugamsajeol (추수감사절): Thanksgiving
chuun (추운): cold
chwejang (췌장): pancreas
chyeodaboda (쳐다보다): to stare
CPU (CPU): central processing unit (CPU)
CT seukaeneo (CT 스캐너): CT scanner

D

da-eumdal (다음달): next month
da-eumju (다음주): next week
dabbyeonhada (답변하다): to answer
dach (닻): anchor
dachida (다치다): to injure
dadda (닫다): to close
daebon (대본): script
daechu (대추): date
daechul (대출): loan
daegagseon (대각선): diagonal
daegi (대기): atmosphere
daegisil (대기실): waiting room
daehaggyo (대학교): university
daehanmingug (대한민국): South Korea
daehyeong teuleog (대형 트럭): lorry
daelyug (대륙): continent
daem (댐): dam
daeman (대만): Taiwan
daemeoli (대머리): bald head

daenamu (대나무): bamboo
daenseo (댄서): dancer
daenseuhwa (댄스화): dancing shoes
daepae (대패): smoothing plane
daesagwan (대사관): embassy
daeseoyang (대서양): Atlantic Ocean
daetonglyeong (대통령): president
daiamondeu (다이아몬드): diamond
daibing (다이빙): diving
daibing maseukeu (다이빙 마스크): diving mask
dajingogi (다진고기): minced meat
dal (달): month, moon
dalag (다락): attic
dalamjwi (다람쥐): squirrel
daleumseutatyum (다름스타튬): darmstadtium
daleunsalam (다른사람): other
dalg (닭): chicken
dalg-gogi (닭고기): chicken
dalgyal huinja (달걀 흰자): egg white
dalgyal noleunja (달걀 노른자): yolk
dali (다리): leg, bridge
dalimipan (다리미판): ironing table
dalimjil hada (다림질 하다): to iron
dalleo (달러): dollar
dallida (달리다): to run
dalligi (달리기): running
dallyeog (달력): calendar
dalpaeng-i (달팽이): snail
dam-yo (담요): blanket
dambae (담배): tobacco, cigarette
dan (단): sweet
danchu (단추): button
dang-geun (당근): carrot
dang-gida (당기다): to pull
dang-gu (당구): billiards
dang-guchae (당구채): cue
dang-yeonhaji (당연하지): of course
dangeoli dalligi (단거리 달리기): sprint
dangnagwi (당나귀): donkey
dangnyobyeong (당뇨병): diabetes
danpungnamu (단풍나무): maple
dasi (다시): again
dateu (다트): darts
dayongdokal (다용도칼): utility knife
deiji (데이지): daisy
deiteo beiseu (데이터 베이스): database
denmakeu (덴마크): Denmark
deo (더): more
deobeulbeiseu (더블베이스): double bass
deobeunyum (더브늄): dubnium
deol (덜): less
deoleoun (더러운): dirty
deonjida (던지다): to throw
deos-sem (덧셈): addition
deoun (더운): hot
desimiteo (데시미터): decimeter
deudda (듣다): to listen
deul-eoollida (들어올리다): to lift
deulda (들다): to carry
deuleom (드럼): drums
deuleseu (드레스): dress
deuleseu saijeu (드레스 사이즈): dress size

deulil (드릴): drilling machine
deuliljilhada (드릴질하다): to drill
deulso (들소): bison
deung (등): back
deungban (등반): climbing
deungdae (등대): lighthouse
deungsan (등산): mountaineering
deungsanhwa (등산화): hiking boots
dijaineo (디자이너): designer
dijei (디제이): DJ
dijel (디젤): diesel
dijeoteu (디저트): dessert
dijiteolkamela (디지털카메라): digital camera
dil (딜): dill
dimseom (딤섬): dim sum
diseupeulosyum (디스프로슘): dysprosium
dobag-eul hada (도박을 하다): to gamble
dobda (돕다): to help
dochag (도착): arrival
dochdae (돛대): mast
dochdanbae (돛단배): sailing boat
dodug (도둑): thief
dog-il (독일): Germany
dog-il-eo (독일어): German
doggam (독감): flu
dogilyu (도기류): pottery
dogseosil (독서실): reading room
dogsuli (독수리): eagle
doje (도제): apprentice
dokki (도끼): axe
dolgolae (돌고래): dolphin
dolo (도로): road
doma (도마): chopping board
domabaem (도마뱀): lizard
domabaembut-i (도마뱀붙이): gecko
dominika (도미니카): Dominica
dominika gonghwagug (도미니카 공화국): Dominican Republic
domino (도미노): dominoes
domitoli lum (도미토리 룸): dorm room
don (돈): money
don-eul beolda (돈을 벌다): to earn
doneos (도넛): doughnut
dong (동-): east
dong-gong (동공): pupil
dong-gul (동굴): cave
dong-uihabnida (동의합니다): I agree
dong-wi wonso (동위 원소): isotope
dongjeon (동전): coin
dongjong-yobeob (동종요법): homoeopathy
donglyo (동료): colleague
dongmaeg (동맥): artery
dongmedal (동메달): bronze medal
dongmul-won (동물원): zoo
dongtimoleu (동티모르): East Timor
doseogwan (도서관): library
dubu (두부): tofu
dubu oesang (두부 외상): head injury
dudeuleogi (두드러기): rash
dugaegol (두개골): skull
duljjae (둘째): second
dung-geun (둥근): round
dutong (두통): headache

duyu (두유): soy milk
DVDpeulleieo (DVD플레이어): DVD player
dwaeji (돼지): pig
dwaejigogi (돼지고기): pork
dwi (뒤): back
dwisjwaseog (뒷좌석): back seat

E

eeobaeg (에어백): airbag
eeokeon (에어컨): air conditioner
eeolobig (에어로빅): aerobics
eeometeuliseu (에어메트리스): air mattress
egseulei sajin (엑스레이 사진): X-ray photograph
ekwadoleu (에콰도르): Ecuador
eliteulea (에리트레아): Eritrea
elkeu (엘크): elk
ellibeiteo (엘리베이터): elevator
elsalbadoleu (엘살바도르): El Salvador
en (엔): yen
eneoji deulingkeu (에너지 드링크): energy drink
enjin (엔진): engine
eobu (어부): fisherman
eobyum (어븀): erbium
eodi (어디): where
eoduun (어두운): dark
eoje (어제): yesterday
eokkae (어깨): shoulder
eokkaeppyeo (어깨뼈): shoulder blade
eol-eum (얼음): ice
eolgullosyeon (얼굴로션): face cream
eolgul maseukeu (얼굴 마스크): face mask
eolgul paudeo (얼굴 파우더): face powder
eolin sutalg (어린 수탉): cockerel
eollugmal (얼룩말): zebra
eolma-eyo? (얼마에요?): How much is this?
eolmana? (얼마나?): how much?
eolyeoun (어려운): difficult
eomeoni (어머니): mother
eomgyeoghan (엄격한): strict
eomji (엄지): thumb
eomma (엄마): mum
eondeog (언덕): hill
eoneu (어느): which
eongdeong-i (엉덩이): bottom
eonieonling (어니언링): onion ring
eonjaenghada (언쟁하다): to argue
eonje (언제): when
eonlon-in (언론인): journalist
eoseon (어선): fishing boat
eotteohge (어떻게): how
eotteohge jinae? (어떻게 지내?): How are you?
eseupeuleso (에스프레소): espresso
eseutonia (에스토니아): Estonia
etiopia (에티오피아): Ethiopia
eukkaen gamja (으깬 감자): mashed potatoes
eum-agga (음악가): musician
eumgyeong (음경): penis
eumhaeg (음핵): clitoris
eumjalipyo (음자리표): clef
eumnang (음낭): scrotum

eumpyo (음표): note
eumseongmesiji (음성메시지): voice message
eun (은): silver
eung-geub (응급): emergency
eung-geubcha (응급차): ambulance
eung-geubsil (응급실): emergency room
eunhaeng-gyejwa (은행계좌): bank account
eunhagye (은하계): galaxy
eunmedal (은메달): silver medal
euntoe (은퇴): retirement

G

ga-eul (가을): autumn
gabal (가발): wig
gabang (가방): bag
gabjagi (갑자기): suddenly
gabong (가봉): Gabon
gabpan (갑판): deck
gabpan uija (갑판 의자): deck chair
gabyeoun (가벼운): light
gadeugchan (가득찬): full
gadigeon (가디건): cardigan
gadollinyum (가돌리늄): gadolinium
gae (개): dog
gaegsil (객실): cabin
gaeguli (개구리): frog
gaejib (개집): kennel
gaemi (개미): ant
gaemihaltgi (개미핥기): ant-eater
gagdo (각도): angle
gagjin (각진): square
gagujeom (가구점): furniture store
gaiana (가이아나): Guyana
gaideu (가이드): tourist guide, tour guide
gajang (가장): most
gaji (가지): aubergine
gajigo gada (가지고 가다): to take
gajogsajin (가족사진): family picture
gajog yobeob (가족 요법): family therapy
gajugsinbal (가죽신발): leather shoes
gakkaun (가까운): close
galade (가라데): karate
galdae (갈대): reed
galkwi (갈퀴): rake
gallyum (갈륨): gallium
galmaegi (갈매기): seagull
galodeung (가로등): street light
galsaeg (갈색): brown
galsaegmeoliui (갈색머리의): brunette
galu (가루): powder
galubinu (가루비누): washing powder
galu seoltang (가루 설탕): icing sugar
gam-og (감옥): prison
gam-yeom (감염): infection
gambia (감비아): The Gambia
gamchosatang (감초사탕): liquorice
gamdog (감독): coach, director
gamgi (감기): cold
gamja (감자): potato
gamjachib (감자칩): chips

gamjasaelleodeu (감자샐러드): potato salad
gan (간): liver
gana (가나): Ghana
gananhan (가난한): poor
ganeuntob (가는톱): handsaw
gang (강): river
gang-ui (강의): lecture
gang-yeonja (강연자): lecturer
gangcheol (강철): steel
gangcheol bim (강철 빔): steel beam
ganghan (강한): strong
gangpan (강판): grater
ganheol oncheon (간헐 온천): geyser
ganhosa (간호사): nurse
ganjil (간질): epilepsy
gansig (간식): snack
gapaleun (가파른): steep
gasa (가사): lyrics
gaseuleinji (가스레인지): cooker
gaseuleinji hudeu (가스레인지 후드): cooker hood
gaseum (가슴): chest
gasu (가수): singer
gaunde songalag (가운데 손가락): middle finger
gawi (가위): scissors
ge (게): crab
geeuleun (게으른): lazy
geleumanyum (게르마늄): germanium
geobug-i (거북이): tortoise
geodda (걷다): to walk
geogjeonghajima (걱정하지마): no worries
geogjeonghaneun (걱정하는): worried
geogjeongma (걱정마): don't worry
geoli (거리): avenue
geomi (거미): spider
geomjeongsaeg (검정색): black
geomsa (검사): prosecutor
geonbae (건배): cheers
geonban (건반): keyboard
geonchoyeol (건초열): hay fever
geonchugga (건축가): architect
geonganghan (건강한): healthy
geonjohan (건조한): dry
geonpodo (건포도): raisin
geonseol nodongja (건설 노동자): construction worker
geosil (거실): living room
geoul (거울): mirror
geowi (거위): goose
gesipan (게시판): bulletin board
geu (그): he
geudeul (그들): they
geudeul-ui hoesa (그들의 회사): their company
geug (극): pole
geugeos (그것): that
geugjang (극장): theatre
geujeokke (그저께): the day before yesterday
geulaem (그램): gram
geulenada (그레나다): Grenada
geuleus (그릇): bowl
geulida (그리다): to paint
geulim (그림): picture, painting, drawing
geulinlandeu (그린란드): Greenland
geuliseu (그리스): Greece

geulja (글자): letter, character
geulladiolleoseu (글라디올러스): gladiolus
geullaideo (글라이더): glider
geulluten (글루텐): gluten
geulujia (그루지아): Georgia
geum (금): gold
geum-aeg (금액): amount
geum-i eunboda deo bissa (금이 은보다 더 비싸): Gold is more expensive than silver
geum-yoil (금요일): Friday
geumbal-ui (금발의): blond
geumgo (금고): safe
geummedal (금메달): gold medal
geumseong (금성): Venus
geumsog (금속): metal
geun-yug (근육): muscle
geundae 5jong gyeong-gi (근대 5종 경기): modern pentathlon
geune (그네): swing
geunyeo (그녀): she
geunyeoui deuleseu (그녀의 드레스): her dress
geuttae (그때): then
geuui cha (그의 차): his car
giab (기압): air pressure
gibseu (깁스): plaster, cast
gicha (기차): train
gicha unjeonsa (기차 운전사): train driver
gichayeog (기차역): train station
giche (기체): gas
gichim (기침): cough
gichim-yag (기침 약): cough syrup
gidalida (기다리다): to wait
gidohada (기도하다): to pray
gigwan (기관): windpipe
gigwancha (기관차): locomotive
gigwansil (기관실): engine room
gihahag (기하학): geometry
gija (기자): reporter
gijeogwi (기저귀): diaper
gijeolhada (기절하다): to faint
gijung-gi (기중기): crane
gijung-gi teuleog (기중기 트럭): crane truck
gileum (기름): oil
gilgeoli eumsig (길거리 음식): street food
gilin (기린): giraffe
gin (긴): long
ginae hyudae suhamul (기내 휴대 수하물): carry-on luggage
gini (기니): Guinea
ginibisau (기니비사우): Guinea-Bissau
ginipigeu (기니피그): guinea pig
ginyeomhada (기념하다): to celebrate
ginyeommul (기념물): monument
ginyeompum (기념품): souvenir
gip-eun (깊은): deep
gipogwansujungi (기포관수준기): spirit level
gis (깃): collar
gisa (기사): article
gisulja (기술자): engineer
gita (기타): guitar
giwa (기와): roof tile
goa (고아): orphan
gobsem (곱셈): multiplication
gobseulgobseulhan (곱슬곱슬한): curly
goche (고체): solid

gocheung-geonmul (고층건물): skyscraper
gochu (고추): chili
gochulyu (고추류): pepper
godegi (고데기): hair straightener
godeunghaggyo (고등학교): high school
goga dolo (고가 도로): overpass
gogaeg (고객): customer
gogeul (고글): swim goggles
gogi (고기): meat
gogseon (곡선): curve
goguma (고구마): sweet potato
gohwan (고환): testicle
gohyeol-ab (고혈압): high blood pressure
gojeoncha (고전차): classic car
golae (고래): whale
golban (골반): pelvis
goldae (골대): goal
golgyeog (골격): skeleton
goljeol (골절): fracture
golmog (골목): alley
golpa (골파): leek, chive
golpeu (골프): golf
golpeuchae (골프채): golf club
golpeugong (골프공): golf ball
golpeujang (골프장): golf course
golsu (골수): bone marrow
gom (곰): bear
gomawo (고마워): thank you
gomuboteu (고무보트): rubber boat
gomudojang (고무도장): rubber stamp
gomujeojkkogji (고무젖꼭지): soother
gomujul (고무줄): rubber band
gong-gan (공간): space
gong-gi peompeu (공기 펌프): air pump
gong-gyeoghada (공격하다): to attack
gong-won (공원): park
gong-yugi (공유기): router
gongbuhada (공부하다): to study
gongchaeg (공책): notebook
gonghang (공항): airport
gongjagsae (공작새): peacock
gongjang (공장): factory
gonglyong (공룡): dinosaur
gongpo yeonghwa (공포 영화): horror movie
gongpyeonghan (공평한): fair
gongsahyeonjang (공사현장): construction site
gongsang gwahag (공상 과학): science fiction
goseumdochi (고슴도치): hedgehog
gosog-yeolcha (고속열차): high-speed train
gosogdolo (고속도로): motorway
gosu (고수): coriander
goyang-i (고양이): cat
goyohan (고요한): silent
goyongju (고용주): employer
GPS (GPS): GPS
gu (구): sphere
gub (굽): heel
gubda (굽다): to bake
gudumitchang (구두밑창): sole
gugga (국가): country
gugja (국자): ladle
guglibgong-won (국립공원): national park

gugmu chongli (국무 총리): prime minister
gugsu (국수): noodle
gujohada (구조하다): to rescue
gulchaggi (굴착기): excavator
guleuda (구르다): to roll
guleum (구름): cloud
guleum kkin (구름 낀): cloudy
guli (구리): copper
gullasi (굴라시): goulash
gulttug (굴뚝): chimney
gumaehada (구매하다): to buy
gumyeongboteu (구명보트): lifeboat
gumyeong bupyo (구명 부표): life buoy
gumyeongjokki (구명조끼): life jacket
gunaesigdang (구내식당): canteen
gutohada (구토하다): to vomit
guun dwaejigogi (구운 돼지고기): roast pork
guun kong (구운 콩): baked beans
guyeog (구역): district
gwabu (과부): widow
gwaenchanh-a? (괜찮아?): Are you ok?
gwaeng-i (괭이): hoe
gwahag (과학): science
gwahagja (과학자): scientist
gwail kkeom (과일 껌): fruit gum
gwail saelleodeu (과일 샐러드): fruit salad
gwail sang-in (과일 상인): fruit merchant
gwan (관): coffin
gwandaehan (관대한): generous
gwang-go (광고): advertisement
gwang-goji (광고지): flyer
gwangaeg (관객): audience
gwangjang (광장): square
gwangwang annaeso (관광 안내소): tourist information
gwangwangmyeongso (관광명소): tourist attraction
gwanjanol-i (관자놀이): temple
gwanjetab (관제탑): control tower
gwanmog (관목): bush
gwanse (관세): customs
gwatemalla (과테말라): Guatemala
gwi (귀): ear
gwigeol-i (귀걸이): earring
gwili (귀리): oat
gwimagae (귀마개): earplug
gwimeogeoliui (귀머거리의): deaf
gwittulami (귀뚜라미): cricket
gwiyeoun (귀여운): cute
gwonchong (권총): gun
gwontu (권투): boxing
gwontujang-gab (권투장갑): boxing glove
gyedan (계단): stairs
gyedansig gang-uisil (계단식 강의실): lecture theatre
gyegipan (계기판): dashboard
gyegog (계곡): valley
gyejwabeonho (계좌번호): account number
gyejwaiche (계좌이체): bank transfer
gyelan (계란): egg
gyeolgwa (결과): result
gyeolhonbanji (결혼반지): wedding ring
gyeolhonhada (결혼하다): to marry
gyeolhonsig (결혼식): wedding
gyeoljang (결장): colon

gyeong-godeung (경고등): warning light
gyeong-gohada (경고하다): to warn
gyeong-yeongdaehag (경영대학): business school
gyeongbiwon (경비원): security guard
gyeongchal (경찰): police, policeman
gyeongchalbong (경찰봉): baton
gyeongchalcha (경찰차): police car
gyeongchalseo (경찰서): police station
gyeongdo (경도): longitude
gyeonghowon (경호원): bodyguard
gyeongjehag (경제학): economics
gyeongjeog (경적): horn
gyeongjuyong jajeongeo (경주용 자전거): racing bicycle
gyeonglyeon (경련): cramp
gyeongsamyeon (경사면): slope
gyeongwa (견과): nut
gyeoul (겨울): winter
gyesandae (계산대): cash register
gyesanhada (계산하다): to calculate
gyobog (교복): school uniform
gyochalo (교차로): intersection
gyogwaseo (교과서): textbook
gyohoe (교회): church
gyojeong-gi (교정기): dental brace
gyooe (교외): suburb
gyosu (교수): professor
gyotongchejeung (교통체증): traffic jam
gyuso (규소): silicon

H

hadeu deulaibeu (하드 드라이브): hard drive
haean (해안): shore
haeanga (해안가): coast
haebalagi (해바라기): sunflower
haebalagiyu (해바라기유): sunflower oil
haebyeon (해변): beach
haeil (해일): tidal wave
haem (햄): ham
haema (해마): sea horse
haembeogeo (햄버거): hamburger
haemeo deonjigi (해머 던지기): hammer throw
haemseuteo (햄스터): hamster
haendeubaeg (핸드백): handbag
haendeu beuleikeu (핸드 브레이크): hand brake
haendeubol (핸드볼): handball
haendeul (핸들): steering wheel
haendeupon (핸드폰): mobile phone
haengboghan (행복한): happy
haengdong chilyo (행동 치료): behaviour therapy
haengseong (행성): planet
haengsil-i baleun (행실이 바른): well-behaved
haepali (해파리): jellyfish
haesanmul yoli (해산물 요리): seafood
haesbich (햇빛): sunshine
haesbyeot-e tam (햇볕에 탐): sunburn
haeseolja (해설자): commentator
haewangseong (해왕성): Neptune
haeyang (해양): ocean
hag-wi (학위): degree
haggi (학기): term

haggyo (학교): school
haggyo undongjang (학교 운동장): schoolyard
hagsa hag-wi (학사 학위): bachelor
haihil (하이힐): high heels
haiking (하이킹): hiking
haipeun (하이픈): hyphen
hajiman (하지만): but
hakiseutig (하키스틱): hockey stick
hallowin (할로윈): Halloween
hama (하마): hippo
hamkke (함께): together
hamonika (하모니카): harmonica
hang-ali (항아리): jar
hang-gong gyotong gwanjesa (항공 교통 관제사): air traffic controller
hang-gongmoham (항공모함): aircraft carrier
hang-gongsa (항공사): airline
hang-gu (항구): harbour
hanghaehada (항해하다): sail
hangmun (항문): anus
hangsaengje (항생제): antibiotics
hangsang (항상): always
hapeu (하프): harp
hapeunyum (하프늄): hafnium
haschokollis (핫초콜릿): hot chocolate
hasdogeu (핫도그): hot dog
hasyum (하슘): hassium
hayansaeg (하얀색): white
hebimetal (헤비메탈): heavy metal
heeobaendeu (헤어밴드): scrunchy
heeo deulaieo (헤어 드라이어): hairdryer
heeo jel (헤어 젤): hair gel
heijeulneos (헤이즐넛): hazelnut
hellikobteo (헬리콥터): helicopter
hellyum (헬륨): helium
helmes (헬멧): helmet
heodeul gyeong-gi (허들 경기): hurdles
heoli (허리): waist
heolikein (허리케인): hurricane
heong-gali (헝가리): Hungary
heopa (허파): lung
heub-ibgi (흡입기): inhaler
heug-yeon (흑연): graphite
heughae (흑해): Black Sea
heulg (흙): soil
heundeul-uija (흔들의자): rocking chair
him (힘): force
himallaya (히말라야): Himalayas
himjul (힘줄): tendon
hobag (호박): pumpkin
hobagbeol (호박벌): bumblebee
hochikiseu (호치키스): stapler
hodu (호두): walnut
hoegye (회계): accounting
hoegyesa (회계사): accountant
hoehyang (회향): fennel
hoejang (회장): chairman
hoejeonmogma (회전목마): carousel
hoeng-gyeongmag (횡경막): diaphragm
hoengdanbodo (횡단보도): pedestrian crossing
hoesaeg (회색): grey
hoesig (회식): business dinner
hoeuisil (회의실): meeting room

hoewon (회원): member
hoewongwon (회원권): membership
hoheubgi (호흡기): respiratory machine
hoju (호주): Australia
hojusig chuggu (호주식 축구): Australian football
hol-abi (홀아비): widower
holang-i (호랑이): tiger
holmyum (홀뮴): holmium
hong-yeog (홍역): measles
hongcha (홍차): black tea
honghae (홍해): Red Sea
honghag (홍학): flamingo
hongkong (홍콩): Hong Kong
hongsu (홍수): flood
hoseu (호스): hose
hoseutel (호스텔): hostel
hosu (호수): lake
hotel (호텔): hotel
huchu (후추): pepper
huingaemi (흰개미): termite
hulaipaen (후라이팬): pan
humchida (훔치다): to steal
humideung (후미등): rear light
hunjang (훈장): medal
hwabun (화분): flower pot
hwachanghan (화창한): sunny
hwacho (화초): houseplant
hwadan (화단): flower bed
hwaga (화가): artist
hwagang-am (화강암): granite
hwahabmul (화합물): chemical compound
hwahag (화학): chemistry
hwahag ban-eung (화학 반응): chemical reaction
hwahag gujo (화학 구조): chemical structure
hwahagja (화학자): chemist
hwajae (화재): fire
hwajaegyeongbogi (화재경보기): fire alarm
hwajangji (화장지): toilet paper
hwajangsil (화장실): toilet
hwajangsil-i eodie iss-eoyo? (화장실이 어디에 있어요?): Where is the toilet?
hwajangsilseullipeo (화장실슬리퍼): bathroom slippers
hwalang (화랑): art gallery
hwaljulo (활주로): runway
hwamul gicha (화물 기차): freight train
hwamulsusong-gi (화물수송기): cargo aircraft
hwan-yeonghabnida (환영합니다): welcome
hwanan (화난): angry
hwang (황): sulphur
hwangsae (황새): stork
hwangso (황소): bull
hwanja (환자): patient
hwasan (화산): volcano
hwasang (화상): burn
hwaseong (화성): Mars
hwassi (화씨): Fahrenheit
hwayoil (화요일): Tuesday
hwibal-yu (휘발유): petrol
hwilcheeo (휠체어): wheelchair
hyangsu (향수): perfume
hyeo (혀): tongue
hyeobbaghada (협박하다): to threaten
hyeobgog (협곡): canyon

hyeol-aeg geomsa (혈액 검사): blood test
hyeong/oppa (형/오빠): big brother
hyeongeum gigye (현금 기계): cash machine
hyeongje (형제): siblings
hyeongsa (형사): detective
hyeongwanmun (현관문): front door
hyeonmigyeong (현미경): microscope
hyeseong (혜성): comet
hyomo (효모): yeast
hyuji (휴지): tissue
hyujitong (휴지통): recycle bin
hyung-gol (흉골): breastbone

I

ib (입): mouth
ibeondal (이번달): this month
ibeonju (이번주): this week
ibeuning deuleseu (이브닝 드레스): evening dress
ibjaga gulg-eun seoltang (입자가 굵은 설탕): granulated sugar
ibsul (입술): lip
icheungchimdae (이층침대): bunk bed
ieopon (이어폰): earphone
igeos (이것): this
igida (이기다): to win
ihon (이혼): divorce
ija (이자): interest
ijibteu (이집트): Egypt
ikonomiseog (이코노미석): economy class
il (일): day
il-yoil (일요일): Sunday
ilakeu (이라크): Iraq
ilan (이란): Iran
ilbangtonghaeng (일방통행): one-way street
ilbon (일본): Japan
ilbon-eo (일본어): Japanese
ildeungseog (일등석): first class
ileum-i mwo-eyo? (이름이 뭐에요?): What's your name?
ilgda (읽다): to read
ilgi (일기): diary
ilhada (일하다): to work
ilidyum (이리듐): iridium
illegteulig gita (일렉트릭 기타): electric guitar
ilsanhwatanso (일산화탄소): carbon monoxide
ilsig (일식): solar eclipse
ima (이마): forehead
imeil (이메일): e-mail
imeiljuso (이메일주소): e-mail address
imi (이미): already
imo (이모): aunt
imsin geomsa (임신 검사): pregnancy test
in (인): phosphorus
in-yonghada (인용하다): to quote
inchi (인치): inch
indo (인도): India
indonesia (인도네시아): Indonesia
indoyang (인도양): Indian Ocean
indyum (인듐): indium
ingkeu (잉크): ink
ingkeu lolleo (잉크 롤러): inking roller
inhuyeom (인후염): sore throat

inhyeong (인형): doll
inhyeong-ui jib (인형의 집): dollhouse
inmyeong gujowon (인명 구조원): lifeguard
insabu (인사부): human resources
inseuteonteu myeonlyu (인스턴트 면류): instant noodles
insyullin (인슐린): insulin
inteon (인턴): intern
ion (이온): ion
ip (잎): leaf
isa (이사): director
isanghan (이상한): strange
isanhwatanso (이산화탄소): carbon dioxide
iseula-el (이스라엘): Israel
itallia (이탈리아): Italy
iteobyum (이터븀): ytterbium
iteulyum (이트륨): yttrium
ius (이웃): neighbour

J

ja (자): ruler
jabcho (잡초): weed
jabda (잡다): to catch
jabji (잡지): magazine
jadong (자동): automatic
jadongcha gyeongju (자동차 경주): car racing
jadu (자두): plum
jae (재): ash
jaebongteul (재봉틀): sewing machine
jaeda (재다): to measure
jaedansa (재단사): tailor
jaeg (잭): jack
jaegpuleuteu (잭푸르트): jackfruit
jaejeu (재즈): jazz
jaem (잼): jam
jaemiissneun (재미있는): funny
jag-eobsil (작업실): workroom
jag-eun (작은): small
jagga (작가): author
jagigongmyeong-yeongsang (자기공명영상): magnetic resonance imaging
jagnyeon (작년): last year
jagung (자궁): uterus, womb
jaibeu (자이브): jive
jajagnamu (자작나무): birch
jajeong (자정): midnight
jajeongeo (자전거): bicycle
jaju (자주): often
jakes (자켓): jacket
jalada (자라다): to grow
jalangseuleoun (자랑스러운): proud
jaleuda (자르다): to cut
jalga (잘가): bye bye
jali (자리): seat
jaljinae (잘지내): take care
jalsaeng-gin (잘생긴): handsome
jam-eul jada (잠을 자다): to sleep
jam-os (잠옷): pyjamas, nightie
jambia (잠비아): Zambia
jameika (자메이카): Jamaica
jamgeuda (잠그다): to lock
jamjali (잠자리): dragonfly

jamong (자몽): grapefruit
jamsubog (잠수복): wetsuit
jamsuham (잠수함): submarine
jandi (잔디): grass
jandikkakk-i (잔디깎이): lawn mower
jang (장): intestine
jang-aemul gyeongju (장애물 경주): show jumping
jang-gab (장갑): glove
jang-gwan (장관): minister
jang-in-eoleun (장인어른): father-in-law
jangdaenop-ittwigi (장대높이뛰기): pole vault
janghaggeum (장학금): scholarship
janghwa (장화): wellington boots
janglyesig (장례식): funeral
jangmi (장미): rose
jangmo (장모): mother-in-law
jangnangam gage (장난감 가게): toy shop
jaoeseon chadanje (자외선 차단제): sunscreen
jaseog (자석): magnet
jebal (제발): please
jegobmiteo (제곱미터): square meter
jenon (제논): xenon
jeobseon (접선): tangent
jeobsi (접시): plate
jeobsudamdangja (접수담당자): receptionist
jeog-eun (적은): few
jeogdo (적도): equator
jeogdo gini (적도 기니): Equatorial Guinea
jeogeum (저금): savings
jeogi (저기): there
jeogpodoju (적포도주): red wine
jeoj-eun (젖은): wet
jeojbyeong (젖병): baby bottle
jeoji (저지): jersey
jeo jom dowajusillaeyo? (저 좀 도와주실래요?): Can you help me?
jeol (절): temple
jeol-yeon teipeu (절연 테이프): insulating tape
jeolbyeog (절벽): cliff
jeoldangi (절단기): loppers
jeolm-eun (젊은): young
jeom-won (점원): shop assistant
jeompeuhada (점프하다): to jump
jeomsimsigsa (점심식사): lunch
jeon-won (전원): power
jeonbanglaiteu (전방라이트): front light
jeonchae yoli (전채 요리): starter
jeondalhada (전달하다): to deliver
jeondanji (전단지): leaflet
jeong-aeg (정액): sperm
jeong-eoli (정어리): sardine
jeong-o (정오): noon
jeong-won (정원): garden
jeong-wonsa (정원사): gardener
jeong-yugmyeonche (정육면체): cube
jeongal (전갈): scorpion
jeongbigong (정비공): mechanic
jeongbogisul (정보기술): IT
jeongchiga (정치가): politician
jeongchihag (정치학): politics
jeonghyeong-oegwa (정형외과): orthopaedics
jeongi babsot (전기 밥솥): rice cooker
jeongi chung-gyeog (전기 충격): electric shock

jeongidalimi (전기다리미): electric iron
jeongigisa (전기기사): electrician
jeongi myeondogi (전기 면도기): shaver
jeongitob (전기톱): chainsaw
jeongmaeg (정맥): vein
jeongmallo (정말로): really
jeongol (전골): hot pot
jeongsagaghyeong (정사각형): square
jeongsin bunseog (정신 분석): psychoanalysis
jeongsingwa (정신과): psychiatry
jeongu (전구): light bulb
jeonhwabeonho (전화번호): telephone number
jeonhwagi (전화기): telephone
jeonhwahada (전화하다): to call
jeonhyeo (전혀): none
jeonja (전자): electron
jeonjaleinji (전자레인지): microwave
jeonlibsaem (전립샘): prostate
jeonyeog (저녁): evening
jeonyeogsigsa (저녁식사): dinner
jeosgalag (젓가락): chopstick
jeteu seuki (제트 스키): jet ski
jeub-i manh-eun (즙이 많은): juicy
jeugseog kamela (즉석 카메라): instant camera
jeugsi (즉시): immediately
jeulgida (즐기다): to enjoy
jeung-geo (증거): evidence
jeung-gi gigwancha (증기 기관차): steam train
jeung-gwon geolaeso (증권 거래소): stock exchange
jeung-gwon jung-gaein (증권 중개인): stockbroker
jeung-in (증인): witness
jewangjeolgae (제왕절개): cesarean
jib (집): house
jib-egaja (집에가자): Let's go home
jibang (지방): province
jibang-i jeog-eun gogi (지방이 적은 고기): lean meat
jibang-i manh-eun gogi (지방이 많은 고기): fat meat
jibbaewon (집배원): postman
jibdan yobeob (집단 요법): group therapy
jibeulolteo (지브롤터): Gibraltar
jibge songalag (집게 손가락): index finger
jibulhada (지불하다): to pay
jibung (지붕): roof
jibuti (지부티): Djibouti
jida (지다): to lose
jido (지도): map
jig-eob (직업): job
jig-eobhaggyo (직업학교): vocational training
jig-won (직원): employee, staff
jigab (지갑): wallet
jigag (지각): earth's crust
jigecha (지게차): forklift truck
jigeum (지금): now
jiggag (직각): right angle
jigjin (직진): straight
jigjinhae (직진해): go straight
jigmoui (직모의): straight
jigsagaghyeong (직사각형): rectangle
jigseon (직선): straight line
jigu (지구): earth
jiguhaeg (지구핵): earth's core
jiha (지하): basement

jiha1cheung (지하1층): first basement floor
jiha2cheung (지하2층): second basement floor
jihacheol (지하철): subway
jihado (지하도): underpass
jihwija (지휘자): conductor
jijin (지진): earthquake
jijunghae (지중해): Mediterranean Sea
jikyeoboda (지켜보다): to watch
jil (질): vagina
jileukonyum (지르코늄): zirconium
jili (지리): geography
jilmunhada (질문하다): to ask
jilso (질소): nitrogen
jiluhan (지루한): boring
jim (짐): luggage
jimbabeuwe (짐바브웨): Zimbabwe
jimun (지문): fingerprint
jin (진): gin
jinandal (지난달): last month
jinanju (지난주): last week
jingongcheongsogi (진공청소기): vacuum cleaner
jinjeonghae (진정해): relax
jinjumoggeol-i (진주목걸이): pearl necklace
jinlyoso (진료소): clinic
jintongje (진통제): painkiller
jipeo (지퍼): zipper
jipye (지폐): note
jisangcheung (지상층): ground floor
jiugae (지우개): rubber
jiyeog (지역): region
jjalb-eun (짧은): short
jjan (짠): salty
jjoli (쪼리): flip-flops
job-eun (좁은): narrow
jogae (조개): shell
jogaghada (조각하다): sculpting
jogjibge (족집게): tweezers
joh-ahada (좋아하다): to like
joh-eun (좋은): good
jojeolpan (조절판): throttle
jojeong (조정): rowing
jojongsa (조종사): pilot
jojongseog (조종석): cockpit
joka (조카): nephew
jokattal (조카딸): niece
jol-eob (졸업): graduation
jol-eobjang (졸업장): diploma
jol-eobsig (졸업식): graduation ceremony
jong-ijeobgi (종이접기): origami
jong-yanghag (종양학): oncology
josansa (조산사): midwife
josu (조수): assistant
joyonghan (조용한): quiet
ju (주): week, state
ju-in (주인): landlord
juchajang (주차장): car park
jucha yogeum miteogi (주차 요금 미터기): parking meter
juchoeja (주최자): host
juda (주다): to give
jug (죽): porridge
jug-eum (죽음): death
jug-ida (죽이다): to kill

juga (주가): share price
jugda (죽다): to die
jugeunkkae (주근깨): freckles
jugiyulpyo (주기율표): periodic table
juhwangsaeg (주황색): orange
jujeonja (주전자): kettle
jul (줄): file
jul-eodeulda (줄어들다): to shrink
juleum (주름): wrinkle
julgi (줄기): trunk, stalk
julja (줄자): tape measure
jumeog (주먹): fist
jumeoni (주머니): pocket
junbiundong (준비운동): warm-up
jung-ang-apeulika gonghwagug (중앙아프리카 공화국): Central African Republic
jung-ang-eobmujigu (중앙업무지구): central business district (CBD)
jung-gopum gage (중고품 가게): second-hand shop
jung-gug (중국): China
jung-uihag (중의학): Chinese medicine
jungdog (중독): poisoning
junghaggyo (중학교): junior school
junghwanjasil (중환자실): intensive care unit
junglyeog (중력): gravity
jungseongja (중성자): neutron
jusagi (주사기): syringe
juseog (주석): tin
jusig (주식): share
juso (주소): address
juyuso (주유소): petrol station
jwahoejeonhae (좌회전해): turn left
jwi (쥐): rat

K

kabobeleude (카보베르데): Cape Verde
kadeugeim (카드게임): card game
kadeumyum (카드뮴): cadmium
kaebsyul (캡슐): capsule
kaelikeochyeo (캐리커쳐): caricature
kaemkodeo (캠코더): camcorder
kaempeujang (캠프장): camping site
kaempeupaieo (캠프파이어): campfire
kaemping (캠핑): camping
kaenada (캐나다): Canada
kaeng-geolu (캥거루): kangaroo
kaesyu (캐슈): cashew
kagteil (칵테일): cocktail
kajaheuseutan (카자흐스탄): Kazakhstan
kajino (카지노): casino
kal (칼): knife
kalamel (카라멜): caramel
kallipoleunyum (칼리포르늄): californium
kallyum (칼륨): potassium
kalsyum (칼슘): calcium
kambodia (캄보디아): Cambodia
kamela (카메라): camera
kamelamaen (카메라맨): camera operator
kamelle-on (카멜레온): chameleon
kamelun (카메룬): Cameroon
kanu (카누): canoe
kanu tagi (카누 타기): canoeing

kapeteu (카페트): carpet
kapuchino (카푸치노): cappuccino
kataleu (카타르): Qatar
kateteo (카테터): catheter
kebab (케밥): kebab
keibeul (케이블): cable
keibeulka (케이블카): cable car
keikeu (케이크): cake
keimaen jedo (케이맨 제도): Cayman Islands
kenya (케냐): Kenya
keob (컵): cup
keol godegi (컬 고데기): curling iron
keoli (커리): curry
keolling (컬링): curling
keonseolteonteu (컨설턴트): consultant
keonsilleo (컨실러): concealer
keonteineo (컨테이너): container
keonteineoseon (컨테이너선): container ship
keopi (커피): coffee
keopimeosin (커피머신): coffee machine
keoseuteodeu (커스터드): custard
keoteun (커튼): curtain
keteul deuleom (케틀 드럼): kettledrum
keulaenbeli (크랜베리): cranberry
keulepe (크레페): crêpe
keulibton (크립톤): krypton
keulikes (크리켓): cricket
keulim (크림): cream
keuliseumaseu (크리스마스): Christmas
keullaesig eum-ag (클래식 음악): classical music
keullalines (클라리넷): clarinet
keulleochi (클러치): clutch
keullib (클립): paperclip
keullibbodeu (클립보드): clipboard
keullobeo (클로버): clover
keuloatia (크로아티아): Croatia
keulomyum (크로뮴): chromium
keulone (크로네): krone
keuloseukeonteuli seuki (크로스컨트리 스키): cross-country skiing
keuloseu teuleineo (크로스 트레이너): cross trainer
keuluasang (크루아상): croissant
keun (큰): big, huge
keunkkamagwi (큰까마귀): raven
kibodeu (키보드): keyboard
kiga jag-eun (키가 작은): short
kiga keun (키가 큰): tall
kileugiseuseutan (키르기스스탄): Kyrgyzstan
kilibasi (키리바시): Kiribati
killogeulaem (킬로그램): kilogram
kipeuloseu (키프로스): Cyprus
kiseu (키스): kiss
kiseuhada (키스하다): to kiss
kiwi (키위): kiwi
kkachi (까치): magpie
kkaekkeushan (깨끗한): clean
kkaemulda (깨물다): to bite
kkalttaegi (깔때기): funnel
kkamagkkachibabnamu yeolmae (까막까치 밥나무 열매): currant
kkamagwi (까마귀): crow
kkeobjil-eul kkada (껍질을 까다): peel
kkeom (껌): chewing gum
kkeuda (끄다): to turn off

kkeulh-ida (끓이다): to boil
kkoch (꽃): flower, blossom
kkoch-ip (꽃잎): petal
kkochbyeong (꽃병): vase
kkochi (꼬치): skewer
kkochkkul (꽃꿀): nectar
kkul (꿀): honey
kkulbeol (꿀벌): bee
kkum-eul kkuda (꿈을 꾸다): to dream
ko (코): nose
koalla (코알라): koala
kobalteu (코발트): cobalt
kokkili (코끼리): elephant
kokoneos (코코넛): coconut
kolla (콜라): coke
kollabi (콜라비): turnip cabbage
kollipeullawo (콜리플라워): cauliflower
kollombia (콜롬비아): Colombia
kollon (콜론): colon
kombain suhwaggi (콤바인 수확기): combine harvester
komidi (코미디): comedy
komolo (코모로): Comoros
kondom (콘돔): condom
kong (콩): bean, soy
kong-go gonghwagug (콩고 공화국): Republic of the Congo
kong-go minju gonghwagug (콩고 민주 공화국): Democratic Republic of the Congo
konkeuliteu (콘크리트): concrete
konkeuliteu honhabgi (콘크리트 혼합기): concrete mixer
konsenteu (콘센트): power outlet
konseoteu (콘서트): concert
kontaegteu lenjeu (콘택트 렌즈): contact lens
kopeleunisyum (코페르니슘): copernicium
kopi (코피): nosebleed
koppulso (코뿔소): rhino
koppyeo (코뼈): nasal bone
koseutalika (코스타리카): Costa Rica
kosgumeong (콧구멍): nostril
kosobo (코소보): Kosovo
koteu (코트): coat
koteudibualeu (코트디부아르): Ivory Coast
kuba (쿠바): Cuba
kug jedo (쿡 제도): Cook Islands
kuki (쿠키): cookie
kuweiteu (쿠웨이트): Kuwait
kwigseuteb (퀵스텝): quickstep
kwilyum (퀴륨): curium
kyeoda (켜다): to turn on

L

labbi (랍비): rabbi
ladieiteo (라디에이터): radiator
ladio (라디오): radio
ladon (라돈): radon
ladyum (라듐): radium
laeb (랩): rap
laekeo (래커): varnish
laelli gyeongju (랠리 경주): rally racing
laempeu (램프): lamp
laepeuting (래프팅): rafting
laibelia (라이베리아): Liberia

laim (라임): lime
laiteo (라이터): lighter
lajanya (라자냐): lasagne
lajeubeli (라즈베리): raspberry
lakeuloseu (라크로스): lacrosse
lama (라마): llama
lamadan (라마단): Ramadan
lamen (라멘): ramen
lanjeli (란제리): lingerie
lantaneom (란타넘): lanthanum
laoseu (라오스): Laos
lateubia (라트비아): Latvia
latin-eo (라틴어): Latin
latin daenseu (라틴 댄스): Latin dance
lebanon (레바논): Lebanon
lege (레게): reggae
legemeoli (레게머리): dreadlocks
legeu peuleseu (레그 프레스): leg press
legingseu (레깅스): leggings
leideo (레이더): radar
leising kateu (레이싱 카트): kart
lekodeu peulleieo (레코드 플레이어): record player
lemon (레몬): lemon
lemoneideu (레모네이드): lemonade
lemongeulaseu (레몬그라스): lemongrass
lenyum (레늄): rhenium
leodeopodyum (러더포듐): rutherfordium
leogbi (럭비): rugby
leom (럼): rum
leosia (러시아): Russia
leosiawo (러시아워): rush hour
leseopanda (레서판다): red panda
leseulling (레슬링): wrestling
leseutolang (레스토랑): restaurant
lesoto (레소토): Lesotho
leuwanda (르완다): Rwanda
libbam (립밤): lip balm
libeomolyum (리버모륨): livermorium
libgeulloseu (립글로스): lip gloss
libia (리비아): Libya
libseutig (립스틱): lipstick
lichi (리치): lychee
lideum chejo (리듬 체조): rhythmic gymnastics
lihitensyutain (리히텐슈타인): Liechtenstein
likyueo (리큐어): liqueur
limokeon (리모컨): remote control
limujin (리무진): limousine
liteo (리터): liter
liteul beullaeg deuleseu (리틀 블랙 드레스): little black dress
lituania (리투아니아): Lithuania
lityum (리튬): lithium
lobi (로비): lobby
lobos (로봇): robot
lodeu lolleo (로드 롤러): road roller
lodyum (로듐): rhodium
loenteugenyum (뢴트게늄): roentgenium
log (록): rock
logkeunlol (록큰롤): rock 'n' roll
lojeumali (로즈마리): rosemary
lokes (로켓): rocket
lolensyum (로렌슘): lawrencium
lolleokoseuteo (롤러코스터): roller coaster

lolleo seukeiting (롤러 스케이팅): roller skating
loseuteuchikin (로스트치킨): roast chicken
loteoli (로터리): roundabout
lubi (루비): ruby
lubidyum (루비듐): rubidium
lugsembuleukeu (룩셈부르크): Luxembourg
luji (루지): luge
lumania (루마니아): Romania
lumba (룸바): rumba
lumseobiseu (룸서비스): room service
lutenyum (루테늄): ruthenium
lutetyum (루테튬): lutetium

M

ma-eul (마을): village
machimpyo (마침표): full stop
madagaseukaleu (마다가스카르): Madagascar
mae (매): falcon
maechunbu (매춘부): prostitute
maeg (맥): tapir
maegbag (맥박): pulse
maegju (맥주): beer
maehyeong (매형): brother-in-law
maeng-in (맹인): blind
maengjang (맹장): appendix
maenhol ttukkeong (맨홀 뚜껑): manhole cover
maenijeo (매니저): manager
maenikyueo (매니큐어): manicure, nail polish
maenikyueo limubeo (매니큐어 리무버): nail varnish remover
maepyogigi (매표기기): ticket vending machine
maepyoso (매표소): ticket office
maeun (매운): hot
mageuma (마그마): magma
mageunesyum (마그네슘): magnesium
mail (마일): mile
maiteuneolyum (마이트너륨): meitnerium
majeoleom (마저럼): marjoram
makao (마카오): Macao
makedonia (마케도니아): Macedonia
maketing (마케팅): marketing
mal (말): horse
malaton (마라톤): marathon
malbeol (말벌): wasp
maleummo (마름모): rhombus
maleun (마른): skinny
malhada (말하다): to talk
mallawi (말라위): Malawi
malleisia (말레이시아): Malaysia
malli (말리): Mali
mallida (말리다): to dry
mallingwail (말린과일): dried fruit
man-yag (만약): if
mandu (만두): dumpling
maneking (마네킹): mannequin
maneul (마늘): garlic
mang-gan (망간): manganese
mang-go (망고): mango
mang-wongyeong (망원경): telescope
mangchi (망치): hammer
mangchijilhada (망치질하다): to hammer

manh-eun (많은): many
manhwa (만화): cartoon
manhwachaeg (만화책): comic book
manjida (만지다): to touch
mannada (만나다): to meet
masaji (마사지): massage
masajileul haejuda (마사지를 해주다): to give a massage
masajisa (마사지사): masseur
maseukala (마스카라): mascara
masida (마시다): to drink
masimello (마시멜로): marshmallow
masyeol jedo (마셜 제도): Marshall Islands
matini (마티니): martini
mauseu (마우스): mouse
mauseupiseu (마우스피스): mouthguard
mayonejeu (마요네즈): mayonnaise
medal (메달): medal
megsiko (멕시코): Mexico
meilham (메일함): inbox
meipeul sileob (메이플 시럽): maple syrup
mellodi (멜로디): melody
mellon (멜론): sugar melon
mendellebyum (멘델레븀): mendelevium
menyupan (메뉴판): menu
meog-ileul juda (먹이를 주다): to feed
meogda (먹다): to eat
meogeukeob (머그컵): cup
meoli (머리): head
meolikalag (머리카락): hair
meolimal (머리말): heading
meolipin (머리핀): barrette
meollittwigi (멀리뛰기): long jump
meon (먼): far
meong (멍): bruise
meopin (머핀): muffin
meoseutadeu (머스타드): mustard
meosjin (멋진): cool
meseu (메스): scalpel
meseukkeoum (메스꺼움): nausea
metan (메탄): methane
meteuliseu (메트리스): mattress
meteulopolliseu (메트로폴리스): metropolis
mettugi (메뚜기): grasshopper
mianhae (미안해): sorry
michin (미친): crazy
mieokaes (미어캣): meerkat
migseogi (믹서기): mixer
migug (미국): The United States of America
migugneoguli (미국너구리): raccoon
mikeulonesia (미크로네시아): Micronesia
mikkeuleomteul (미끄럼틀): slide
mil (밀): wheat
milda (밀다): to push
milgalu (밀가루): flour
milkeusweikeu (밀크쉐이크): milkshake
milkeuti (밀크티): milk tea
milliliteo (밀리리터): milliliter
millimiteo (밀리미터): millimeter
min-yo (민요): folk music
minaliajaebi (미나리아재비): buttercup
mindeulle (민들레): dandelion
miniba (미니바): minibar

minteu (민트): mint
misig chuggu (미식 축구): American football
misigchuggugong (미식축구공): football
misoleul jisda (미소를 짓다): to smile
misul (미술): art
miteo (미터): meter
miteubol (미트볼): meatball
mitjul (밑줄): underscore
miyeog (미역): seaweed
miyongsa (미용사): hairdresser
mochalella (모차렐라): mozzarella
model (모델): model
modeun (모든): every
modeunsalam (모든사람): everybody
modu (모두): all
mog (목): neck
mog-yoggaun (목욕가운): bathrobe
mog-yogsugeon (목욕수건): bath towel
mog-yoil (목요일): Thursday
mogbal (목발): crutch
mog bohodae (목 보호대): neck brace
mogcha (목차): table of contents
mogdeolmi (목덜미): nape
moggeol-i (목걸이): necklace
mogi (모기): mosquito
mogmaleun (목마른): thirsty
mogsegong (목세공): woodwork
mogseong (목성): Jupiter
mogsu (목수): carpenter
moja (모자): hat, sun hat
mojambikeu (모잠비크): Mozambique
moka (모카): mocha
molae (모래): sand
molae sangja (모래 상자): sandbox
moldibeu (몰디브): Maldives
moldoba (몰도바): Moldova
mole (모레): the day after tomorrow
molisyeoseu (모리셔스): Mauritius
molitani (모리타니): Mauritania
molla (몰라): I don't know
mollibeudeneom (몰리브데넘): molybdenum
moloko (모로코): Morocco
molta (몰타): Malta
mom-eul tteolda (몸을 떨다): to shiver
monako (모나코): Monaco
mong-gol (몽골): Mongolia
moniteo (모니터): screen
monoleil (모노레일): monorail
monopolli (모노폴리): Monopoly
monselateu (몬세라트): Montserrat
montenegeulo (몬테네그로): Montenegro
mos (못): nail
mos-saeng-gin (못생긴): ugly
moseukeu (모스크): mosque
moteo (모터): motor
moteokeuloseu (모터크로스): motocross
MP3peulleieo (MP3플레이어): MP3 player
mu (무): radish
mudae (무대): stage
mudangbeolle (무당벌레): ladybird
mudeom (무덤): grave
mueos (무엇): what

mugeoun (무거운): heavy
muhwagwa (무화과): fig
mujeongi (무전기): walkie-talkie
mujigae (무지개): rainbow
mul (물): water
mul-eumpyo (물음표): question mark
mulbyeong (물병): water bottle
muleup (무릎): knee
mulgogi (물고기): fish
mullichilyo (물리치료): physiotherapy
mullichilyosa (물리치료사): physiotherapist
mullihag (물리학): physics
mullihagja (물리학자): physicist
mullin sangcheo (물린 상처): bite
mulppuligae (물뿌리개): water can
mulso (물소): buffalo
mun (문): door
mun-eo (문어): octopus
mundan (문단): paragraph
munhag (문학): literature
munja mesiji (문자 메시지): text message
munsonjab-i (문손잡이): door handle
mupeuti (무프티): mufti
myeochgae? (몇 개?): how many?
myeondogi (면도기): razor
myeondonal (면도날): razor blade
myeondoyong geopum (면도용 거품): shaving foam
myeoneuli (며느리): daughter-in-law
myeong-wangseong (명왕성): Pluto
myeongham (명함): business card
myeongsang (명상): meditation
myeonjeog (면적): area
myoji (묘지): cemetery
myujeulli (뮤즐리): muesli

N

na (나): I
nab (납): lead
nabang (나방): moth
nabi (나비): butterfly
nabinegtai (나비넥타이): bow tie
nachimpan (나침판): compass
nachyo (나쵸): nachos
naebog (내복): thermal underwear
naebunbihag (내분비학): endocrinology
nae gang-aji (내 강아지): my dog
naegihada (내기하다): to bet
naegwauisa (내과의사): physician
naeil (내일): tomorrow
naembi (냄비): pot
naemsae matda (냄새 맡다): to smell
naengdongsil (냉동실): freezer
naengjang-go (냉장고): fridge
naengjeonghan (냉정한): sober
naenyeon (내년): next year
naeyong (내용): content
nag-yeobsong (낙엽송): larch
naghasan (낙하산): parachuting, parachute
nagta (낙타): camel
na igeo gajgo sip-eo (나 이거 갖고 싶어): I want this

na igeo pil-yohaeyo (나 이거 필요해요): I need this
naijilia (나이지리아): Nigeria
naillon (나일론): nylon
naiobyum (나이오븀): niobium
naiteukeulleob (나이트클럽): night club
naj-eun (낮은): low
najung-e boja (나중에 보자): see you later
nakksileul hada (낚시를 하다): to fish
nalang gat-i gaja (나랑 같이 가자): Come with me
nalda (날다): to fly
nalgae (날개): wing
nalgeos-ui (날것의): raw
nalssinhan (날씬한): slim
nam (남): south
nam-apeulika gonghwagug (남아프리카 공화국): South Africa
nambangu (남반구): southern hemisphere
namdongsaeng (남동생): little brother
namgeug (남극): South Pole
namibia (나미비아): Namibia
namja (남자): man
namjachingu (남자친구): boyfriend
nampyeon (남편): husband
namseong-yong sagag suyeongbog (남성용 사각 수영복): swim trunks
namsudan (남수단): South Sudan
namu (나무): tree
namu bim (나무 빔): wooden beam
namusgaji (나뭇가지): branch
namu sudgalag (나무 숟가락): wooden spoon
nanbang (난방): heating
nan deo wonhae (난 더 원해): I want more
nan gaeleul kiwoyo (난 개를 키워요): I have a dog
nan ige silh-eoyo (난 이게 싫어요): I don't like this
nan ihaega andwae (난 이해가 안돼): I don't understand
nanja (난자): ovum
nan neoga joh-ayo (난 너가 좋아요): I like you
nanso (난소): ovary
nanuda (나누다): to share
nanus-sem (나눗셈): division
napalgwan (나팔관): oviduct
nappeun (나쁜): bad
na salanghae? (나 사랑해?): Do you love me?
nateulyum (나트륨): sodium
naulu (나우루): Nauru
ne-odimyum (네오디뮴): neodymium
ne-on (네온): neon
nebtunyum (넵투늄): neptunium
nedeollandeu (네덜란드): Netherlands
negeullije (네글리제): negligee
ne goyang-i (네 고양이): your cat
negtai (넥타이): tie
neo (너): you
neodobamnamu (너도밤나무): beech
neoga geuliwo. (너가 그리워.): I miss you
neohuideul (너희들): you
neolb-eun (넓은): broad
neoui tim (너의 팀): your team
nepal (네팔): Nepal
nesjjae (넷째): fourth
neteu (네트): net
neteuwokeu (네트워크): network
neugdae (늑대): wolf
neuggol (늑골): rib

neukkimpyo (느낌표): exclamation mark
neulg-eun (늙은): old
neulin (느린): slow
nijeleu (니제르): Niger
nikalagwa (니카라과): Nicaragua
nikel (니켈): nickel
niue (니우에): Niue
nobellyum (노벨륨): nobelium
noe (뇌): brain
noejintang (뇌진탕): concussion
noejoljung (뇌졸중): stroke
noeu (뇌우): thunderstorm
nogcha (녹차): green tea
nohda (놓다): to put
nohwabangji keulim (노화방지 크림): antiwrinkle cream
no jeosneun bae (노 젓는 배): rowing boat
nol-igong-won (놀이공원): theme park
nol-iteo (놀이터): playground
nolaehada (노래하다): to sing
nolangsaeg (노랑색): yellow
nolda (놀다): to play
noleudig boghab (노르딕 복합): Nordic combined
noleuwei (노르웨이): Norway
nollan (놀란): surprised
nong-aja (농아자): mute
nong-gu (농구): basketball
nong-gu goldae (농구 골대): basket
nongbu (농부): farmer
nongdam (농담): joke
nongjang (농장): farm
nonmun (논문): thesis
nop-eun (높은): high
nop-i (높이): height
nop-ittwigi (높이뛰기): high jump
noteubug (노트북): laptop
nubda (눕다): to lie
nuga (누가): nougat
nugu (누구): who
nuleuda (누르다): to press
nun (눈): eye, snow
nuna/eonni (누나/언니): big sister
nunsseob (눈썹): eyebrow
nyeon (년): year
nyujillaendeu (뉴질랜드): New Zealand
nyukalledonia (뉴칼레도니아): New Caledonia
nyuseu (뉴스): news
nyuseuleteo (뉴스레터): newsletter

O

obeun (오븐): oven
obo-e (오보에): oboe
oda (오다): to come
odumag (오두막): shed
oebakwi sonsule (외바퀴 손수레): wheelbarrow
oeeum jeolgaesul (외음 절개술): episiotomy
oegwa (외과): surgery
oegwauisa (외과의사): surgeon
oehal-abeoji (외할아버지): grandfather
oehalmeoni (외할머니): grandmother
oelaehwanja (외래환자): outpatient

oeloun (외로운): lonely
oenjjog (왼쪽): left
og (옥): jade
ogsusu (옥수수): corn
ogsusugileum (옥수수기름): corn oil
ohu (오후): afternoon
ohu dusi (오후 두시): two o'clock in the afternoon
oi (오이): cucumber
oil paseutel (오일 파스텔): oil pastel
oil peinteu (오일 페인트): oil paint
ojeon (오전): morning
ojing-eo (오징어): squid
okeseuteula (오케스트라): orchestra
okeu (오크): oak
okeula (오크라): okra
olaedoen (오래된): old
olegano (오레가노): oregano
olenji (오렌지): orange
olenji juseu (오렌지 주스): orange juice
oleuda (오르다): to climb
oleugan (오르간): organ
oleunjjog (오른쪽): right
olh-eun (옳은): correct
olhae (올해): this year
oli (오리): duck
olibal (오리발): fin
ollibeu (올리브): olive
ollibeuyu (올리브유): olive oil
olola (오로라): aurora
oman (오만): Oman
ondo (온도): temperature
ondulaseu (온두라스): Honduras
oneul (오늘): today
onseu (온스): ounce
onsil (온실): greenhouse
opal (오팔): opal
opela (오페라): opera
oseumyum (오스뮴): osmium
oseuteulia (오스트리아): Austria
osjang (옷장): wardrobe
oteumil (오트밀): oatmeal
otobai (오토바이): motorcycle
otobai gyeongju (오토바이 경주): motorcycle racing

P

pa (파): spring onion
pab (팝): pop
pabkon (팝콘): popcorn
pada (파다): to dig
paegseu (팩스): fax
paenkeig (팬케익): pancake
paenti (팬티): panties, underpants
paentilaineo (팬티라이너): panty liner
paentiseutaking (팬티스타킹): pantyhose
pai (파이): pie
pail (파일): file
pain-aepeul (파인애플): pineapple
pakiseutan (파키스탄): Pakistan
pal (팔): arm
palagwai (파라과이): Paraguay

palangsaeg (파랑색): blue
palasol (파라솔): parasol
palesteu (파렛트): pallet
paleumesan chijeu (파르메산 치즈): parmesan
palgaghyeong (팔각형): octagon
palgubhyeo pyeogi (팔굽혀 펴기): push-up
pali (파리): fly
paljji (팔찌): bracelet
palkkumchi (팔꿈치): elbow
palladyum (팔라듐): palladium
pallau (팔라우): Palau
palleseutain (팔레스타인): Palestine
palleteu (팔레트): palette
panama (파나마): Panama
panda (판다): panda
panmaehada (판매하다): to sell
pansa (판사): judge
papaya (파파야): papaya
papeulika (파프리카): paprika
papuanyugini (파푸아뉴기니): Papua New Guinea
paudeo peopeu (파우더 퍼프): powder puff
paundeisyeon (파운데이션): foundation
paundeu (파운드): pound
pedikyueo (페디큐어): pedicure
peinteu (페인트): paint
peleumyum (페르뮴): fermium
pellikeon (펠리컨): pelican
pelo jedo (페로 제도): Faroe Islands
pelu (페루): Peru
pen (펜): pen
penchi (펜치): pincers
peng-gwin (펭귄): penguin
pensing (펜싱): fencing
peog (퍽): puck
peojeul (퍼즐): puzzle
peonchi (펀치): hole puncher
peongkeu (펑크): punk
peoti (퍼티): putty
peta (페타): feta
peteuli jeobsi (페트리 접시): Petri dish
peulangseu (프랑스): France
peulangseulyeong pollinesia (프랑스령 폴리네시아): French Polynesia
peulansyum (프란슘): francium
peulase-odimyum (프라세오디뮴): praseodymium
peulejenteisyeon (프레젠테이션): presentation
peulenchi holeun (프렌치 호른): French horn
peulenchi peulai (프렌치 프라이): French fries
peulinteo (프린터): printer
peuliseutail seuki (프리스타일 스키): freestyle skiing
peullaesi (플래시): flash
peullaseutig (플라스틱): plastic
peullelobyum (플레로븀): flerovium
peulleogeu (플러그): plug
peullib chateu (플립 차트): flip chart
peulloliseuteu (플로리스트): florist
peulluoleu (플루오르): fluorine
peulluteu (플루트): flute
peullutonyum (플루토늄): plutonium
peulogeulaemeo (프로그래머): programmer
peulojegteo (프로젝터): projector
peulometyum (프로메튬): promethium
peuloteuagtinyum (프로트악티늄): protactinium

piano (피아노): piano
pibugwa (피부과): dermatology
pigo (피고): defendant
pigonhan (피곤한): tired
pigyeo seukeiting (피겨 스케이팅): figure skating
piim-yag (피임약): birth control pill
pija (피자): pizza
piji (피지): Fiji
pikeunig (피크닉): picnic
pilamideu (피라미드): pyramid
pildeuhaki (필드하키): field hockey
pilgi (필기): note
pillateseu (필라테스): Pilates
pillipin (필리핀): Philippines
pilteo (필터): filter
piltong (필통): pencil case
pinlandeu (핀란드): Finland
pipes (피펫): pipette
piseutachio (피스타치오): pistachio
pisi aen chibseu (피시 앤 칩스): fish and chips
pituseong-iui (피투성이의): bloody
piuda (피우다): to smoke
piuija (피의자): suspect
pobog (포복): to crawl
podo (포도): grape
pog (폭): width
pogpo (폭포): waterfall
pogpung (폭풍): storm
pohwandeonjigi (포환던지기): shot put
pojang (포장): package
pokeo (포커): poker
pokeu (포크): fork
pokeullaendeu jedo (포클랜드 제도): Falkland Islands
poldeo (폴더): folder
poleutugal (포르투갈): Portugal
pollandeu (폴란드): Poland
pollieseuteleu (폴리에스테르): polyester
pollo (폴로): polo
pollonyum (폴로늄): polonium
pollosyeocheu (폴로셔츠): polo shirt
pomyulleo won (포뮬러 원): Formula 1
poniteil (포니테일): ponytail
poteupollio (포트폴리오): portfolio
ppaelsem (뺄셈): subtraction
ppaleun (빠른): quick
ppalgansaeg (빨간색): red
ppallae (빨래): laundry
ppallaejibge (빨래집게): peg
ppallaetong (빨래통): laundry basket
ppang (빵): bread
ppuli (뿌리): root
ppyam (빰): cheek
ppyeo (뼈): bone
puding (푸딩): pudding
pueleutoliko (푸에르토리코): Puerto Rico
pujuhan (푸주한): butcher
pul (풀): glue
punglyeog baljeonso (풍력 발전소): wind farm
pungsu (풍수): feng shui
pus (풋): foot
pyeheo (폐허): ruin
pyeondutong (편두통): migraine

pyeonghaengsabyeonhyeong (평행사변형): rhomboid
pyeongmyeon hwamyeon (평면 화면): flat screen
pyeongpyeonghan (평평한): flat
pyeonji (편지): letter
pyesucheolijang (폐수처리장): sewage plant
pyo (표): ticket
pyobeom (표범): leopard

R

RAM (RAM): random access memory (RAM)

S

sa-eobga (사업가): entrepreneur
sab (삽): shovel
sachon (사촌): cousin
sadali (사다리): ladder
sadalikkol (사다리꼴): trapezoid
saeabeoji (새아버지): stepfather
saebyeog hansi (새벽 한시): one o'clock in the morning
saeeomeoni (새어머니): stepmother
saeg-yeonpil (색연필): coloured pencil
saegsopon (색소폰): saxophone
saehae (새해): New Year
saekkidwaeji (새끼돼지): piglet
saekki songalag (새끼 손가락): little finger
saelleodeu (샐러드): salad
saeloun (새로운): new
saendeul (샌들): sandals
saendeuwichi (샌드위치): sandwich
saeng-gaghada (생각하다): to think
saeng-gang (생강): ginger
saeng-il (생일): birthday
saeng-ilkeig (생일케익): birthday cake
saeng-ilpati (생일파티): birthday party
saengjwi (생쥐): mouse
saengkeulim (생크림): whipped cream
saenglidae (생리대): sanitary towel
saengmulhag (생물학): biology
saengseon (생선): fish
saengseongage (생선가게): fish market
saengseon gasi (생선 가시): fishbone
sageon (사건): case
sago (사고): accident
sagwa (사과): apple
sagwa juseu (사과 주스): apple juice
sagyeog (사격): shooting
sagyo daenseu (사교 댄스): Ballroom dance
sahala (사하라): Sahara
saida (사이다): cider
saideu diswi (사이드 디쉬): side dish
saideumileo (사이드미러): wing mirror
saikeulling (사이클링): cycling
sailen (사이렌): siren
saja (사자): lion
sajeon (사전): dictionary
sajincheob (사진첩): photo album
sajinjagga (사진작가): photographer
sake (사케): sake
salang (사랑): love

salanghada (사랑하다): to love
salanghae (사랑해): I love you
salda (살다): to live
salgu (살구): apricot
sallami (살라미): salami
salm-eun (삶은): boiled
salm-eungyelan (삶은계란): boiled egg
salsa (살사): salsa
samag (사막): desert
samagwi (사마귀): praying mantis
samalyum (사마륨): samarium
samba (삼바): samba
samchon (삼촌): uncle
samgagdae (삼각대): tripod
samgaghyeong (삼각형): triangle
samkida (삼키다): to swallow
samoa (사모아): Samoa
samsibbun (삼십분): half an hour
samusil (사무실): office
san (산): mountain
san-ag jajeongeo tagi (산악 자전거 타기): mountain biking
san-eobjigu (산업지구): industrial district
san-ultali (산울타리): hedge
sanbu-ingwa (산부인과): gynaecology
sanchaeglo (산책로): promenade
sang-eo (상어): shark
sang-gwan-eobs-eo (상관없어): doesn't matter
sangcheo (상처): wound
sangchu (상추): lettuce
sangdaeseong ilon (상대성 이론): theory of relativity
sangsabyeong (상사병): lovesickness
sangsog-in (상속인): heir
sangtume peulinsipe (상투메 프린시페): São Tomé and Príncipe
sanhocho (산호초): coral reef
sanmaeg (산맥): mountain range
sanmalino (산마리노): San Marino
sanso (산소): oxygen
sansu (산수): arithmetic
sapaieo (사파이어): sapphire
saseo (사서): librarian
saseum (사슴): deer
saseumgogi (사슴고기): game
sasib-obun (사십오분): three quarters of an hour
satang (사탕): candy
satangmu (사탕무): sugar beet
satangsusu (사탕수수): sugar cane
saudialabia (사우디아라비아): Saudi Arabia
sauna (사우나): sauna
sawi (사위): son-in-law
sawo (사워): sour
sawokeulim (사워크림): sour cream
secha (세차): car wash
seda (세다): to count
segeum (세금): tax
segseu (섹스): sex
segsihan (섹시한): sexy
segye gilog (세계 기록): world record
seilling (세일링): sailing
seinteubinsenteu geulenadin (세인트빈센트 그레나딘): Saint Vincent and the Grenadines
seinteukicheu nebiseu (세인트키츠 네비스): Saint Kitts and Nevis
seinteulusia (세인트루시아): Saint Lucia
seisyel (세이셸): Seychelles

sejegobmiteo (세제곱미터): cubic meter
seleubia (세르비아): Serbia
sellenyum (셀레늄): selenium
selleoli (셀러리): celery
selyum (세륨): cerium
semikollon (세미콜론): semicolon
semyeongi (세면기): basin
senegal (세네갈): Senegal
sentimiteo (센티미터): centimeter
seo (서): west
seobeo (서버): server
seobssi (섭 씨): centigrade
seobu (서부): western film
seoda (서다): to stand
seog-yeong (석영): quartz
seoghoeseog (석회석): limestone
seogsa hag-wi (석사 학위): master
seogtan (석탄): coal
seojeom (서점): bookshop
seokis teuleining (서킷 트레이닝): circuit training
seolab (서랍): drawer
seolsa (설사): diarrhea
seolsangcha (설상차): snowmobile
seoltang (설탕): sugar
seolyucheol (서류철): folder
seolyugabang (서류가방): briefcase
seom (섬): island
seomun (서문): preface
seomyeong (서명): signature
seon-injang (선인장): cactus
seonbag (선박): ship
seonban (선반): shelf
seong (성): castle
seongbyeol (성별): gender
seongdang (성당): cathedral
seongeullaseu (선글라스): sunglasses
seongnyang (성냥): match
seonjang (선장): captain
seonlo (선로): railtrack
seonmul (선물): present
seonpung-gi (선풍기): fan
seonsaengnim (선생님): teacher
seontaeghada (선택하다): to choose
seoping (서핑): surfing
seopingbodeu (서핑보드): surfboard
sesjjae (셋째): third
sessangdung-i (세쌍둥이): triplets
sesyum (세슘): caesium
setaggi (세탁기): washing machine
seubdo (습도): humidity
seubji (습지): marsh
seubjin (습진): eczema
seudoku (스도쿠): Sudoku
seukaeneo (스캐너): scanner
seukaenhada (스캔하다): to scan
seukandyum (스칸듐): scandium
seukapeu (스카프): scarf
seukeiteu (스케이트): skates
seukeiteubodeu tagi (스케이트보드 타기): skateboarding
seukelleton (스켈레톤): skeleton
seukeulaembeuldeu egeu (스크램블드 에그): scrambled eggs
seukeulin (스크린): screen

seukeulolba (스크롤바): scrollbar
seukeulyu deulaibeo (스크류 드라이버): screwdriver
seukeulyu lenchi (스크류 렌치): screw wrench
seuki (스키): skiing, ski
seukibog (스키복): ski suit
seuki jeompeu (스키 점프): ski jumping
seuki jiyeog (스키 지역): ski resort
seuki seutig (스키 스틱): ski pole
seukulbeoseu (스쿨버스): school bus
seukuteo (스쿠터): motor scooter
seukwoteu (스쿼트): squat
seulgaegol (슬개골): kneecap
seulilangka (스리랑카): Sri Lanka
seulilleo (스릴러): thriller
seullipeo (슬리퍼): slippers
seullobakia (슬로바키아): Slovakia
seullobenia (슬로베니아): Slovenia
seulpeun (슬픈): sad
seumateupon (스마트폰): smartphone
seumudi (스무디): smoothie
seuneeo deuleom (스네어 드럼): snare drum
seung-gangjang (승강장): platform
seung-in (승인): ok
seung-yongcha (승용차): car
seungmuwon (승무원): stewardess
seunobodeu (스노보드): snowboarding
seunukeo (스누커): snooker
seunukeo teibeul (스누커 테이블): snooker table
seupageti (스파게티): spaghetti
seupakeulling wain (스파클링 와인): sparkling wine
seupein (스페인): Spain
seupein-eo (스페인어): Spanish
seupeulei (스프레이): spray
seupideu seukeiting (스피드 스케이팅): speed skating
seupikeo (스피커): loudspeaker
seupocheubeula (스포츠브라): jogging bra
seupocheu yongpumjeom (스포츠 용품점): sports shop
seuponji (스폰지): sponge
seusi (스시): sushi
seutaking (스타킹): stocking
seuteikeu (스테이크): steak
seuteuleching (스트레칭): stretching
seuteuleseu (스트레스): stress
seuteulontyum (스트론튬): strontium
seutul (스툴): stool
seuwajillandeu (스와질란드): Swaziland
seuweden (스웨덴): Sweden
seuweteo (스웨터): sweater
seuwichi (스위치): light switch
seuwiseu (스위스): Switzerland
si (시): hour
sib-ijijang (십이지장): duodenum
sib-obun (십오분): quarter of an hour
sibjamalpul-i (십자말풀이): crosswords
sibnyeon (십년): decade
sibogyum (시보귬): seaborgium
sibumo (시부모): parents-in-law
siche (시체): corpse
sicheong (시청): town hall
sielalion (시에라리온): Sierra Leone
siga (시가): cigar
siganpyo (시간표): timetable

sigcho (식초): vinegar
sigdo (식도): oesophagus
sigeumchi (시금치): spinach
siggidogu (식기도구): cutlery
siggisecheoggi (식기세척기): dishwasher
sigminji (식민지): colony
sigmul-won (식물원): botanic garden
sigtag (식탁): table
sigtagbo (식탁보): tablecloth
sigye (시계): clock
siheom (시험): exam
sijang (시장): market
sikkeuleoun (시끄러운): loud
silheomsil (실험실): laboratory
silia (시리아): Syria
siljelo (실제로): actually
sillopon (실로폰): xylophone
sillyehabnida (실례합니다): excuse me
silnae undong-yong jajeongeo (실내 운동용 자전거): exercise bike
silpaehada (실패하다): to fail
simbeoljeu (심벌즈): cymbals
simenteu (시멘트): cement
simenteu honhabgi (시멘트 혼합기): cement mixer
simjang (심장): heart
simjanghag (심장학): cardiology
simjang mabi (심장 마비): heart attack
simji (심지): pit
simlichilyo (심리치료): psychotherapy
simpan (심판): referee
simponi (심포니): symphony
sin-yongkadeu (신용카드): credit card
sinae (시내): stream
sinagogeu (시나고그): synagogue
sinamon (시나몬): cinnamon
sinbaljang (신발장): shoe cabinet
sinbal kkeun (신발 끈): lace
sinbu (신부): bride, priest
sing-gapoleu (싱가포르): Singapore
singkeudae (싱크대): sink
singyeong (신경): nerve
singyeong-gwa (신경과): neurology
sinho (신호): signal
sinhodeung (신호등): traffic light
sinhon-yeohaeng (신혼여행): honeymoon
sinjang (신장): kidney
sinlang (신랑): groom
sinmun (신문): newspaper
sin paedeu (신 패드): shinpad
sinseonghan (신성한): holy
sinu-i (시누이): sister-in-law
soagwa (소아과): paediatrics
sobang-gwan (소방관): firefighters, firefighter
sobangcha (소방차): fire truck
sobangseo (소방서): fire station
sodogje (소독제): antiseptic
soegogi (쇠고기): beef
soeseulang (쇠스랑): pitchfork
sogdogye (속도계): speedometer
sogdojehan (속도제한): speed limit
sogeum (소금): salt
sognunsseob (속눈썹): eyelashes
sogsag-ida (속삭이다): to whisper

sogsyeocheu (속셔츠): undershirt
sohaengseong (소행성): asteroid
sohwagi (소화기): fire extinguisher
sohwajeon (소화전): hydrant
sohyeong beoseu (소형 버스): minibus
sojang (소장): small intestine
solijileuda (소리지르다): to shout
sollomon jedo (솔로몬 제도): Solomon Islands
som (솜): cotton
somae (소매): sleeve
somallia (소말리아): Somalia
somsatang (솜사탕): candy floss
son (손): hand
sonamu (소나무): pine
sonbadag (손바닥): palm
song-ajigogi (송아지고기): veal
songalag (손가락): finger
songjang (송장): bill
songjeonseon (송전선): power line
sonja (손자): grandson
sonjeondeung (손전등): torch
sonju (손주): grandchild
sonmog (손목): wrist
sonmogsigye (손목시계): watch
sonnim (손님): guest
sonnyeo (손녀): granddaughter
sonsil (손실): loss
sontob (손톱): fingernail
sontob dadeumneun jul (손톱 다듬는 줄): nail file
sontobgawi (손톱가위): nail scissors
sontobkkakk-i (손톱깎이): nail clipper
sonyeo (소녀): girl
sonyeon (소년): boy
sopa (소파): sofa
sopo (소포): parcel
soseol (소설): novel
sosiji (소시지): sausage
sosyeol midieo (소셜 미디어): social media
ssal (쌀): rice
ssan (싼): cheap
ssangdung-i (쌍둥이): twins
ssauda (싸우다): to fight
sseolmae (썰매): sledge
sseuda (쓰다): to write
sseulegitong (쓰레기통): garbage bin
sseulgae (쓸개): gall bladder
ssias (씨앗): seed
ssilieol (씨리얼): cereal
ssisda (씻다): to wash
ssoda (쏘다): to shoot
su-ig (수익): profit
suaeg (수액): infusion
subag (수박): water melon
su chilyobeob (수 치료법): hydrotherapy
sudal (수달): otter
sudan (수단): Sudan
sudgalag (숟가락): spoon
sudo (수도): capital
sudokkogji (수도꼭지): tap
sudoseung (수도승): monk
sudosmul (수돗물): tap water
sudu (수두): chickenpox

sueob (수업): lesson
sueun (수은): mercury
sugab (수갑): handcuff
sugeon (수건): towel
sugje (숙제): homework
sugu (수구): water polo
suhag (수학): mathematics
sujoggwan (수족관): aquarium
sujub-eun (수줍은): shy
sujung balle (수중 발레): synchronized swimming
sulchwihan (술취한): drunk
sulihada (수리하다): to fix
sulinam (수리남): Suriname
suljib (술집): bar
sulyeogbaljeonso (수력발전소): hydroelectric power station
sum-eul swida (숨을 쉬다): to breathe
sumda (숨다): to hide
sumyeonje (수면제): sleeping pill
sumyeon maseukeu (수면 마스크): sleeping mask
sunyeo (수녀): nun
sup (숲): forest
supeu (수프): soup
supil (수필): essay
supyo (수표): cheque
susangseuki (수상스키): waterskiing
suseong (수성): Mercury
suseonhwa (수선화): daffodil
suso (수소): hydrogen
susul (수술): surgery
susulsil (수술실): operating theatre
suuisa (수의사): vet
suyeong (수영): swimming
suyeongbog (수영복): swimsuit
suyeonghada (수영하다): to swim
suyeongjang (수영장): swimming pool
suyeongmo (수영모): swim cap
suyoil (수요일): Wednesday
swaegol (쇄골): collarbone
swida (쉬다): to rest
swimpyo (쉼표): comma
swiun (쉬운): easy
syampein (샴페인): champagne
syampu (샴푸): shampoo
syawogi (샤워기): shower
syawojel (샤워젤): shower gel
syawokaeb (샤워캡): shower cap
syawokeoteun (샤워커튼): shower curtain
syawoleul hada (샤워를 하다): to take a shower
syeocheu (셔츠): shirt
syeoteulkog (셔틀콕): shuttlecock
syopingbaguni (쇼핑바구니): shopping basket
syopingkateu (쇼핑카트): shopping cart
syopingsenteo (쇼핑센터): shopping mall
syoteuteulaeg (쇼트트랙): short track
syupeomakes (슈퍼마켓): supermarket

T

taea (태아): foetus
taegsi (택시): taxi
taegsigisa (택시기사): taxi driver

taegug (태국): Thailand
taegwondo (태권도): taekwondo
taembeolin (탬버린): tambourine
taeng-go (탱고): tango
taengkeu (탱크): tank
taepung (태풍): typhoon
taepyeong-yang (태평양): Pacific Ocean
taeuda (태우다): to burn
taeyang (태양): sun
taeyang jeonjipan (태양 전지판): solar panel
taggu (탁구): table tennis
taggu teibeul (탁구 테이블): table tennis table
tagja (탁자): coffee table
taieo (타이어): tyre
tail (타일): tile
taitanyum (타이타늄): titanium
tajikiseutan (타지키스탄): Tajikistan
tajo (타조): ostrich
tal-uisil (탈의실): changing room
talae song-gos (타래 송곳): corkscrew
talantyulla (타란튤라): tarantula
taleu (타르): tar
tallyum (탈륨): thallium
tam-yogseuleoun (탐욕스러운): greedy
tampon (탐폰): tampon
tanjania (탄자니아): Tanzania
tansaeng (탄생): birth
tansansu (탄산수): soda
tanso (탄소): carbon
tantalleom (탄탈럼): tantalum
tatu (타투): tattoo
tawon (타원): ellipse
teipeu (테이프): adhesive tape
tekeunetyum (테크네튬): technetium
tekilla (테킬라): tequila
telaseu (테라스): terrace
tellebijeon (텔레비전): TV set, TV
tellulyum (텔루륨): tellurium
teniseu (테니스): tennis
teniseu chae (테니스 채): tennis racket
teniseu gong (테니스 공): tennis ball
teniseukoteu (테니스코트): tennis court
tenteu (텐트): tent
teobyum (터븀): terbium
teog (턱): chin
teogbad-i (턱받이): bib
teogppyeo (턱뼈): jawbone
teogsuyeom (턱수염): beard
teoki (터키): Turkey
teongseuten (텅스텐): tungsten
teteuliseu (테트리스): Tetris
teulaeg saikeulling (트랙 사이클링): track cycling
teulaegteo (트랙터): tractor
teulaem (트램): tram
teulaempeollin (트램펄린): trampoline
teulaiaeng-geul (트라이앵글): triangle
teuleilleo (트레일러): trailer
teuleiningbaji (트레이닝바지): sweatpants
teuleoggisa (트럭기사): lorry driver
teuleombon (트럼본): trombone
teuleompes (트럼펫): trumpet
teuleongkeu (트렁크): rear trunk

teuleopeul (트러플): truffle
teulihauseu (트리하우스): tree house
teulinidadeu tobago (트리니다드 토바고): Trinidad and Tobago
teullin (틀린): wrong
teulopi (트로피): cup
tib (팁): tip
tibi silijeu (티비 시리즈): TV series
tipaenti (티팬티): thong
tisyeocheu (티셔츠): T-shirt
tob (톱): saw
tobjilhada (톱질하다): to saw
togo (토고): Togo
tokki (토끼): rabbit
tolyum (토륨): thorium
tomato (토마토): tomato
tomatososeu (토마토소스): tomato sauce
ton (톤): ton
toneido (토네이도): tornado
toneo (토너): facial toner
tong-ga (통가): Tonga
tonghaenglyo (통행료): toll
tongjolim (통조림): tin
tongtonghan (통통한): plump, chubby
toseong (토성): Saturn
toseuteo (토스터): toaster
toyoil (토요일): Saturday
ttaelida (때리다): to hit
ttagttaghan (딱딱한): hard
ttal (딸): daughter
ttaleuda (따르다): to follow
ttalgi (딸기): strawberry
ttallang-i (딸랑이): rattle
ttamheubsubaendeu (땀흡수밴드): sweatband
ttangkong (땅콩): peanut
ttangkong-gileum (땅콩기름): peanut oil
ttangkongbeoteo (땅콩버터): peanut butter
ttatteushan (따뜻한): warm
tteol-eojida (떨어지다): to fall
ttoneun (또는): or
tuballu (투발루): Tuvalu
tuja (투자): investment
tuleukeumeniseutan (투르크메니스탄): Turkmenistan
tullyum (툴륨): thulium
tupyoleul hada (투표를 하다): to vote
twigida (튀기다): to fry
twiginsosiji (튀긴소시지): fried sausage
twiniji (튀니지): Tunisia
tyuba (튜바): tuba
tyullib (튤립): tulip

U

ubi (우비): raincoat
uchegug (우체국): post office
uganda (우간다): Uganda
ugi (우기): monsoon
uhoejeonhae (우회전해): turn right
uibus-adeul (의붓아들): stepson
uibusttal (의붓딸): stepdaughter
uichi (의치): dental prostheses
uija (의자): chair

uisa (의사): doctor
ujeubekiseutan (우즈베키스탄): Uzbekistan
ujubog (우주복): space suit
uju jeong-geojang (우주 정거장): space station
uju wangbogseon (우주 왕복선): space shuttle
ukeulaina (우크라이나): Ukraine
ukullelle (우쿨렐레): ukulele
ulanyum (우라늄): uranium
ulda (울다): to cry
uli (우리): we
ulieunha (우리은하): Milky Way
uli jib (우리 집): our home
ulim (우림): rainforest
ultali (울타리): fence
ulugwai (우루과이): Uruguay
undongbog (운동복): tracksuit
undonghwa (운동화): trainers
unseog (운석): meteorite
upyeonbeonho (우편번호): zip code
upyeonham (우편함): mailbox
upyo (우표): stamp
URL (URL): url
usan (우산): umbrella
USB peullaesi deulaibeu (USB 플래시 드라이브): USB stick
usda (웃다): to laugh
uyu (우유): milk

W

wa (와): and
wae (왜): why
waenyahamyeon (왜냐하면): because
wain (와인): wine
waipeo (와이퍼): windscreen wiper
walcheu (왈츠): waltz
wanchung-gi (완충기): shock absorber
wandukong (완두콩): pea
wang-gwan (왕관): crown
wapeul (와플): waffle
wateu (와트): watt
webkaem (웹캠): webcam
websaiteu (웹사이트): website
wedingdeuleseu (웨딩드레스): wedding dress
weding keikeu (웨딩 케이크): wedding cake
weiteo (웨이터): waiter
wejigamja (웨지감자): potato wedges
wi (위): stomach, above
wian (위안): yuan
wido (위도): latitude
windeu seoping (윈드 서핑): windsurfing
wiseong (위성): satellite
wiseongbangsong susin antena (위성방송 수신 안테나): satellite dish
wiseuki (위스키): whiskey
wismom il-eukigi (윗몸 일으키기): sit-ups
wol-yoil (월요일): Monday
wolgeub (월급): salary
wolsig (월식): lunar eclipse
won (원): circle
wonban deonjigi (원반 던지기): discus throw
wongidung (원기둥): cylinder
wonja (원자): atom

wonja beonho (원자 번호): atomic number
wonjalyeogbaljeonso (원자력발전소): nuclear power plant
wonppul (원뿔): cone
wonsung-i (원숭이): monkey
woteopakeu (워터파크): water park
woteo seullaideu (워터 슬라이드): water slide

Y

yadeu (야드): yard
yaggug (약국): pharmacy
yaghan (약한): weak
yaghon (약혼): engagement
yaghonbanji (약혼반지): engagement ring
yaghonja (약혼자): fiancé
yaghonnyeo (약혼녀): fiancée
yagsa (약사): pharmacist
yagsongalag (약손가락): ring finger
yagu (야구): baseball
yagu bangmang-i (야구 방망이): bat
yagu geulleobeu (야구 글러브): mitt
yagu moja (야구 모자): baseball cap
yajasu (야자수): palm tree
yang (양): sheep
yang-gogi (양고기): lamb
yang-gung (양궁): archery
yangbog (양복): suit
yangchisigmul (양치식물): fern
yangcho (양초): candle
yangdong-i (양동이): bucket
yangmal (양말): sock
yangmo (양모): wool
yangpa (양파): onion
yangseongja (양성자): proton
yat-eun (얕은): shallow
yemen (예멘): Yemen
yeobseo (엽서): postcard
yeodongsaeng (여동생): little sister
yeogdo (역도): weightlifting
yeoggi (역기): barbell
yeogi (여기): here
yeogsa (역사): history
yeogwon (여권): passport
yeohaeng-eul hada (여행을 하다): to travel
yeohaengsa jig-won (여행사 직원): travel agent
yeohaeng teuleilleo (여행 트레일러): caravan
yeoja (여자): woman
yeojachingu (여자친구): girlfriend
yeol (열): row, fever
yeolda (열다): to open
yeoldae (열대): tropics
yeoleum (여름): summer
yeolgigu (열기구): hot-air balloon
yeolsoe (열쇠): key
yeolsoegoli (열쇠고리): key chain
yeolsoegumeong (열쇠구멍): keyhole
yeomsaegmeoli (염색머리): dyed
yeomso (염소): goat, chlorine
yeon-eo (연어): salmon
yeong-eo (영어): English
yeong-eob (영업): sales

yeong-gug (영국): United Kingdom
yeongeug (연극): play
yeongeun (연근): lotus root
yeonghwagwan (영화관): cinema
yeongigamjigi (연기감지기): smoke detector
yeonglihan (영리한): clever
yeongol (연골): cartilage
yeongto (영토): territory
yeongu (연구): research
yeonlagseon (연락선): ferry
yeonmos (연못): pond
yeonpil (연필): pencil
yeonpilkkakk-i (연필깎이): pencil sharpener
yeonseubhada (연습하다): to practice
yeop (옆): beside
yeopmun (옆문): side door
yeoseong-yong jigab (여성용 지갑): purse
yeou (여우): fox
yeouwonsung-i (여우원숭이): lemur
yeyag (예약): reservation, booking, appointment
yoga (요가): yoga
yogeum (요금): fare
yogjo (욕조): bathtub
yogsil (욕실): bathroom
yoguleuteu (요구르트): yoghurt
yoleudan (요르단): Jordan
yolihada (요리하다): to cook
yolisa (요리사): cook
yong-am (용암): lava
yong-gamhan (용감한): brave
yoodeu (요오드): iodine
yoteu (요트): yacht
yua (유아): infant
yuayong anjeonsiteu (유아용 안전시트): child seat
yubang (유방): bosom
yuchaessiyu (유채씨유): rapeseed oil
yuchiwon (유치원): kindergarten
yuchiwon seonsaengnim (유치원 선생님): kindergarten teacher
yudo (유도): judo
yudu (유두): nipple
yueon (유언): testament
yugdugu (육두구): nutmeg
yuggaghyeong (육각형): hexagon
yugol danji (유골 단지): urn
yuhyogigan (유효기간): expiry date
yujoeui (유죄의): guilty
yukallibtuseu (유칼립투스): eucalyptus
yulamseon (유람선): cruise ship
yulikeob (유리컵): glass
yulo (유로): euro
yulopyum (유로퓸): europium
yumocha (유모차): pushchair
yunhwalje (윤활제): lubricant
yunipom (유니폼): uniform
yusan (유산): heritage, miscarriage

www.ingramcontent.com/pod-product-compliance
Lightning Source LLC
La Vergne TN
LVHW010012120325
805731LV00035B/1633

* 9 7 8 1 9 7 7 8 2 9 0 4 7 *